THE MEDIA AND HUMAN RIGHTS

In recent years there has been an explosion in the usage and visibility of the language of human rights, but what does this mean for the role of the media? For evolving ideas about human rights? And for the prospect of shared cosmopolitan values?

Ekaterina Balabanova argues that in order to answer these questions there needs to be a deconstruction of monolithic ways of thinking about the media and human rights, incorporating the spectrum of political arguments and world views that underpin both.

Ten case studies are presented which illustrate many of the problems and challenges associated with the relationship between the media and human rights. The examples range from cases of humanitarian intervention to analysis of global human rights campaigning on refugee issues; from immigration and asylum to genocide, freedom of speech and torture.

Anchored in an appreciation of the political conflicts and compromises at the heart of international human rights agreements, *The Media and Human Rights* is an invaluable resource for students studying media and human rights, international politics, security studies and political communication.

Ekaterina Balabanova is a Senior Lecturer in Political Communication in the Department of Communication and Media, University of Liverpool, UK. She is the author of *Media, Wars and Politics: Comparing the Incomparable in Western and Eastern Europe*.

THE MEDIA AND HUMAN RIGHTS

The Cosmopolitan Promise

Ekaterina Balabanova

 Routledge
Taylor & Francis Group

LONDON AND NEW YORK

First published 2015
by Routledge
2 Park Square, Milton Park, Abingdon, Oxon, OX14 4RN

and by Routledge
711 Third Avenue, New York, NY 10017

Routledge is an imprint of the Taylor & Francis Group, an informa business

British Library Cataloguing in Publication Data
A catalogue record for this book is available from the British Library

Library of Congress Cataloging in Publication Data
Balabanova, Ekaterina, 1975–
The media and human rights : the cosmopolitan promise / Ekaterina Balabanova.
pages cm
Includes bibliographical references and index.
1. Human rights. 2. Mass media. 3. Cosmopolitanism. I. Title.
JC571.B336 2014
070.4'49323044–dc23
2014011351

ISBN: 978-0-415-62311-7 (hbk)
ISBN: 978-0-415-62312-4 (pbk)
ISBN: 978-0-203-10543-6 (ebk)

Typeset in Bembo
by Taylor and Francis Books

CONTENTS

ACKNOWLEDGEMENTS

The idea for this book appeared a few years ago when I first decided to link two of my areas of interest and introduced my students to the subject of media and human rights. The discussions that have taken place in classes since then and the students' incredible level of interest are the reasons for the publication of this book. So, thank you to the students who took my course on Media and Human Rights and made it such a success. Thanks also to everyone in the Department of Communication and Media at the University of Liverpool for making possible the research leave during which this book was completed. I would also like to acknowledge the help of Leigh Foster, Head of Events, Campaigns and Goodwill Ambassadors at UNHCR, and the financial support of the University of Liverpool for the knowledge exchange project that made the study of the 2012 Dilemmas World Refugee Day campaign possible.

My thanks also go to the two anonymous reviewers whose very useful comments and suggestions have been extremely helpful and encouraging. Thanks also to Natalie Foster and Sheni Kruger at Routledge for their understanding and support throughout the writing of the book.

Finally, as ever, thanks to my family for their love and support – my sister, my parents and my granny. My biggest thanks and love go to my husband Alex. His comments and copy-editing have been extraordinary, and his support, patience and encouragement invaluable.

ABBREVIATIONS

ACHPR	African Charter on Human and Peoples' Rights
ACTA	Anti-Counterfeiting Trade Agreement
AI	Amnesty International
AMIS	African Union Mission in Sudan
AU	African Union
BNP	British National Party
CAT	Convention against Torture and Other Cruel, Inhuman or Degrading Treatment or Punishment
CIA	Central Intelligence Agency
CoE	Council of Europe
EC	European Commission
ECHR	Convention for the Protection of Human Rights and Fundamental Freedoms/European Convention on Human Rights
ECtHR	European Court of Human Rights
EU	European Union
FRY	Federal Republic of Yugoslavia
GCHQ	Government Communications Headquarters
HRW	Human Rights Watch
ICC	International Criminal Court
ICCPR	International Covenant on Civil and Political Rights
ICESCR	International Covenant on Economic, Social and Cultural Rights
ICHRP	International Council on Human Rights Policy
ICISS	International Commission on Intervention and State Sovereignty
ICRC	International Committee of the Red Cross
IICK	Independent International Commission on Kosovo
IPPR	Institute for Public Policy Research
ITUC	International Trades Union Congress

JEM	Justice and Equality Movement
KLA	Kosovo Liberation Army
KPI	Key performance indicators
MOU	Memorandum of Understanding
NATO	North Atlantic Treaty Organization
NGO	Non-governmental organization
NSA	National Security Agency
NUJ	National Union of Journalists
OAU	Organization of African Unity
OLC	Office of Legal Counsel
OSCE	Organization for Security and Co-operation in Europe
PDD	Presidential Decision Directive
PIPA	Preventing Real Online Threats to Economic Creativity and Theft of Intellectual Property Act
PM	Prime Minister
PSA	Public service announcement
R2P	Responsibility to Protect
RPF	Rwanda Patriotic Front
RTLM	Radio-Télévision Libre des Milles Collines
SC	Security Council
SLA	Sudan Liberation Army
SOPA	Stop Online Piracy Act
UDHR	Universal Declaration of Human Rights
UN	United Nations
UNAMID	African Union/UN Hybrid Operation in Darfur
UNAMIR	United Nations Assistance Mission for Rwanda
UNHCR	United Nations High Commissioner for Refugees
UPR	Universal Periodic Review
WRD	World Refugee Day

INTRODUCTION

When addressing the assembled international media following the appearance of Russian troops in Crimea, then a part of Ukraine, Russian Foreign Minister Lavrov claimed: 'this is a question of defending our citizens and compatriots, and ensuring human rights' (cited in *Telegraph* 2014). While Lavrov's account and defence of the intervention was disputed by Ukraine, the United States and the European Union, it demonstrates both the ubiquity of the language of human rights in contemporary international relations and the importance of the global media in attempts to control the narrative of political disputes.

Human rights issues have indeed become a prominent feature of media coverage: usage and visibility of the term 'human rights' have increased dramatically since the 1990s. Is this evidence of a growing cosmopolitanism fuelled by the extraordinary expansion of media channels and coverage? As Cmiel (2004: 117) notes, 'Few political agendas have seen such a rapid and dramatic growth'. When, in 1993, Ovsiovitch examined human rights discourses in the *New York Times*, *Time* magazine and the *CBS Evening News* between 1978 and 1987, he concluded that 'there [was] very little coverage of human rights' (Ovsiovitch 1993: 685). Caliendo, Gibney and Payne's (1999) analysis of the *New York Times* in 1985 and 1995 found that attention to human rights had increased since Ovsiovitch's study, but that coverage was still 'seriously lacking'. A more recent analysis of human rights coverage in the media by Cole (2010) established that attention to human rights had increased 'dramatically' in the *New York Times* and the *Washington Post* between 1980 and 2000, with the number of articles referencing human rights doubling. Similar trends were observed for the media outside of the US. A study based on the coverage of *The Economist*, *Newsweek* and four American and European dailies – the *New York Times*, *Guardian*, *Le Monde* and *Frankfurter Allgemeine Zeitung* – discovered a growing use by the Northern media of the term 'human rights' from 1986 to 2000 (Ramos *et al.* 2007). In its report *Journalism, Media and the Challenge of Human Rights Reporting*, the International Council on Human Rights Policy (ICHRP 2002: 5), while acknowledging being 'biased in a distinctly Northern perspective', drew on experiences of journalists, editors, producers and media consultants in parts of Sub-Saharan Africa, Latin America, South-Eastern Europe and South Asia. The report, which is one of very few attempts to examine present-day human rights reporting internationally, noted that 'the media are more receptive to human rights issues today than at any time in the modern history of the media' (ICHRP 2002: 32). It claimed that

> In recent years, it has become apparent to observers as well as practitioners of mass communications that human rights is more newsworthy than it was. The media have become interested not only in violations of human rights, but in the institutional apparatus that has been designed to promote and protect human rights.
>
> *(ICHRP 2002: 16)*

What should we make of the changing ways in which human rights appear in the media? What does this tell us about the changing role of the media in society and international relations? What does it tell us about the system of human rights itself? What does it tell us about shared values and principles in a globalizing world? These are the overarching questions that animate the rest of this book.

In order to answer them and to understand the meaning and significance of the explosion of interest in human rights, the problematic and monolithic ways of thinking about the topic need to be deconstructed. 'Human rights' and 'the media' are vague labels – there are many different types of both. On the one hand, they are real, material, facts; on the other hand, they are concepts that contain powerful, and therefore contentious, normative assumptions and dilemmas. These include a range of questions about what is and what ought to be. The parallel interest in cosmopolitanism in the humanities and social sciences has emerged in part as a reaction to, and in part as a means of analysing, these questions; but it likewise risks being used as a monolithic concept when there are significant disagreements over its meaning and the ways in which it can speak to social, political and economic problems.

The proposal here is to unpack these three elements to mutual benefit by:

1 Considering more carefully the ways in which the media plays a role in enabling the implementation of, and shaping our perceptions of, international human rights.
2 Developing a more contingent and critical perspective on the varied purchase of different kinds of human rights in the international sphere in practical and conceptual terms.
3 Relating both of the above to a more nuanced and historically informed understanding of the different cosmopolitan and non-cosmopolitan ideas and arguments; and using these to make sense of contemporary human rights debates.

As such, the book offers a critical perspective on how different kinds of human rights – ranging from genocide and the practice of humanitarian intervention to torture; from freedom of speech to asylum and immigration – are covered by the media, and relates these to cosmopolitan arguments about international politics.

The range of case studies offered is wide, with each carefully selected to demonstrate a different dimension or aspect of the link between media and human rights. The book introduces new topics and subject areas to the media–human rights debate, such as immigration and asylum. Traditionally, most analyses exploring the role of media in promoting and protecting human rights have dealt primarily with cases of humanitarian intervention and human suffering or explored freedom of speech, which in itself is both a human right and a particularly powerful role of the media. The argument put forward here is for an expansion of this rather narrow focus and inclusion and examination of a wider range of human rights. Importantly, the book relates debates about the role of the media to a solid understanding of the complexities of the human rights framework itself, including introduction to the political conflicts and compromises which are embedded within the international agreements. It is argued that to understand the media's role in relation to specific human rights issues, an awareness of the key debates and tensions shaping the issue at stake is vital. To achieve this, the book provides a clear explanation of sometimes complex theoretical arguments and illustrates them through empirical examples. It also links with the growing interdisciplinary interest in cosmopolitanism and provides a clear explanation of how this relates to media–human rights debates.

Table 0.1 summarizes the main questions and the analytical approach which this book adopts to address them. This introductory chapter continues by exploring in more detail the so-called 'explosion' in human rights reporting. What immediate explanations can we identify for this phenomenon, and what are the main criticisms of the media's role when it comes to human rights?

TABLE 0.1 Making sense of contemporary human rights debates

Question: What do contemporary human rights debates tell us about:	Analytical approach: How can these questions be addressed?
(1) The changing role of the media in society and international relations?	Consider the ways in which the media plays a role in enabling the implementation of, and shaping our perceptions of, international human rights.
(2) The state of the system of human rights itself?	Develop a critical perspective on the varied purchase of different kinds of human rights in the international sphere – as both concept and practice.
(3) Shared values and principles in a globalizing world?	Relate (1) and (2) to a more nuanced and historically informed understanding of the different cosmopolitan and non-cosmopolitan ideas and arguments.

Explaining the explosion in human rights reporting

The increased salience of human rights issues in media coverage is not accidental, but rather the cumulative effect of at least seven interrelated developments. First, there is the growing international web of agreements over human rights and organizations that seek to implement, evaluate or assess them. Ever since the Universal Declaration of Human Rights (UDHR) in 1948 governments across the world have increasingly referred to and integrated human rights principles into their policies and laws; numerous international protocols and conventions have been ratified; and ever more human rights 'watchdogs' that promote human rights, monitor human rights violations, investigate abuses and publish information have emerged (Benhabib 2004; Dunne and Hanson 2013; Internews 2012; Kaldor 2003; ICHRP 2002; Tsutsui and Wotipka 2004). Second, there is a discursive shift whereby the language of human rights has gained salience in political and public discourses – governments and political leaders and their critics refer to human rights more often both in their formal statements of policy and in political rhetoric (Beitz 2009). Third, this discursive shift has a political dimension as ever more issues are framed as human rights issues – such as children's issues, HIV/AIDS, sexual and reproductive health, ageing, poverty and housing.

Fourth, human rights are now part of 'high politics'. They are not just discussed during local and national elections but also serve as justifications for 'humanitarian interventions' internationally (Chandler 2006; Hehir 2010; Internews 2012; ICHRP 2002). The many humanitarian crises of the 1990s which took place in Africa and South-Eastern Europe in particular pushed human rights to the foreground and contributed to the increased media coverage. The United Nations' monitoring system has become more visible and international tribunals have taken place (e.g. on Rwanda and Former Yugoslavia), with new permanent ones created, such as the International Criminal Court (ICC), set up in 2002 to prosecute individuals for genocide, crimes against humanity, war crimes, and the new crime of aggression. Fifth, these changes were accompanied by a reduction in state control over the media. The end of the Cold War signalled a new freedom for the media to report more independently on issues of their choice, significantly facilitated by the technological developments that challenged government dominance as a news source (Robinson 2002). This was seen by the radical technological optimists as an opportunity to mould a 'cosmopolitan global consciousness' (Carruthers 2000: 201), transforming the whole world into a single 'imagined community' (Hannerz 1996: 121; Ignatieff 1997: 27) and creating a 'global village' (McLuhan 1964). Sixth, and connecting to the previous point, mobile and internet technology, alongside social-networking platforms like Twitter and Facebook and content-sharing sites such as Vine, Instagram, Flickr and YouTube, has increased the means of receiving information about human rights by adding more sources and more alerts. It has also created new ways of reporting human rights violations and developing connections or networks between people living in distant places (Internews 2012).

Seventh, unpredicted political crises have brought human rights to the fore. The recent uprisings in the Middle East and North Africa are good examples of events that have brought together many of the above factors. Facilitated to a degree (rather than caused) by networked communication technologies that disrupted the traditional and established media models, these events led to news sourced from Facebook, Twitter and Flickr to be incorporated into the way the story of the Arab Spring was explained to the outside world.

These changes in the global geopolitical and media landscape have affected the work of journalists, media content and the news agenda, all of which have had an impact on the way in which the media deal with the subject of human rights, as will be demonstrated in later chapters and case studies.

Gaps, problems, criticisms

While there is broad agreement on the increase in interest in human rights in the media – and perhaps even on explanations for why this has happened – there is no such consensus in terms of assessments of either the quantity or quality of coverage. Despite the increased frequency and salience of these topics in media coverage, there are many aspects which remain under-reported, and the media has been roundly criticized for the manner in which it covers human rights. This was particularly so during the Cold War period when Ovsiovitch (1993: 685) observed that 'information is incomplete, thus skewing the public's perception of human rights around the world'. In addition, some of the more general concerns in this era (which, it should be said, were not always based on any systematic examination of media coverage) included that coverage of human rights concerns was sporadic (Berry and McChesney 1988), that it was biased against both 'open' (Reisman 1984) and communist societies (Herman and Chomsky 1988) and that it was racially skewed (Robinson, cited in Ovsiovitch 1993: 672). Almost ten years later, referring to the post-Cold War era, the ICHRP (2002: 16) similarly identified problems with human rights reporting and concluded:

> Issues that are less visible, or slow processes, are covered rarely. Human rights are still taken largely to mean political and civil rights, and the importance of economic, social and cultural rights is ignored widely by the media in their coverage of economic issues, including the international economy, poverty, inequity and social and economic discrimination.

The media has suffered a wave of criticism in the post-9/11 era. The lack of critical analysis of the prosecution of the 'war on terror' prompted many to claim that the US press was 'in crisis', turning a 'blind eye' (Umansky 2006) and completely failing to fulfil its role as a check on state power (Bennett *et al.* 2006). In their analysis of the coverage of torture (see Chapter 8), Graber and Holyk (2009) list seven main criticisms of the media:

- incomplete coverage of events;
- avoidance of labels that denote human rights issues;

- dependence on government version of events;
- avoidance of counter-arguments;
- failure to highlight patterns of abuse;
- dependence on official sources; and
- a lack of investigative journalism.

The ICHRP (2002) identified three main issues that lay beneath the suboptimal state of human rights reporting. Perhaps rather disappointingly, these same issues were echoed by Internews (2012) ten years later in its toolkit for reporting on human rights issues, *Speak up, Speak out*, which suggests that these challenges are deep and persistent. The first issue that these critiques point to is the knowledge gap, leading to an 'inadequate understanding' (even 'ignorance') of human rights. According to both reports, there is a 'serious lack of knowledge' of what human rights are, how they are created, how they are promoted and enforced, and what governments' responsibilities are as well as 'a superficial grasp of the institutional apparatus of human rights'. Many journalists seem to be unfamiliar with the UDHR and the international human rights treaties and mechanisms that 'are taken to be rather arcane and specialist territory' (Internews 2012: 62; ICHRP 2002: 19, 114). While the ICHRP acknowledges that this lack of knowledge applies not only to journalists but also to many politicians and other actors in civil society, this still has negative repercussions for the quality of human rights reporting, with human rights often wrongly regarded as relevant only to the reporting of conflict.

There is certainly evidence to suggest that the Western human rights agenda, in particular, focuses more heavily on civil and political rights rather than abuses of social and economic rights (Ramos *et al.* 2007). In Africa, the International Federation of Journalists (1999) found considerable ignorance and lack of awareness about human rights, with few journalists or public officials able to identify even a small number of the rights outlined in the UDHR or in the African Charter on Human and Peoples' Rights (ACHPR). Internews (2012: 62) adds that, as a result, 'journalists miss stories or ways of reporting issues. This affects the quality of journalism and the public's right to information.'

The second concern, identified by both the ICHRP and Internews, relates to the media's understanding of where the main challenges to human rights take place. The media are predisposed to think that human rights violations occur abroad, so any issues that relate to their own governments or other powerful interests in their own societies are not placed in the context of the international human rights regime and national responsibilities following on from it. Therefore, while human rights issues are covered, they are not presented as such, but rather as national or local crime or politics.

> For the Western media, human rights are almost always seen as a dimension of foreign policy. Issues that have a strong human rights element may be addressed extensively in a domestic context but are seldom categorized in terms of rights. Child abuse, refugees and immigration, unemployment,

sexual and racial discrimination and a host of other issues that are the daily staple of the media are generally covered in a manner that suggests that there are no external or commonly agreed standards to which governments must adhere.

(ICHRP 2002: 19)

According to both the ICHRP (2002) and Internews (2012), this inevitably weakens the media's 'watchdog' role, as they do not hold their governments and other powerful institutions to account. Cole's (2010: 321) study of human rights coverage in the American press between 1980 and 2000 provides further empirical support for this claim by discovering that 'different kinds of rights might also be conceptualized in different ways internationally and domestically'. In the US, citizenship rights garnered more attention in the national or local sections of the newspapers, whereas the phrase 'human rights' appeared more frequently in the international or world sections. American newspapers also reported certain kinds of abuse more than others, 'perhaps reflecting an ideological bias in favor of civil and political rights and against socioeconomic rights' (Cole 2010: 321).[1] Interestingly, a case study of Mexican newspapers revealed that human rights there are contextualized as part of the relationship between the citizenry and the government and as such have a domestic focus, in contrast to the foreign focus that is often found in the Western media (McPherson 2012).

The third problem concerns the quality of reporting. The media tend to miss the historical, political, social and local context of human rights stories (ICHRP 2002) and fail to provide in-depth and detailed analysis (Internews 2012). 'As a result, human rights violations seem to be isolated instances or new events even when they are only the latest in a history of similar violations' (Internews 2012: 62).

Media complicity and guilt in human rights abuses

Internews (2012) identifies one more weakness of contemporary human rights reporting. It sees the media as sometimes perpetrating human rights abuses itself by invading privacy (e.g. the *News of the World* phone-hacking scandal in the UK), perpetuating bias and stereotypes (e.g. in the reporting of immigration, asylum and refugee issues), not calling governments to account, or even deepening an existing conflict. Supporting this, in a 2003 special report, the United States Institute of Peace concluded that 'across the globe, media have been used as tools to inflame grievances and accelerate the escalation towards violence' (Frohardt and Temin 2003: 1).

This notion of the media as responsible or complicit in human rights abuses is often linked to recent examples where it has been claimed that the media has been used to incite violence, murder and genocide, as in Rwanda, Somalia and the Former Yugoslavia. According to Schimmel (2009: 444), 'the media facilitates, often inadvertently and unconsciously, the efforts of governments engaged in human rights abuses to deny and cover up their actions, and shield them from public knowledge and scrutiny'.

These key problems in reporting human rights are exacerbated by the very nature of human rights and the controversies and challenges posed by them as subject matter. The tensions regarding the universal applicability of human rights, for example, have an impact on how journalists in different parts of the world cover the topic. It is likely that many journalists hold cultural beliefs and act in ways that do not conform to all universal human rights ideals.

Finally, the role of the state in controlling or regulating the media needs to be acknowledged. The reluctance of sovereign states to allow international monitoring and enforcement of human rights may allow governments – in times of crisis – to introduce laws that violate human rights. This issue is particularly relevant with reference to the freedom of speech/expression discussed in Chapter 7. Arguably, states have the power to influence mainstream media significantly (Bennett 1990; Hallin 1986; Herman and Chomsky 1988), and in countries where the media is controlled by the state this could even take the form of shutting down the internet or censoring its content, with China, Bahrain, Iran, Cuba, Burma and Tunisia among the worst offenders (*The Economist* 2013; Pearlman 2012). Human rights have become the language of criticism in the international system (Beitz 2009); they therefore often work against powerful political and economic interests, and the threat of repercussions for reporting on them can be significant (Internews 2012). This means that more often than not the victims of human rights violations are unable or unwilling to look to the media as a means to address their problems.

This brief introduction to existing research into the quantity and quality of media coverage of human rights issues, and the reasons accounting for that, provides an important context for the subsequent analysis offered in this book. It is, however, just a starting point. There is a general lack of work that has developed a broad understanding of the nexus between human rights and the media, partly because of disciplinary boundaries. There is a tendency for scholars from law or political science to pay little regard to the media as an actor, or factor, when it comes to examining questions relating to human rights. Likewise, criticisms from media and communication studies scholars are, as one might expect, very media-centric, with little in the way of detailed examination of the historical and institutional variables which have underpinned the construction of the international human rights system. There is thus ample scope and space to deepen our understanding of the nexus of the media and human rights by offering a more granular and grounded approach. This book achieves this by delving deeper into the nature and complex dimensions of the human rights issues themselves and identifying nuances and variations in the media's coverage across a wide spectrum of topics.

Shape of the book

The book is organized into three parts. Part I provides the overall context by introducing the concept of human rights, their historical evolution and the key contemporary debates and challenges. Part II consists of two chapters that develop the questions and the analytical approach (summarized in Table 0.1). These chapters also introduce the key themes and topics that are explored in subsequent chapters. Part III introduces a series of real-world examples that illustrate the policy and practice of human rights and the media. It is organized on the basis of specific human rights problems and issues and uses contemporary case studies (two in each chapter) to illustrate key characteristics of the human rights–media relationship. The intention is that every chapter can be read independently or in a different sequential pattern from the one followed in the book.

The first chapter sets out in a systematic way the range of understandings around human rights in order to provide a context for analysing the book's case studies. It looks at definitions, questions relating to universality, and the international regime for monitoring and enforcement. It also traces historical roots and the role of the UN and post-1945 legislation. Chapter 2 looks at the relationship between information, media and power. It begins the task of developing the analytical focus for the rest of the book by critically challenging understandings of the role of the media with respect to human rights and connecting this with the function of the media within state and society.

Completing the second part of the book, Chapter 3 develops a normative approach to the analysis of the media and human rights. It does this through an exploration of the roots and contemporary ideas around cosmopolitanism. It ends by providing an analytical framework for the rest of the book which rests on the notion that understandings of the media and human rights can be thought of as lying within two main dimensions: a continuum between 'stronger' and 'weaker' forms of cosmopolitanism; and a continuum between more 'optimistic' and 'pessimistic' views of the role of the media in constructing shared values on issues such as human rights.

The chapters in Part III cover topics that could be described as 'traditional' concerns of those studying the nexus between the media and human rights but also areas that are less usually linked, such as immigration. They also explore the different aspects of this nexus, beyond the usual focus on freedom of speech and awareness-raising, to explore the importance of context and intention, for example through news values and framing, and employing different techniques, such as case studies, content analysis, and investigations of human rights campaigning. Beginning with humanitarian intervention, Chapter 4 considers the quest to legitimize war and the role of public opinion and the media. It examines the problems in defining and agreeing when an intervention is humanitarian and the current focus on the Responsibility to Protect (R2P) doctrine. The media's role is explored through an examination of theories around the 'CNN effect' and 'compassion fatigue', illustrated in the case studies of Kosovo (1999) and Libya (2011).

Continuing the theme of humanitarian intervention, Chapter 5 focuses on genocide as the human rights violation that has been fundamental in developing practice around armed intervention. Genocide is prohibited by international law and is recognized as an international crime, but it still happens. This chapter considers the international human rights norms with regard to genocide and examines the media's coverage of such gross human rights violations. The two specific case studies explored here are Rwanda (1994) and Darfur (2003–present).

Chapter 6 looks at how the media deals with asylum, refugee and immigration issues as contemporary human rights concerns. It shows how these discussions reflect different cosmopolitan positions over global justice and the prioritization of different groups in societies. Of particular interest is the importance of the role of language in representation, and the way that the issue can be 'framed'. The first of the case studies demonstrates these issues of representation and framing through analysis of UK press coverage of immigration and asylum. The second adopts a different approach by exploring how an international organization (UNHCR) uses the media to spread its (cosmopolitan) message about refugees.

Chapter 7 examines freedom of expression as a human right, taking into consideration the international documents and provisions that establish it, before considering specific instances where it is limited and the arguments that are employed to support this. It shows how, despite optimism around new technologies, self-censorship and continued restrictions on media freedom are justified on the basis of other rights, such as freedom from discrimination, and how the state employs security or 'societal cohesion' arguments to limit freedom of expression. The two case studies analysed here are the Danish cartoons of Prophet Mohammed and the 'whistle-blowing' of Edward Snowden.

Chapter 8 is concerned with torture, a key aspect of human rights abuse that is particularly relevant to the 'war on terror'. There are many parallels with the earlier chapter on genocide because torture is prohibited by international law and recognized as an international crime. However, it continues to be employed by many states around the world. The chapter explores the international human rights norms with regard to torture and examines the media's coverage of such gross human rights violations. The two case studies focus on the use of torture at the Abu Ghraib prison and the practice of rendition.

General conclusions are drawn in the final chapter. The questions posed at the start of the book are revisited and key themes are discussed. Findings from each of the case studies in Part III are summarized and compared with respect to the issues identified in the first two parts of the book. The nexus between the media and human rights is revisited, as is the relationship between cosmopolitanism and the media (introduced in Chapter 2). The cosmopolitan 'promise' presented by the combination of new global media technologies and the forces of globalization is contrasted with the cosmopolitan 'deficit' identified on closer inspection of the actual performance of the media on key human rights issues.

Note

1 Historically, economic and social rights have been considered un-American, collectivist and 'alien in spirit and philosophy to the principles of a free economy' (Alston 1990: 383).

PART I

1

HUMAN RIGHTS

Key issues

Introduction

For those in the developed world, human rights violations and the resultant suffering are often things that happen to people far away and on a massive scale. Both Mother Teresa and Joseph Stalin, coming from two completely opposite moral positions, talked about the significance of scale in relation to suffering. The former said, 'If I look at the mass, I will never act. If I look at one, I will' (cited in Slovic 2007: 80). Stalin's statement is more notorious: 'One death is a tragedy. One million deaths is a statistic' (cited in Moeller 1999: 36).

There are myriad misunderstandings, myths and misconceptions when it comes to public discussions around human rights. Some of these are relatively unimportant. For example, when talking about the human right of freedom of expression, many over the years have been tempted to quote Voltaire: 'I disapprove of what you say, but I will defend to the death your right to say it.' However, the French philosopher did not even say these words. In surely one of the most widely misattributed quotations in history, the true source is Evelyn Beatrice Hall (1906), who attributed this attitude to Voltaire, not the actual words.

Other mistakes are more serious. The Human Rights Blog, run by the 1Cor (One Crown Office Row) barristers' chambers, lists some of the more egregious errors in human rights reporting in the UK.[1] These range from straightforward (and quite common) mistakes, such as confusing the EU with human rights law (Wagner 2013a), to more misleading 'facts' about the costs of human rights court cases (Wagner 2012), or stories about the creation of 'new' human rights that already exist (Wagner 2013b).

The rest of this chapter is designed to provide some background about the history and basis for human rights and introduce some of the key questions and debates, such as: are human rights national or international? What role is played by the UN? What are the 'problems' around cultural relativism, enforcement and monitoring?

Are human rights national or international?

The contemporary human rights regime demonstrates an important shift about arguments over human rights from the national to the international sphere. Before the Second World War human rights were not a subject of international relations. The exceptions were very few, such as the nineteenth-century efforts to end the slave trade and the twentieth-century work on eradicating slavery. These campaigns resulted in a number of international treaties on the abolition of slavery, such as the Treaty of Washington, 1862, and conferences on the subject in Brussels, 1867 and 1890, and Berlin, 1885. Another area of international cooperation was the development of laws regarding the conduct of war, such as the Declaration of Paris, 1856, the first and second Geneva Conventions, 1864 and 1906, and the Hague Conventions, 1899 and 1907. The International Committee of the Red Cross (ICRC) was created in 1864 and thereafter contributed to efforts to persuade Western governments to adopt treaties obligating them to correct injustices (such as stopping the slave trade from Africa and providing neutral medical assistance to the sick and wounded in war). After the First World War treaties and declarations were signed in Central and Eastern Europe in which individuals from minority groups were afforded certain rights of petition to international bodies in order to try to prevent discrimination by the national majority. However, the League of Nations – the first universal intergovernmental organization, created after the First World War, and predecessor of the UN – remained silent about human rights as a system of universal norms, and debates on this topic were largely excluded from inter-war international relations.

The present system of international human rights norms, as distinct from what had existed previously, emerged only in the 1940s. On an intellectual level, President Franklin D. Roosevelt's famous 'four freedoms' speech of 1942 provided an impetus. In it he explicitly linked the war effort with the freedoms of speech, of religion, from want, and from fear. These freedoms were later an essential component of the International Bill of Rights. But it was the reactions to the atrocities of the Second World War that marked the start of the current 'era of human rights', for they ended the view that it was up to individual states to determine how to treat their citizens. In the nineteenth and early twentieth centuries violations of the human rights of a country's own nationals were not considered matters of international concern. However, there were 56 million military and civilian deaths in the Second World War, including six million European Jews, Roma, homosexuals, disabled people and others who were considered a threat or 'unworthy of life' killed as part of a programme of deliberate extermination – the Holocaust. The war led to huge numbers of refugees in Europe, while Japan was seriously affected by the detonation of two atomic bombs over Hiroshima and Nagasaki – many died instantly and tens of thousands of initial survivors suffered later as a consequence of radiation exposure.

Arguably for the first time, the human impacts of state action or inaction – as a result of the war crimes committed in the war – became of central importance, and human rights became a central concern. The International Military Tribunal at Nuremberg (1945–6) prosecuted Nazis under the then novel charge of 'crimes against humanity' – German soldiers and officials were held liable for offences committed against individual citizens, not states, and individuals who were often fellow nationals, not foreigners. This is significant, and it was revolutionary because it made human rights an international issue, rather than the almost exclusively national concern they had been up to that point. Also, the idea that all individuals have fundamental rights in peace and war was furthered, notwithstanding some well-founded criticism of bias and 'victor's justice'.

Have we always had human rights?

In the words of Mother Teresa, 'Human rights are not a privilege conferred by government. They are every human being's entitlement by virtue of his humanity' (Teresa 1994). Although apparently benign, this is a deeply political statement. From Mother Teresa's perspective, human rights are the natural-born rights of every person, and they are equal rights because every human being has them equally and may claim them irrespective of who they are, what they do or where they live. As Hamelink (1994: 58) puts it, human rights provide a 'universally available set of standards for the dignity and integrity of all human beings'. They are, according to this definition, essential for everyone to enjoy a life of dignity; and, as such, violations of human rights deny a person's humanity.

According to this view, the ideas behind human rights have always been present throughout history in different societies and civilizations, but they have evolved and have been called various things at different times. Contemporary human rights concepts can be traced to the so-called 'Age of Enlightenment and Reason' of the seventeenth and eighteenth centuries, which provided a favourable socio-structural context. Political philosophers of the time developed the notion that citizens enjoy certain rights – mainly civil or political in nature – in relation to the state. John Locke is associated with the idea of natural rights – the rights of freedom and equality. However, the enjoyment of these rights was seen as fragile, which meant the society and the state were essential devices to guarantee them. The legitimacy of the government depended on its protection of natural rights through positive law and practice. These ideas were further developed by Jean-Jacques Rousseau, who put forward the idea of a 'social contract' whereby the individual surrendered some of his or her natural rights to the state machinery in return for personal safeguards and assistance in the protection of property.

Such theories gained purchase in the eighteenth century and eventually found their expression in two important documents: the French Declaration of the Rights of Man and of the Citizen (1789); and the American Bill of Rights (1791), which forms part of the current US Constitution. The French declaration proclaimed 17 rights as 'the natural, inalienable and sacred rights of man', but did not correct the pre-existing inferior legal status of women. The Bill of Rights was based on the idea of universal equality, but in practice created legal protection only for land-owning white men. Thus, the rights that these two documents guaranteed were far from 'universal', as they were limited on the grounds of gender, skin colour and/or wealth; nor were they comprehensive, as they addressed only civil and political issues. Still, because they asserted individual rights, the two documents can be seen as the precursors to many of today's human rights declarations.

The difficulties with this view emerge when we recognize that human rights are not given to man by some higher force but rather arise from human action. The problem with Mother Teresa's claim about entitlement is that 'human rights' are not 'innate' or 'natural' qualities of all human societies but instead represent a social practice 'founded on a particular conception of "being human", implemented by particular kinds of mechanisms' (Donnelly 2013b: 17).

'Nonsense upon stilts' was the famous response of Jeremy Bentham to the notion that there were such things as natural rights or natural laws that were absolute or inalienable (see, e.g., Schofield 2003). For Bentham, rights could exist only on the basis of proper legislative processes carried through by governments; they were not innate to humanity. It is important to note this, because a narrative which presents human rights as things that have always existed – simply waiting to be discovered – is open to question. According to the conservative thinker Edmund Burke (arguing against the French Revolution), rights are not universal; rather, societies must fight for them and win them before passing them on to future generations. This was why Burke felt that the freedoms enjoyed by Eng-lishmen did not flourish outside that country's borders: they were specific to England and related to its unique historical experience – from the Magna Carta in the thir-teenth century through to the so-called 'Glorious Revolution' in the seventeenth (Burke 2006 [1790]).

Human rights and the UN: a world government-in-waiting?

Modern differences over the concept of human rights have moved on since discussion over the innate nature of rights and the merits of the French Revolution. In one sense the system put in place in the twentieth century as a response to the events of the Second World War represents a fairly resounding defeat for the Burkean narrative around universality, at least at the rhetorical level. However, various aspects of the contemporary regime continue to provoke discussion and disagreement.

The first formal and authoritative expression of the twentieth-century human rights 'movement' was the UN Charter. Ever since this point the UN has remained the dominant international institution dedicated to elaborating international human rights standards. After a series of meetings, the UN Charter was adopted in San Francisco on 26 June 1948. From that moment onwards, all of the UN member states agreed to take certain measures to protect and promote human rights. However, the Charter does not directly address human rights. Rather, the provisions mentioning human rights tend to be promotional or programmatic in character as they refer to the purposes or goals of the UN or to the competences of its various organs. For example, the Charter states that the fundamental objectives of the UN are 'to save succeeding generations from the scourge of war' and 'to reaffirm faith in funda-mental human rights, in the dignity and worth of the human person and in the equal rights of men and women'. Article 1 outlines international cooperation in 'promoting and encouraging respect for human rights and for fundamental freedoms for all without distinction as to race, sex, language or religion' as one of the primary aims of the organization. As a treaty, the Charter is a legally binding document and all member states must fulfil their obligations under it to promote the observance of human rights and to cooperate with the UN to achieve this. However, the language of obligation is nowhere to be found, human rights are not specified, and no concrete mechanism to ensure member states' implementation of them is established.

Despite this, the UN Charter is the first treaty in world history to recognize universal human rights, and it can be seen as a philosophical, historical, moral and legal document (Carey *et al.* 2010). The human rights were vaguely endorsed, but they were to be pursued by traditional state diplomacy. All individuals had these rights and sover-eign states had to respect them, which was quite revolutionary. But neither the UN itself nor any other organization has ever been given clear supranational authority to enforce the respect of human rights. So, in a way, universal human rights were affirmed and state sovereignty over domestic social issues was reaffirmed by the UN Charter.

The formal codification of the contemporary human rights regime happened via the so-called International Bill of Human Rights, which is the collective name for the Universal Declaration of Human Rights (UDHR), adopted in 1948 by the UN General Assembly, and the two international human rights covenants – the International Covenant on Civil and Political Rights (ICCPR) and the Interna-tional Covenant on Economic, Social and Cultural Rights (ICESCR). As with all documents created by humans at particular points in history, they are imperfect, and affected by the historical, economic, political, cultural and social conditions of their times. Also, as with all international agreements drawn up by diplomats, politicians and experts from diverse backgrounds and cultures, they represent and reflect a series of complicated negotiations and compromises, all of which were embedded in (rather than resolved by) the legal and institutional structures that were built with the intention of putting the concept of human rights into practice.

Out of the three main human rights documents mentioned above, the UDHR is the most important. It is often referred to as the 'Magna Carta' of human rights instruments and makes the bold claim that it sets 'a common standard for achievement for all peoples and all nations'. Indeed, it is the first international document to state that all people have human rights and to specify exactly what those human rights are. As Nickel (2007: 9) puts it, the UDHR 'has been amazingly successful in establishing a fixed meaning for the idea of human rights'. But, for some, it 'generated a hyperinflation of rights that can only destroy the value of rights altogether' (Dun 2001: 2).

One problem arises from the broad scope and range of rights which were included in the document. It contains 30 principles that encompass a range of political and civil, as well as economic, social and cultural rights. Some of these rights are similar to those of earlier documents that refer to the 'rights of man', such as the US Bill of Rights and the French Declaration of the Rights of Man and of the Citizen. Others, particularly the economic, social and cultural rights, clearly depend upon delivery by the state (e.g. Article 26 – the right to education) and are contingent upon political membership/citizenship (e.g. Articles 20 and 21 – freedom of peaceful assembly and association and the right to take part in the government of a country) (Dun 2001: 4–6). This has prompted much discussion over the indivisibility of human rights: can there be a hierarchy; and, if so, which are the most important 'basic' or 'essential' rights?

The precise status of the human rights regime inaugurated by the UDHR is also ambiguous. The document set in motion the whole international human rights regime and established the pattern for the numerous human rights treaties that followed. Nonetheless, according to Eleanor Roosevelt – chair of the UN Human Rights Commission when the declaration was drafted – the UDHR is a statement of aspirations (cited in Forsythe 2012: 50). It is a recommendatory document, not a legally binding treaty. Despite this, the distinction between binding and recommendatory has blurred over the years, and the UDHR has acquired the status of a customary international law. The standard practice is for states to accept its norms and treat them as rules by which they should abide.

The actual international human rights regime that has existed since 1948 has been neither static nor universal. The system that was initiated with the 30 principles of the UDHR has not stopped developing, and the number of states that have signed up to the new treaties varies significantly depending on which categories of rights are involved. Perhaps the most important additions were the two subsequent basic treaties which attempted to address some of the issues left untouched or unresolved by the UDHR: the ICCPR and the ICESCR. These two covenants are the only universal treaties that include broad coverage of human rights topics. They develop in more detail the different categories of rights – civil and political; and economic, social and cultural – that figure in the Universal Declaration but include additional rights, too. By 2013 most UN states had become parties to the ICCPR – 167 parties, with 74 signatories pending ratification. In the case of the ICESCR, 160 countries were parties and a further seven had signed but not yet ratified the covenant. Unlike the UDHR, both covenants bind the parties in accordance with their terms subject to reservations that may be made when ratifying the document.

The range of personal, legal, civil, political, subsistence, economic, social and cultural rights has been expanded through single-issue treaties and declarations on genocide, refugees, political rights of women, racial discrimination, torture, children's rights, migrant workers, enforced disappearances and people with disabilities. Thus, there are currently eleven core UN human rights treaties:

- 1948 Convention on the Prevention and Punishment of the Crime of Genocide (entered into force 1951);
- 1951 Convention Relating to the Status of Refugees (entered into force 1954);
- 1966 International Covenant on Civil and Political Rights (entered into force 1976);

- 1966 International Covenant on Economic, Social and Cultural Rights (entered into force 1976);
- 1984 UN Convention against Torture and Other Cruel, Inhuman or Degrading Treatment or Punishment (entered into force 1987);
- 1979 Convention on the Elimination of All Forms of Discrimination against Women (entered into force 1981);
- 1965 International Convention on the Elimination of All Forms of Racial Discrimination (entered into force 1969);
- 1990 UN Convention on the Rights of the Child (entered into force 1990);
- 1990 UN Convention on the Protection of the Rights of All Migrant Workers and Members of Their Families (entered into force 2003);
- 2006 UN Convention for the Protection of All Persons from Enforced Disappearances (entered into force 2010); and
- 2006 UN Convention on the Rights of Persons with Disabilities (entered into force 2008).

Many aspects of this system and these agreements will be examined in greater detail in later chapters, but at this point it is useful to make an initial observation regarding the variation in the 'success' of these treaties (i.e. how many states sign up to, ratify and enforce their contents), which demonstrates how difficult it is to maintain the claim that human rights are 'innate' and 'universal'. The evidence shows that state interests and political issues repeatedly shape and influence both the scope and the implementation of human rights. Very few countries have signed up to the UN Convention on the Protection of the Rights of All Migrant Workers and Members of Their Families (1990), for example: only 47 out of 193 UN member states had ratified the Convention as of 2014. Signatories also comprise migrant 'sending' (source) rather than 'receiving' (host) countries, which is where the human rights issues for migrants occur. The ILO Conventions on Forced Labour have been much more successful in terms of signatories: the 1930 Forced Labour Convention and the 1957 Abolition of Forced Labour Convention had been ratified by 177 and 174 of the 185 ILO members, respectively, as of 2013. However, one country that has signed both documents is Qatar, a Middle East country that has come under severe criticism over its migration recruitment system, sometimes referred to as the Kafala system. Indeed, it has been claimed that it is difficult to distinguish the Kafala system from contemporary forms of slavery; elsewhere, such practices are seen as the serious criminal offence of human trafficking (Vlieger 2012).

The contemporary human rights regime: key debates

Universality and cultural diversity[2]

The view that people have rights simply because they are human suggests that human rights are intrinsic and cannot be either earned or lost during one's life. They are universal in that they take no account of race, sex or colour. The UN

Charter states that human rights are 'for all without distinction'. According to Article 2 of the UDHR, human rights 'belong to all humans regardless of race, colour, sex, language, religion, political or other opinion, national or social origin, property, birth or other status'. Since 'all human beings are born free and equal in rights and dignity' (Article 1), human rights treat all people as equal and acknowledge that all people deserve the same opportunities and treatment, while simultaneously their different cultures and traditions, political persuasion, sexuality, social origin, status and so forth should be respected.

In terms of content, human rights encompass fundamental principles of humanity. They are underpinned by core values such as fairness, respect, equality, dignity, autonomy, universality and participation that can be found in almost every culture and civilization, religion and philosophical tradition. Most societies and cultures have practised human rights throughout most of their history. However, despite the historical universality of values across time and cultures, no society, culture or civilization prior to the seventeenth century had a widely endorsed practice of equal and inalienable human rights.

Many rights are absolute – they can never be limited or restricted and no country can override them under any circumstances. This confirms that the ideas behind human rights transcend political and theological concepts. Such absolute rights are the right to life, freedom from slavery and freedom from torture. However, the majority of human rights are *not* absolute, which means they can be limited or restricted in certain circumstances. In such instances, certain specific limits may be placed upon them. This is clarified within the international conventions themselves. For example, the authors of hate speech who incite violence against an ethnic group may find their freedom of expression limited in order to ensure the safety of others.

Given the nature of human rights, their promotion and protection are not limited to national boundaries. The ideals that they illustrate apply all over the world. States are accountable for meeting the conditions which satisfy the requisite promotion, protection and respect of human rights. Thus, responsibility for protecting human rights rests not just with individual states but effectively overrides notions of state sovereignty. And while most states have found it desirable to give at least formal endorsement to the notion of universal human rights, expressed through the ratification and acceptance of the key international human rights documents, human rights remain a contested concept. Their alleged universal validity has been challenged by those who disagree that there can be only one legitimate version of the human rights doctrine, with views ranging from those suggesting that human rights should be thought of not so much as a single, unified doctrine but as a number of significantly different moral and cultural outlooks to those that completely dismiss the very idea of universality.

Cultural relativism asserts that human values are not universal and vary according to different cultural perspectives. As a result, human rights can be interpreted differently within various cultural, ethnic and religious traditions, which makes them culturally relative rather than universal. Cultural relativism is based on the idea that there are no objective standards by which others can be judged. It often implies that traditional culture is sufficient to protect human dignity and therefore universal human rights are unnecessary. They are seen as potentially intrusive and disruptive to the traditional protection of human life, liberty and security, and even as a threat to the very identity of a culture. These claims have been voiced by countries such as China, Cuba, Syria, Iran, Vietnam, Pakistan, Malaysia, Singapore, Yemen and Indonesia. They see human rights, as currently defined, as based on Western morality and therefore feel they should not be imposed as norms on non-Western societies in disregard of those societies' historical and economic development and their cultural differences and perceptions of what is right and wrong. The very imposition of one standard on another culture is seen as unjust and imperialist (see, e.g., Zakaria 1994; Mutua 2001, 2002).

Those who defend universal human rights suggest that the promotion and protection of human rights perceived as culturally relative would be left to state discretion, rather than subject to an international legal imperative, which might well lead to dictators using them to justify an 'anything-goes' approach – 'an excuse that can be used to cover a multitude of sins', in the words of the former president of Sri Lanka, Chandrika Kumaratunga (cited in Franck 2001: 197). For universalists, traditional culture is not a substitute but rather a cultural context in which human rights are established, integrated, protected and promoted. This is based on the idea that universal human rights do not impose one cultural standard but rather a single legal standard of minimum protection necessary for human dignity. They are not representative of, or oriented towards, one culture to the exclusion of others. Rather, they are sufficiently flexible to respect and protect cultural diversity and integrity. This flexibility is achieved through the establishment of minimum standards and the incorporation of cultural rights into the Universal Declaration and then the ICESCR. Human rights are not deeply rooted in Western culture; rather, they are a product of developments, such as universal education, industrialization, urbanization, the rise of the middle classes, advances in transportation and communications, and the spread of new information technology, all of which first took place in the Western world. But these processes and trends have since occurred everywhere, albeit at different speeds, and they are the key factors that have driven and generated the move to global human rights.

A way of avoiding the extremes of universality and cultural relativism has been Donnelly's (2007, 2013a, 2013b) notion of 'relative universality'. He advocates 'universal rights, not identical practices': 'Human rights are (relatively) universal at the level of the *concept* ... Particular rights concepts, however, have multiple defensible *conceptions*. Any particular conception, in turn, will have many defensible *implementations*' (Donnelly 2007: 298; emphasis in original). Here, Donnelly is effectively proposing a three-level approach to universality, where concepts set a range of plausible variations among conceptions, which in turn restrict the range of practices that can plausibly be considered implementations of a particular concept and conception.

Importantly, the key international documents that engaged with the contested universal validity of human rights have stood by the universality. The World Conference on Human Rights in Vienna, 1993, is particularly significant in this respect as it became the forum that agreed the Vienna Declaration and Programme of Action reaffirming universal human rights. While the basic differences were not resolved, the final declaration reiterated 'universal respect for and observance of human rights and fundamental freedoms for all … The universal nature of these rights and freedoms is beyond question.' But it also asserted:

> While the significance of national and regional particularities and various historical, cultural and religious backgrounds must be borne in mind, it is the duty of states, regardless of their political, economic and cultural systems, to promote and protect all human rights and fundamental freedoms.

The defence of universal human rights is weakened by past and present violations committed by countries that have long championed this universal validity. Most US states, for example, including Texas, Oklahoma, Virginia and Florida, still practise the death penalty, despite the universally proclaimed right to life and the United States' leadership in the cause of universal human rights. The arguments used to defend such violations are very similar to those put forward by cultural relativists: for instance, that states have a sovereign right to do what they want within their own borders and should not be judged by international human rights standards. Mutua (2001) takes this point further by talking about a lack of Western self-examination and self-criticism. He suggests that Western institutions vigorously expose the horrors committed in 'savage' societies, but at the same time are unwilling or unable to recognize their own wrongdoing. And while there are clear inconsistencies and hypocrisy in the concept of human rights and its application, using this as an excuse for doing nothing about human rights violations, regardless of where they take place, is far from convincing.

Responsibility for upholding human rights

The fact that all people have human rights does not mean that these rights are always respected. Violations of at least some human rights occur in all states, although which rights are violated differs from country to country, and some states are far more culpable than others in refusing to implement – or grossly and systematically violating – most internationally recognized human rights.

This is where one of the key contradictions in the international human rights regime lies. Internationally recognized human rights are implemented nationally, leaving the enforcement almost entirely to sovereign states (the exceptions are genocide, crimes against humanity, some war crimes and torture). The UN Charter and the International Bill of Human Rights require that all states must recognize, establish, protect and enforce human rights at global, regional, national and local levels. Thus, they affirm universal human rights, but they also reaffirm state sovereignty over domestic social issues.

The state is indeed a guarantor and protector of human rights according to international law, and the principle of non-interference in the internal affairs of another state is central to the UN Charter. Article 2(7) stipulates: 'Nothing contained in the present Charter shall authorize the United Nations to intervene in matters which are essentially within the domestic jurisdiction of any state or shall require the Members to submit such matters to settlement under the present Charter.' An allowance for a global rule of law to deal with the human rights violations of others would by default restrict the freedom of every individual country and highlight any potential human rights issues and problems within its borders. A strong international legal regime for human rights would inevitably restrict national decisions. In reality, states refuse to allow much international enforcement, or even monitoring, of their performance in fulfilling their human rights obligations, and consequently the domestic practice often falls short of the ideal. There is a significant disjunction between promise and reality in the realm of human rights – between the rights proclaimed by international human rights instruments and the reality of violations of those rights around the world. And, because of the weaknesses of the enforcement and protection of human rights, the rights themselves are sometimes dismissed as unrealistic or utopian (Carey *et al.* 2010).

Nevertheless, human rights issues are raised within the UN system and the UN Charter recognizes that peace and stability among nations are related to the recognition of and respect for human rights. In 1992 the UN Security Council declared that the international community 'no longer can allow advancement of fundamental rights to stop at national borders' (Pease and Forsythe 1993: 296), effectively returning to and reaffirming the starting principles of the international human rights regime in the aftermath of the Second World War. Thus, although most political decisions are left in the hands of national leaders, human rights do set minimum standards that impose significant constraints on legislation, policy-making and official behaviour.

International monitoring and enforcement of human rights

The institutionalized procedures to protect and effectively enforce human rights demonstrate the gap between the promotion of human rights, on one hand, and their protection, on the other. Global enforcement of human rights in the form of international court judgements and other forms of direct international responsibility for the application of human rights happens rarely. Not the International Court of Justice, nor any other international court, nor the Security Council generally assumes direct responsibility in making sure that universal human rights norms prevail. This is especially the case outside Europe. However, an argument has been made that since the end of the Cold War the existing multilateral procedures are being used more vigorously and to greater effect (see Malone 2004).

The norms for the global human rights regime are provided by the Universal Declaration and the two international covenants, which altogether entail weak supervisory and enforcement mechanisms. The main organs of this regime are the Security Council, the UN Human Rights Council (which replaced the UN Commission on Human Rights in 2006) and the Human Rights Committee.

Initially the Commission on Human Rights was perceived to be the most important body, but since the end of the Cold War the significance of the Security Council has increased because, if it establishes a connection between human rights and international peace and security, it becomes the most important and authoritative UN forum for human rights. Until 2005, the Commission was the centre for traditional, routine human rights diplomacy. For instance, the International Bill of Human Rights was drafted there. The Commission consisted of representatives of states, and consequently it initially 'avoided specific enquiries about specific rights in specific countries', as Forsythe (2012: 92) puts it. From the end of the 1960s, the Commission engaged in more protection activities, pressuring states into complying with internationally recognized human rights through reviews of state behaviour on rights and in response to private petitions. Overall, however, no further action ever followed its proceedings and the whole process tended to be time-consuming and not very transparent (Carey *et al.* 2010). It was disappointment with this state of affairs that led to the Commission being replaced by the Human Rights Council. The Commission was seen as having become too 'politicized' and a place where some of the worst violators of human rights in the world were elected to serve while representatives of the US, for example, were not (Alston 2006).

The biggest innovation introduced with the creation of the Human Rights Council was the Universal Periodic Review (UPR). Under this procedure, every UN member state is subjected to a review of its fulfilment of its human rights obligations every four years. By 2012 all UN member states had been reviewed under the UPR mechanism. The early assessments of the first review cycle suggested that the 'UPR is a compromise, born out of the need to have a meaningful instrument to promote universal human rights norms while respecting the reality of a consensus-based decision-making process' (Mcmahon 2012: 3). There are clear benefits and strengths to the new approach, including the very high level of state participation, heightened communication and dialogue between governments and non-state actors, and the baseline set of evaluations created. However, key weaknesses include the actual level of commitment demonstrated by individual states and the lack of any willingness to see the UPR develop into a robust mechanism.

The Human Rights Committee was established by the ICCPR to review and comment on obligatory state reports and to process individual petitions alleging violations of human rights under the covenant. It consists of 18 independent experts, nominated and elected by states that are party to the covenant. However, these individuals act in a personal capacity, not on behalf of their respective states. The Committee was divided over its proper role during the Cold War. According to the minimalist view, its function was simply to facilitate dialogue among sovereign states. According to the maximalist view, it was to pronounce on whether a state had reported correctly and whether that state was in compliance with its legal obligations. Since the end of the Cold War, the Committee has followed the latter path, introducing new procedures towards more effective examination of state reports and follow-up measures. Since 2001, after examining a state report, the Committee can identify specific concerns as priorities and request a response from the state in question. If a state does not submit a report, the Committee may examine a report based on information obtained from other sources. Still, the Committee's power remains limited, as it cannot proceed beyond public criticism of a state because it possesses no mechanism through which to enforce its views legally. This is a clear example of the previously identified contradiction in the international human rights regime – the protection of so-called universal human rights depends upon compliance at the national level. An argument can be made, however, that most (although not all) governments are generally sensitive to public exposure of their human rights performance and even in the absence of a genuine will to fulfil their obligations under the covenant they may do so 'out of respect for the Committee' and to enhance their international image (Levin 2012).

The Security Council has responsibility for the maintenance of international peace and security under the provisions of the UN Charter. On security issues, the Council can take legally binding decisions under Chapter VII. On economic, social, cultural and humanitarian issues, it can make recommendations under Chapter VI. Human rights issues could be seen as both different from security and linked to it, since threats to peace could arise from violations of human rights. Hence, human rights issues have been raised before the Council. Even during the Cold War it dealt with such issues as racism giving rise to violence (South Africa), human rights abuses in armed conflicts, armed intervention across national boundaries, and armed supervision of elections. After the end of the Cold War, the Security Council has expanded the notion of international peace and security, and now the dividing line between human rights issues and security issues is blurred. Overall, the Security Council has more potential for systematic action on human rights issues, although the international community has remained indecisive and largely inactive when called upon to guarantee human security.

At the regional level there are five main human rights regimes: the European, Inter-American, African, Asian and Middle Eastern regimes. Regional standards and organizations are stronger in Europe, the Americas and Africa, and weaker in the Middle East and Asia. The European regime, in particular, is seen as very strong as a result of its decision-making procedures. The Convention for the Protection of Human Rights and Fundamental Freedoms, commonly known as the European Convention on Human Rights (ECHR), was adopted under the auspices of the Council of Europe (CoE) in 1950 to protect human rights and fundamental freedoms. All CoE member states are party to the Convention and new members are expected to ratify it at the earliest opportunity. The ECHR established the European Court of Human Rights. Its significance stems from the fact that any individual who feels his or her rights under the Convention have been violated by a state party can bring a case before the Court. (State parties may bring cases against other state parties before the Court, but this power is rarely used.) It is also noteworthy that the judgements of the Court are legally binding, and it has the power to award damages. As Fabbrini (2007: 298) points out,

> The establishment of a Court to protect individuals from human rights viola-
> tions is an extremely innovative feature for an international convention on

human rights, as it gives the individual an active role on the international arena … The European Convention is still the only international human rights agreement providing such a high degree of individual protection.

Conclusions

Ideas about human rights have appeared and reappeared throughout history, but the formal system that currently exists is related to a very specific set of circumstances which existed after the end of the Second World War. The concepts that had existed previously were formed in the context of the nation-state and thus did not have international agreement or recognition. These earlier versions also tended to exclude women, the poor and other supposedly 'inferior' groups. The current system is by far the most universal and comprehensive of all attempts to codify human rights. However, it is full of compromises, definitional ambiguities and weaknesses, particularly when it comes to implementation and enforcement.

As mentioned in the Introduction and at the start of this chapter, the media has often been accused of inaccuracy, misunderstandings and systemic problems when it comes to reporting human rights. The next two chapters explore the role of the media and provide the conceptual framework upon which the analysis presented in the rest of the book is based. Chapter 2 aims to provide an essential understanding of the way that the media operates within its institutional, organizational and societal context. Chapter 3 introduces a normative dimension to the debate by linking both the ideas about human rights and the role of the media to the notion of cosmopolitanism.

Questions

- What are the key differences between the 'rights of man' declared during the French Revolution and the human rights system of today?
- Have human rights always existed?
- Is the UN system the most effective means of protecting human rights?
- Can the universality of human rights be maintained in light of criticisms from cultural relativism?

Notes

1 http://ukhumanrightsblog.com/category/blog-posts/poor-reporting/.
2 As one of the key debates in the field of human rights, this topic has been studied extensively. See, for example, Bell 1996; Donnelly 2007, 2013b; Goodhart 2003; Mutua 2002; O'Sullivan 2000; Kim Dae 1994; Zakaria 1994.

Further reading

Donnelly, J. 2013. *International Human Rights: Dilemmas in World Politics*, 4th edn. Boulder, CO: Westview Press.

Forsythe, D. P. 2012. *Human Rights in International Relations*, 3rd edn. Cambridge: Cambridge University Press.

Ignatieff, M. (ed.). 2001. *Human Rights as Politics and Idolatry*. Princeton: Princeton University Press.

Lauren, P. G. 1998. *The Evolution of International Human Rights: Visions Seen*. Philadelphia: University of Pennsylvania Press.

Mutua, M. 2001. 'Savages, victims, and saviours: the metaphor of human rights', *Harvard International Law Journal* 42(1): 201–45.

Mutua, M. 2002. *Human Rights: A Political and Cultural Discourse*. Philadelphia: University of Pennsylvania Press.

Osiatyński, W. 2009. *Human Rights and Their Limits*. Cambridge: Cambridge University Press.

Shue, H. 1996. *Basic Rights: Subsistence, Affluence and US Foreign Policy*, 2nd edn. Princeton, NJ: Princeton University Press.

Useful websites

www.un.org (UN)
www.un.org/en/sc (UN Security Council)
www.un.org/en/documents/udhr/index.shtml (UDHR)
www.ohchr.org/en/hrbodies/hrc (Human Rights Council)
www.icrc.org (International Committee of the Red Cross)
http://hub.coe.int (Council of Europe)
www.iidh.org/home.html (International Institute of Human Rights)
www.echr.coe.int (European Court of Human Rights)

PART II

2

INFORMATION, MEDIA AND POWER

Introduction

There is a problem in the way that communication and the role of the media are discussed, related to what Michael Reddy has described as the 'conduit metaphor' (Reddy 1994). This is the notion that information can be passed from one person to another in a straightforward way – as a message, via media, from sender to receiver. This idea became foundational to the positivist approach to communication that was popularized in the information sciences of the 1940s and 1950s, when knowledge and information were 'understood as intentional, self-evident, and quantitative entities' (Day 2000: 811). When it comes to thinking about how the contemporary media works, one might imagine that most people would dismiss this as a simplistic and outdated model of communication. However, there is evidence that the conduit metaphor does structure popular understandings about the role of the media, for example in relation to international terrorism (Harrison *et al.* 2008).

Since Harold Lasswell's (1948) attempt to model the role of the mass media in society, a range of research programmes have developed. Among other things, these have explored how information is mediated and the ways in which this mediation connects with power and politics (Hodkinson 2011). In the twenty-first century – the era of the internet and the supposed 'age of transparency' – what does coverage of human rights say about the relationship between information, media and power? For some, there is an uncomplicated relationship between greater transparency and an opportunity for human rights to flourish. The extraordinary rise to prominence of WikiLeaks, founded in 2006 and set up to allow whistle-blowers to disseminate information and make it available to a global audience, has led to many claims: that we are witnessing a transformation in journalism; that this will challenge 'dominant articulations of power' and usher in 'a new generation of social movement and online activism' (Brevini *et al.* 2013: 4). While this sounds rather like the language of a 'paradigm shift', the way in which the story actually played out was more like 'business as usual' for the information–power relationship.

The WikiLeaks project was driven, initially at least, by the philosophy of Julian Assange, who made a very simplistic link between information and power, reminiscent of the conduit metaphor. He completely overlooked the importance of mediation in communication practices in the public sphere. The basic argument was that authoritarian regimes need to suppress freedom of expression to maintain their power, so the free movement of information would potentially threaten, and even ultimately destroy, the very basis of that power. However, as we now know, WikiLeaks (and Edward Snowden several years later) ended up being completely dependent on older forms of media. This was not just to spread the information it had obtained, but to make sense of it, to frame it, and to pick out those pieces that would grab the public's attention (Beckett and Ball 2012).

The lesson here is that if we wish to explain the meaning and significance of human rights in the media we first have to develop a clear understanding of how ideas about media–state relations and concepts such as 'news values', 'agenda-setting' and 'framing' impact on the way that human rights issues are influenced, transmitted and transformed by the media.

Human rights and newsworthiness

A significant set of challenges for the reporting of human rights issues is linked to the very nature of news media and their driving principles. This explains why it is not always easy to fit breaking news into a human rights format and why, as Heinze and Freedman (2010: 491) argue, 'Situations of egregious abuse are often overshadowed by those which receive attention for reasons extraneous to any specific concern for human rights.' In the current competitive media environment, 'selling' human rights stories that are not headline news but rather relate to ongoing problems – such as poor health services, lack of water or inadequate education – could be a challenge (Internews 2012). Similarly, human rights news is usually about their violation rather than any respect for them (McPherson 2012). Pressures to attract reader/viewer interest and to respond to the most topical and controversial issues are powerful considerations. Today's media has a clear preference for stories that are relatively simple, graphically compelling and easily photographable. In that sense, human rights reporting is affected by the same values and factors that influence the coverage of any international news story, and it is also closely linked to the 'societal values and expectations of the way the world operates' (Ovsiovitch 1993: 685).

News selection is driven by what is perceived to be newsworthy. Galtung and Ruge's (1965) seminal study, while later revisited and expanded upon (Allern 2002; Golding and Elliot 1979; Harcup and O'Neill 2001), still provides the 'most influential explanation' (McQuail 1994: 270) of news values. They help to explain why some phenomena are identified as worthy of coverage and why some of these are later selected to become news. The media is likely to cover conflicts, crises, natural disasters (particularly if the scale of destruction and human loss is very high or a local/national angle is evident), instances of torture, genocide and so on as they all meet the criteria of being extreme and dramatic. Such events may also be novel, timely, unexpected, relevant to the audience, culturally proximate, and involve elite nations or elite people among others. Finally, as McPherson (2012: 96) points out, if newsworthiness is established, the more a particular piece of information is also 'in line with a newspaper's journalistic, economic, and political aims relative to other bits of information, the more likely it is to be published'.

However, not all human rights stories fit these criteria, and this leads to what Schimmel (2009) labels 'human rights repetition compulsion'. Certain human rights abuses receive extensive media coverage at the expense of other human rights stories that remain largely undocumented and unexplored. While Guantanamo Bay has attracted significant media attention, the spotlight has never consistently stayed on Darfur or the Democratic Republic of the Congo. While China's hosting of the 2008 Olympic Games became a worldwide media story, the ongoing systemic violations of human rights within that country both before and after the Games have largely failed to make it on to the news agenda. The coverage of humanitarian crises in general is uneven, with some regions, such as Africa, covered significantly less than others. Hawkins (2008) introduces the term 'stealth conflicts' and provides evidence of decreasing coverage of ongoing major conflicts in Angola, Congo, Ethiopia, Eritrea and Sierra Leone at a time when the conflict in Kosovo was receiving ever more coverage in the run-up to the 1999 NATO intervention there (Hawkins 2004). A subsequent study undertaken in 2009 similarly found that 'most of the world's conflicts take place largely unreported by the media and the deadliest conflicts are among those ignored' (Hawkins 2011: 55). Galtung and Ruge (1965) themselves acknowledged the limitations of the prevailing news factors and suggested that journalists should include more background and context in their reports, focus more on long-term issues and less on 'events', pay more attention to complex and ambiguous issues and give more coverage to non-elite people and nations. These general shortcomings of media reporting clearly apply to human rights reporting as well.

Gaining access to countries or to specific locations within them where human rights violations occur also contributes to the variance in media attention. Some of the countries that are among the worst human rights violators – such as Sudan, Congo, Burma, Sri Lanka and North Korea – are not fully open to journalists and are characterized by repressive conditions with high levels of political terror. This often makes the conditions of reporting from them, even if access is allowed, too dangerous and unstable. As a rule, human rights violators do not want their activities reported, foreign journalists are generally not well received and the fear of retribution makes it very difficult to find credible and reliable sources. Consequently, as Schimmel (2009: 443) points out, 'there is an enormous gap between the knowledge that the general public can glean from the media about human rights abuses taking place around the world, and the actual gravity and extent of these human rights abuses'.

The decline in the number of foreign correspondents, the use of local reporters (stringers) and 'parachute journalism' are all realities of human rights reporting that arguably limit the information that is being reported to the public. Major stories might still receive considerable attention, but day-to-day issues, such as chronic human rights violations, can go unreported (Caliendo *et al.* 1999; Sandvig 1988).

Media–state relations and human rights

The media's role in relation to human rights reporting follows from its presumed roles in a democratic society: to inform and educate about the issues of the day; and to provide a platform for public political discourse, facilitating the formation of public opinion and feeding that opinion back to the public (Curran 2005; McNair 2011; Negrine and Stanyer 2007). The latter is commonly referred to as the 'public sphere' (Habermas 1989). The media also has an important duty to act as a 'watchdog', a check on the power of the state, to report government misconduct and expose abuses of public authority. In addition to these roles, the media in most advanced democracies could be expected to 'act for inclusive discussions', 'mobilise citizens' interest, engagement and participation in public discussions' and 'foster public discussions characterised by rationality, impartiality, intellectual honesty and equality' (Strömbäck 2005: 341).

The extent to which contemporary media organizations deliver on these functions has been contested, with criticisms concentrating on their agendas, content and style. Herman and Chomsky (1988), for example, have argued consistently that instead of democratic scrutiny and accountability of the political elite, the media is managed and manipulated by the state in order to 'manufacture consent' for policy among the population. Their propaganda model suggests that the 'media operate on the basis of a set of ideological premises, depend heavily and uncritically on elite information sources and participate in propaganda campaigns helpful to elite interests' (Herman 2003). The information must pass through five filters – ownership, sources, advertising, ideology and flak – that individually and often in combination influence media choices and ensure that only news that is fit to print gets through.

Another criticism of the media's role in democracy stems from the argument that competitive pressures on the media and the consequent commercialization have driven the standards of journalism down and thus undermined democracy. The views here range from more sanguine accounts about what we can expect of the media (Graber 2003b) to rather critical assessments that discuss 'dumbing down' (Franklin 1997), 'infotainment' or 'tabloidisation' (McNair 2009), 'simplifying of a subject towards the lowest common denominator' (Temple 2006: 259) and 'news as spectacle' (Louw 2010). Anderson (2007a: 67) is particularly pessimistic in his assessment of the future of journalism, arguing that 'it is increasingly unlikely that much of the future news provision in the UK will meet the informational needs of a democracy'.

Finally, in terms of content, there has been considerable scholarly and public criticism of the media's increasing reliance on public relations material and news agency stories, and the simultaneous decline in fact-checking as a result of newsroom pressure. Arguably, this has had serious implications for journalistic independence and has led to a 'compromised fourth estate' (Lewis *et al.* 2008a, 2008b). The chapters in Part III of this book touch upon these debates when assessing the media's performance in relation to the specific human rights issues examined.

Earlier studies about the role of human rights reporting have highlighted its significance in terms of education, protection of rights and the development of foreign policy (Berry and McChesney 1988; Reisman 1984; UNCHR 1989). It has been argued that the media can influence public opinion to such an extent that the public in turn might motivate legislators and other policy-makers to consider human rights when developing foreign policy. This line of reasoning is particularly well developed in relation to the media's coverage of war and conflict and the presumed effects this reporting has had on foreign policy formulation and decisions to carry out humanitarian interventions (Balabanova 2007; Gilboa 2005; Robinson 2002). And, while parts of Ovsiovitch's (1993: 685) claim that 'News coverage of human rights shapes public opinion, influences foreign policy development, and serves as an informal means of documenting abuse' may need further research and empirical support, the importance of the media's coverage of human rights is widely accepted.

The centrality of a free and open media for the promotion and protection of human rights is recognized internationally through provisions in two key human rights documents. Article 19 of the UDHR explicitly states that 'Everyone has the right to freedom of opinion and expression', a right that is reiterated by Article 19 (2) of the ICCPR. This is closely linked to the understanding that the media can disseminate human rights information, clarify human rights abuses, mobilize human rights NGOs, strengthen popular participation in civil society, promote tolerance, and shine a light on government activity (Apodaca 2007; Hammarberg 2011; McPherson 2012; Metzl 1996; Pruce 2012).

Raising awareness, restraining the state?

Apodaca's (2007) study of the effect of press freedom on the achievement of human rights reveals that an increase in press censorship is associated with an increase in human rights abuses. A free and open media is seen to act as a constraint on a state by exposing abuses of public authority, thus fulfilling the expectation of it as a watchdog or a fourth estate preventing abuses by those in positions of power by monitoring how they exercise that power. For example, McPherson's (2010) study of human rights reporting in Mexico highlights how journalists work with the national and state human rights commissions[1] by publishing their recommendations for redressing human rights violations issued to infringing institutions and thus hold the state to account through the generation of public moral pressure. The media can also provide news, information, political opinion, propaganda and ideological slants from both sides of a conflict as well as international opinions:

> The ability of the press to serve as an avenue for free expression, allowing dissenting opinions to be heard, providing alternative information, and coordinating independent explanations and analysis … benefits human rights.
> *(Apodaca 2007: 156)*

Arguably, if human rights are to be respected, journalists, policy-makers and the general public all need to be knowledgeable about them in the first place. Hence the media has a vital role to play in a democratic society, as reasoned and rational choices on the important issues facing that society can be made only with access to accurate information. As Anderson (2007b: 43) argues, 'high-quality, independent news journalism which provides accurate and thoughtful information and analysis about current events is crucial to the creation of an enlightened citizenry that is able to participate meaningfully in society and politics'. Considering that people do not acquire much of their political knowledge from personal experience – or, as Walter Lippmann (1922: 18) noted, 'the world that [people] have to deal with politically is out of reach, out of sight, out of mind' – the media becomes a key source of information and contact with the political environment. This opens the possibility for the media to 'wield significant influence over citizens' perceptions, opinions and behaviors' (Entman *et al.* 2009: 179).

However, as discussed earlier, although the media is now providing more information than ever before about human rights, there are still some significant gaps. For instance, the International Federation of Journalists (1999: 3) concluded that in the case of Africa:

> The African Charter needs to be more widely known and discussed and needs to be made meaningful to citizens. People need to know what this home grown Charter says, how it can protect them and how they can assert their rights through the African Commission on Human and People's Rights.

Setting the agenda, framing the debate?

The media can create greater awareness of human rights and shine the spotlight on any violations that are taking place. This information can be empowering and the resultant human rights knowledge can be deployed to the advantage of citizens in relation to their state. As a journalist interviewed as part of the human rights reporting in Mexico project claimed, 'If people know their rights, they can organize to defend them or even just to demand that they be respected' (quoted in McPherson 2012: 110). Internews (2012: 5) highlights a similar point:

> Both professional journalists and citizen reporters and human rights activists who do 'advocacy journalism' are in a unique position to shed light on human rights violations. Their reporting can put pressure on governments and international organizations to take action. It can also help inform the public about their rights and how to access remedies for violations of these rights.

This particular role of the media relates to its presumed ability to set the agenda for public discussion. As a concept, agenda-setting refers to how the media, by focusing on certain issues rather than others, directs people to think only about these issues (Lang and Lang 1966; McCombs and Shaw 1972). The more coverage an issue receives, the more the public will perceive it to be important. As Cohen (1963: 13) remarked, the press 'may not be successful much of the time in telling people what to think, but it is stunningly successful in telling its readers what to think about'. Some argue that this is 'an inadvertent by-product of the necessity to focus' rather than the result of pre-planned activities by journalists (McCombs 2004: 19). The limited amount of space and time different media have at their disposal and the ensuing need to edit guided by agreed-upon news values lead to public attention being directed to a few issues and topics as the most important of the day. Following this line of reasoning, if no information about human rights violations is available, it is unlikely that people will see such issues as important; and if human rights issues are not important to the public, then political elites are unlikely to devote much time to them either (Caliendo *et al.* 1999). Some earlier studies have found that the increased media coverage of human rights issues is 'at least partially responsible for the increased awareness of, and support for, human rights found in the US public' (Pritchard 1991: 138).

The idea that issues emphasized by the media become the issues that the public thinks are important focuses only on the amount of media coverage an issue receives. While media attention is obviously essential, the way in which the media discusses an issue is equally, if not more, significant. This is where the concept of agenda-setting, particularly its 'second-level' interpretation, comes very close to the notion of framing. While there is a considerable variety of definitions of news frames in both theoretical and empirical contributions, frames are generally perceived as devices for seeing the world in a particular way and making sense of its complicated nature. They 'organize everyday reality' (Tuchman 1978: 193), 'provide meaning to an unfolding strip of events' (Gamson and Modigliani 1987: 143) and promote 'particular definitions and interpretations of political issues' (Shah *et al.* 2002). Gitlin (1980: 7) defines them as 'persistent patterns of cognition, interpretation, and presentation, of selection, emphasis and exclusion by which symbol handlers routinely organize discourse'. De Vreese (2005: 53) builds on this by arguing that 'frames are parts of political arguments, journalistic norms, and social movements' discourse. They are alternative ways of defining issues, endogenous to the political and social world.' By framing an issue in a certain way, the media organizes and structures its presentation of that issue. In this process it both includes and excludes ideas and arguments and thus effectively produces a coherent construction of the issue (Pan and Kosicki 1993). By emphasizing some elements of a topic at the expense of others, frames also provide a way to understand an event or issue. Thus, frames 'define problems', 'diagnose causes', 'make moral judgments' and 'suggest remedies' (Entman 1993). In the words of Entman (2004: 5) framing is 'selecting and highlighting some facets of events or issues, and making connections among them so as to promote a particular interpretation, evaluation, and/or solution'. If we are talking about a problem, the way in which we frame that problem points us towards potential solutions and limits alternative courses of action. Repeated exposure to a particular frame over a period of time is likely to increase the probability of particular responses in the future at the expense of potentially relevant alternatives.

In general, consistent, coherent and oft-repeated frames, tailored to specific audiences, are seen as the most successful (Chong 2012). This understanding of the concept suggests that framing in news production is inevitable because journalists have to adapt stories into limited space or time and present them in ways that can help the audience categorize, label, interpret and evaluate information. Overall, both agenda-setting and framing allude to the fact that the media decides what to cover and which issues or aspects of a story to highlight. By making these decisions, it has power over what we know and do not know about human rights. These selective processes affect how the public view different issues (Brewer and Gross 2005; Lecheler and de Vreese 2010). In the words of Chong (2012: 124), 'framing strategies attempt to "mediate atrocity" by making us aware of, sympathetic to, and actively engaged in the daily, and often unseen, suffering of others'. Pasackow (cited in Borer 2012b: 21–22) highlights the significance of media choices by arguing that:

> The language employed by the media is far from neutral and powerless; on the contrary, biases and stereotypes, omissions and emphases, syntax and diction build a frame in which post-disaster narratives are presented. More than simply reporting, media outlets have the power to indirectly determine emergency responses and disaster priorities.

Media and the politics of information

Once the news media places human rights abuses on the front page or makes them a lead story in a newscast, it engages in so-called 'information politics' (Cole 2010; Ron *et al.* 2005). On the one hand, negative press coverage has the potential to embarrass or shame countries into either changing their practices or – the more pessimistic scenario – concealing them more effectively. A state that violates established human rights norms may attract the disapproval of other states or international organizations as well as that of international and national audiences. Being labelled an abusive regime can have negative effects on legitimacy and reputation (Apodaca 2007; Pruce 2012). Apodaca (2007) offers the example of the revelation of the involvement of European countries in the CIA's extraordinary rendition activities. After this story was published (first in the *Washington Post*), special investigations were launched by the Council of Europe and the European Parliament in 2005, citizen protests were organized in the named countries, politicians backtracked and there was global outrage. Advances in communication, including satellite and cable TV, the internet and social media, were instrumental here.

Arguably, in the current context of available and accessible 24/7 information, it is extremely difficult, if not impossible, to fully control the dissemination of knowledge, thus forcing a degree of transparency on state actions. In the case of human rights violations, even if full secrecy is maintained initially, the information almost always becomes public later. McCorquodale and Fairbrother (1999: 759) advance this view by stating that 'the globalised communication system reduces the ability of government to hide their activities, including acts which violate human rights, from public scrutiny'. Images from Abu Ghraib, for example, which were taken by the guards themselves using digital cameras, provided indisputable evidence of what was happening in the prison. They were not fully controlled by the government elite and, if anything, they challenged the official interpretation of the war on terror as a fight between 'good' and 'evil' (Bennett *et al.* 2006; Hersh 2004a).

On the other hand, media coverage can strengthen existing domestic and international groups devoted to promoting human rights or, by informing local populations about their governments' abuses, encourage the formation of social or civil movements and awaken moral outrage in the public (McPherson 2012; Pruce 2012; Thomas 2001):

> [The] globalised communications system can provide human rights groups with information, assistance, and support in their resistance to oppression … When people know about human rights and are aware of human rights abuses, they are more likely to seek to protect them … and exposure can lead to changes in policy by the state concerned.
>
> *(McCorquodale and Fairbrother 1999: 759)*

The news media can also serve as an informal means of documenting human rights violations (Ovsiovitch 1993), just as it can be used by human rights activists and NGOs to publicize human rights violations in order to pressurize perpetrators and even force them to change their behaviour (Cmiel 2004; Ramos *et al.* 2007). Park's (2002) study of Argentina highlights how important the media was in enabling NGOs to transmit information about human rights abuses and generate open debate about the 'free pass' given to violators during Argentina's dirty war. This confirms earlier findings that 'advances in information technology benefit human rights movements by enabling rapid transmission of information to monitor and respond to human rights violations' (Metzl 1996: 705). Although the Arab Spring demonstrated that technological advances alone are not enough to cause social change, and while not only protesters but repressive regimes and counter-insurgents have proved adept at using it, social media has become a valuable resource for human rights activists because of its potential to influence public opinion, generate international support, disseminate information rapidly and globally, and facilitate messaging between activists (Kessler 2012; Lindsey 2013).

The link between the media and NGOs works in the opposite direction as well. It is often organizations such as Amnesty International and Human Rights Watch that investigate and report human rights violations and raise attention for human rights issues in the public sphere. These organizations have been successful in putting these issues on the public, media and political agendas (Dhir 2007; Soh 1996) and they have had an impact on human rights performance as well (Murdie 2009).

Media strategies and human rights

Apart from framing, three other media strategies can arguably make a difference to the media's ability to grab audiences' attention and provoke action: the use of shock, celebrities and social media (Borer 2012b).

Using graphic and disturbing images and prose to try to shock readers into taking action on a particular human rights issue may work on some occasions, but this tactic can also do more harm than good by actually reinforcing anti-cosmopolitan and pro-national sentiments (Borer 2012a). Images of suffering – commodified to raise funds as well as awareness – and one-dimensional (and sometimes offensive) images of the 'other' have raised concerns over 'disaster pornography' (Omaar and Waal 1993) as well as ethical anxiety over the selectivity of the death and suffering to which Western readers and viewers, in particular, are exposed.

We tend to associate specific human rights issues with individual celebrities, such as Bono and foreign aid, Angelina Jolie and refugees and sexual violence in war zones, and George Clooney and Darfur. Some commentators believe that such celebrity involvement raises attention for particular issues, and sometimes even influences policy and public consciousness (Dittrich 2009; Valley 2009). Cooper and Turcotte (2012: 201) argue, 'Celebrity diplomats can help to set and frame an agenda in the public consciousness and then promote that agenda to global leaders in the hope that the issue will be addressed.' Their work is most effective – and can establish and promote sustained effort, involvement and institutions that encourage change – when celebrities work together with a network of NGOs or civil society organizations (Cooper and Turcotte 2012). However, there are limits to what celebrities can do beyond raising money and consciousness. Critics accuse them of oversimplification – as Dieter and Kumar (2008: 260) put it, 'the world [gets] painted in black and white and good is pitted against evil. Nuance is inevitably lost' – drowning out alternative voices from the global South and anti-globalization voices from the North (Valley 2009); incompetence; and a lack of representativeness (Dieter and Kumar 2008).

Finally, the arrival of social media has introduced a large debate over the significance of digital activism in combating human rights violations around the world. Opinions again are divided. It is argued that the lack of both strong ties among activists and a hierarchical organization that would make it possible to take on powerful and well-organized entities limits the potential of digital activism (Gladwell 2010). Internet-based groups are vulnerable to problems of control, decision-making and collective identity (Bennett 2003). Their activism can easily become 'slacktivisim' (Naidoo 2010), understood as largely insignificant actions undertaken by individuals with the main aim of making them feel good about themselves. Despite this, while social media does not cause revolutions, it has certainly begun to revolutionize the way in which activists approach them (Kessler 2012; Lindsey 2013). As Kessler (2012: 206) argues,

> the social media are beginning to shift the world of activism from one in which organizations and centralized movements are the most effective change agents to one in which individuals and decentralized collections of individuals are equally effective or more effective at completing activists tasks.

Conclusions

This chapter has assessed the assumption that awareness of human rights violations as a result of media exposure has a mobilizing effect on audiences and leads to actions to halt them. While some might consider this a reasonable causal argument, for many there is not enough evidence to support such a conclusion. It also overlooks some of the complexities of the three key themes presented here: information, media and power. When it comes to the media–information relationship, it is rather naïve to expect the media to provide comprehensive awareness about all violations of human rights taking place around the world (not least due to the sheer number). And in the media–politics relationship, it is also unrealistic to expect that knowledge of human rights crises through media coverage means that anybody will be in a position to do something about them politically. This has to be considered in the context of declining coverage of foreign affairs since the end of the Cold War, with many arguing that this trend has not been reversed (Hoge 1994; Jones 2008). As Seib (2002:17) observes about the United States, 'relatively few news executives appear willing to gamble that the American news audience might be interested in the rest of the world'. This again brings to the fore the question of newsworthiness, confirming that the media tends to be 'myopic to those who are culturally, geographically and psychologically close' (Tai 2000: 351). On the other hand, the cases of Rwandan genocide (1994), the civil war in Sierra Leone (1999) and the famine in Somalia (2011) – to name just a few recent examples – are powerful illustrations that detailed information about and knowledge of human rights abuses do not guarantee effective – or timely – international action.

Unfortunately, this conclusion gets us no closer to understanding the significance of having more or fewer human rights stories in the media. It seems to suggest that while the media can provoke action in response to viewing and reading about human rights violations, it can also desensitize its audience to the suffering, overwhelm them with the magnitude of violence and make them feel helpless about a situation they perceive as hopeless. These feelings can result in inactivity or even indifference (Borer 2012b). As Pruce (2012: 235) concludes, 'graphic news coverage of atrocity may be a necessary condition for awareness, but awareness is not a sufficient condition for action'.

How can we explain the urge towards action or inaction? As will be seen in the next chapter on cosmopolitanism, the elusive connection between knowledge of and action on human rights depends to a large part on underlying values and attitudes towards distant others, and the role of the media in furthering or undermining the sharing of such values.

Questions

- Which human rights get most media coverage and why?
- To what extent are new information technologies affecting the quality of media presentation of human rights issues?
- Does the media report consistently and accurately about human rights?
- What is the best strategy for human rights organizations to adopt when trying to utilize the media?

Note

1 These are semi-autonomous, government-funded commissions established during the negotiations for the North American Free Trade Agreement mainly as a way to allay US concerns about the Mexican government's human rights record.

Further reading

Beckett, C. and J. Ball. 2012. *WikiLeaks: News in the Networked Era*. Cambridge: Polity Press.
Borer, T. A. (ed.). 2012. *Media, Mobilization, and Human Rights: Mediating Suffering*. London: Zed Books.
Entman, R. 2004. *Projections of Power: Framing News, Public Opinion, and US Foreign Policy*. Chicago: University of Chicago Press.
Galtung, J. and M. H. Ruge. 1965. 'The structure of foreign news: the presentation of the Congo, Cuba and Cyprus crises in four Norwegian newspapers', *Journal of Peace Research* 2(1): 64–90.
Herman, E. and N. Chomsky. 1988. *Manufacturing Consent: The Political Economy of the Mass Media*. London: Vintage.
International Council on Human Rights Policy (ICHRP). 2002. *Journalism, Media and the Challenge of Human Rights Reporting*. Geneva: ICHRP.
Negrine, R. and J. Stanyer (eds). 2007. *The Political Communication Reader*. Abingdon: Routledge.
Street, J. 2011. *Mass Media, Politics and Democracy*, 2nd edn. Basingstoke: Palgrave Macmillan.
Wahl-Jorgensen, K. and T. Hanitzsch (eds). 2009. *The Handbook of Journalism Studies*. London: Routledge.

3

THE NORMATIVE DIMENSION

Cosmopolitanism

Introduction

In the previous chapter, different connections were explored between the media, information (or knowledge) about human rights, and power (or politics). The analysis demonstrated that simply knowing about human rights atrocities could not help to predict the effects of such knowledge. Indeed, it proved to be exceptionally difficult to support or deny the causal argument that increased media coverage would necessarily lead to any action to address human rights issues. The reason for this is that the way in which such information is packaged and understood is itself contingent upon the underlying values which inform the way we think about human rights in the first place. As Ignatieff (1997: 11–12) puts it, 'Images of human suffering do not assert their own meaning; they can only instantiate a moral claim if those who watch understand themselves to be potentially under obligation to those they see.' This is why it is necessary to look beyond mechanistic models of how information flows in society and consider in a more systematic way the normative dimension.

Norms are ideas about what is right and what is wrong, so understanding normative ideas is crucial when analyzing the way in which the media attempts to make sense of information, the way in which that information is received by audiences, and what effects this might have. This leads to a range of questions. When people receive news about human rights, how is the idea of human rights represented and framed in these discussions? Who is held responsible and accountable for breaches in which human rights? Which remedies are suggested, and why?

Using the concept of cosmopolitanism means linking the ways in which human rights are discussed and understood to the approach to global suffering in general. Does one hold a weak or a strong cosmopolitan position? Should we just aim to secure a basic range of human rights (weak) or should global equality (strong) – a more demanding objective – be the ultimate goal? How does this affect the way in which the role played by the media is viewed? Does such motivation come from a sense of global justice or from humanitarian/charitable duty? What does this mean for the system of enforcement that exists, or should exist? How, in turn, does this affect the role of the UN and other national, regional and international agencies, organizations and institutions? The rest of the chapter explores these questions by examining the history and contemporary emergence of cosmopolitan ideas.

Cosmopolitanism

On some level in the contemporary era there is fairly broad agreement on one aspect of cosmopolitanism – namely, that all human beings are morally equal – but this was not always the case, and even today this agreement is sometimes only surface deep. There remains a very real question over the extent to which the requirements of equality and justice should be limited to the national level, and on what basis non-nationals should be excluded. On the one hand, if the duty towards one another derives from common humanity, then it makes sense that duties exist towards everyone. If, however, we believe that we have duties only towards those who share our membership of an association or a political community, then there is no duty of justice beyond our own borders/fellow nationals – aside, perhaps, from a rather minimal humanitarian one (Brock 2013: 4–6).

In the last decade or two there has been growing interest in cosmopolitanism across a range of disciplines and particularly in media and communication studies. From Ulrich Beck to Jürgen Habermas and from David Held to Onora O'Neill, there are a number of political theorists whose arguments and claims are based either entirely or loosely on one form of cosmopolitanism or another. Likewise, in the field of communication studies, cosmopolitanism has become central to theoretical debates about the role of the media in society. The system of international human rights, as conceived, detailed and set out in myriad conventions and agreements (discussed in Chapter 1), can be seen as the classic cosmopolitan project. Indeed, most contemporary cosmopolitan thinkers would endorse international human rights; the language of human rights has become the main tool of criticism for activists seeking to reform the existing international order (Beitz 2009). So, can we say that human rights are synonymous with cosmopolitanism?

Cosmopolitanism is an old concept that is now used in a variety of ways that can sometimes be confusing and disorientating to the uninitiated. A key objective of this book is to clarify the main threads and strands in debates over cosmopolitanism in communication and media studies, and fashion these ideas into an ordered and usable analytical 'map' that can then be applied systematically to the analysis of human rights. A good way to start such a task is to consider the historical and philosophical roots of the concept.

Historical and philosophical roots

Cosmopolitanism has been described as many things, partly because it is a concept that has appeared and reappeared in some of the key intellectual traditions in the Western philosophical canon. This makes it a rich but complex notion that is constantly evolving; or, as Skrbiš *et al.* (2004: 115) put it, 'its Stoic parentage, Kantian upbringing and postmodern spoiling have made it a robust but somewhat confused adolescent'. It is perhaps natural that the gathering forces of globalization should prompt reflection over moral implications and questions of governance, directing us towards cosmopolitanism as a global political theory (Brown and Held 2010: 1). Indeed, for some, 'Cosmopolitanism is today one of the most important ways of making sense of the contemporary world' (Delanty 2009: 18).

The Greek origins of the word 'cosmopolitan' (*kosmopolitês*) betray its classical roots. It was Diogenes of Sinope (b. 412 BC) who famously declared, 'I am a citizen of the world' (the literal translation of *kosmopolitês*), and he has since been referred to as the first 'cosmopolitan'. While such a statement would seem a relatively uncontroversial thing to say in the context of the twenty-first century, in Diogenes' time this was quite a radical departure from mainstream thinking. Classical teaching about citizenship was very much concerned with the connection between the individual and the political community to which he belonged – that is, the city-state – and the duties and responsibilities that this might entail. Such duties and responsibilities were not extended to other communities outside the city-state's boundaries. Thinking of oneself as a cosmopolitan therefore challenged the conventional understandings of citizenship because of its implications of attachment to the whole world, rather than a specific political community. But Diogenes was not calling for a world state; rather, his declaration was a rejection of any special responsibilities to his own political community.

It was the Greek and Roman thinkers known as the 'Stoics' who built a more positive vision of cosmopolitanism as serving others outside one's own political community. Their ideas were founded on the principle that everyone is part of the whole of humankind and should therefore be treated as a fellow citizen. The basis for this common humanity is reason: the ability to be rational and moral. For Seneca, Cicero and other Stoics, recognition of the universal qualities of humanity did not mean giving up local affiliations. Rather, it meant life should be seen as comprising concentric circles: starting with the self and the immediate family, and ending with the largest circle of all – humanity (Nussbaum 2010: 30–31).

The rise and fall of empires in the Graeco-Roman period has been associated with an environment that saw a flourishing of cosmopolitan ideas (Delanty 2009: 23). Early Christianity also found these ideas relevant and helpful in separating the authority of 'earthly' local politics from that which joins all of mankind to God (filtered and interpreted by the Church, of course). This was crystallized by Augustine's notion of two citizenships – that of the particular city or state where one lives and the 'heavenly city' that includes citizens of all nations. Cosmopolitanism also emerged in the natural law theories that developed in the sixteenth and seventeenth centuries, in which the laws of natural justice were seen as deriving from humanity's divine creation.

Although there are clear linkages in the use of the concept over at least two millennia, it is probably the cosmopolitanism outlined by Immanuel Kant in the Enlightenment era which has become the key reference point for most contemporary discussions (Fine 2003). Kant was much influenced by the thinking of the Stoics (Nussbaum 2010), but he rejected their metaphysics and developed a more substantial and systematic version of cosmopolitanism that was based on law. Writing at the time of the French Revolution, he was dismayed by the anarchy in international relations, which he felt had led to a Hobbesian state of nature, pitting 'all against all' (Fine 2003: 613).

According to Brown (2010: 45–46), there are three (interrelated) elements to Kant's cosmopolitanism:

1 'individuals represent the unit of ultimate moral concern equally' and 'human capacities can only be fully developed within a condition of universal justice';
2 the achievement of universal justice requires a cosmopolitan civil society – that is, one based on humanity rather than nationality or local allegiance; and
3 cosmopolitan right is about the 'fundamental normative principles that underwrite a cosmopolitan constitution'.

It should be noted that when Kant talked about 'cosmopolitan right', he was referring to what we would now call 'international law' (Waldron 2000: 229).

Kant has been criticized on a number of fronts, but one significant area is his supposedly teleological philosophy of history and human progress. He saw both international trade and warfare (its aftermath and the desire to avoid it) as inevitably leading to legal relationships that broaden and ultimately produce a cosmopolitan matrix (Brown 2010: 50–51). It should also be noted that the conventional narrative (indulged here) of cosmopolitanism – which traces the idea from the Stoics through Kant to the contemporary era (e.g. Delanty 2009; Nussbaum 2010) – has been accused of 'Eurocentricism' (Dussel 2000). It would also overlook the backlash against cosmopolitanism led by Marx's critique of capitalism in the nineteenth century.

The Marxist perspective, and subsequent critical theoretical approaches, argue that no matter how peaceful and humanist the cosmopolitan concept claims to be, it is ultimately an ideology that is deeply complicit in national and global power dynamics (Beardsworth 2011: 128–129). For Marx, cosmopolitanism is a dangerously moralizing discourse that conveniently facilitates the economic liberalism of Adam Smith and others, thereby ignoring the causal linkages between capitalism, exploitation and empire. The whole cosmopolitan project comes too soon for Marx in historical terms: it is a 'top-down' ideology that misses out the important first stage of achieving social solidarity (e.g. through revolution). It therefore unintentionally provides cover for the powerful to continue their exploitation of the world's resources and people's labour.

Many of the political ideologies of the nineteenth and twentieth centuries – particularly nationalism and communism – attacked cosmopolitan ideas and employed the label in a highly derogatory way. Nationalists, of course, have a clear logic in distrusting cosmopolitans because of their perceived lack of loyalty to the nation – something that is even more dangerous than rival nationalisms (Gellner 1994: 112). The fascistic nationalisms of the first half of the twentieth century adopted the word for a darker purpose by associating it with the rampant anti-Semitism of Europe of the nineteenth and twentieth centuries. It is well known that the Nazis saw the Jews as archetypal cosmopolitans – rootless, nationless and therefore highly suspicious. Berlin was seen as a highly 'cosmopolitan' city in 1920s Germany, and it is still viewed as a city of foreigners (Richie 1998). But this was not just a German phenomenon – the discursive connection with cosmopolitanism was made wherever there was anti-Semitism across Europe. Russia, and later the Soviet Union, with its long history of anti-Semitism often linked cosmopolitanism with unwanted groups. The 'anti-cosmopolitan' campaigns of the 1940s and 1950s, for example, unequivocally connected 'rootless cosmopolitanism' with Jewish identity (Azadovskii and Egorov 2002).

While it is easy to dismiss fascism, Nazism and Stalinism as horribly twisted, racist and discredited ideologies, it was no accident that they were able to utilize popular antipathy towards cosmopolitanism in their highly effective propaganda campaigns. This was because they could frame it as a threat, both politically and culturally. They successfully drew on feelings of fear and envy by evoking the stereotype of a cosmopolitan as a privileged individual who could afford to travel the world, pick and choose which identity to adopt, and would take according to his desires but give back to the state only what he must. In short, the cosmopolitan was defined as a parasite on society (Scruton 1982: 100). Those seeking to rehabilitate cosmopolitanism in the late twentieth and early twenty-first centuries have sought to reject these stereotypes and rediscover the moral, political and institutional projects of various thinkers – particularly Kant. The next section charts some of the main trajectories in these contemporary debates over cosmopolitanism.

Contemporary debates

The usual reason given for the spectacular proliferation of books and articles on cosmopolitanism since the 1990s is very straightforward and can be summed up in one word: globalization (e.g. Brown and Held 2010: 3). Fleshing this out a little further, the political context at the turn of the century – the end of the Cold War – perhaps should be added, as should the rise of various technological developments that have facilitated an expansion in international movement and communication. Whatever the reason or reasons, however, it seems accurate to say that 'cosmopolitanism has never been so popular' (Robbins 2012: 2).

This popularity means there are multiple areas of interest that feature cosmopolitan concepts, and an almost endless number of adjectives associated with different types of cosmopolitanism. For instance, cosmopolitan thought is commonly divided into moral, political, cultural and economic strands, while Brown and Held (2010: 9–13) see cosmopolitan ideas applied through five related themes: global justice, and cultural, legal, political and civic cosmopolitanism. Other typologies identify dozens of different types (for a long list, see Skrbiš and Woodward 2013: 4–5).

Despite the obvious difficulties in summarizing all of these, there have been some attempts to generalize about what is common to all forms of contemporary cosmopolitanism. Delanty (2006: 28), for example, points out that all types of cosmopolitanism are in some way moral because the concept begins with an ethic of universalism. Pogge (1994: 89–90) claims that all cosmopolitan positions share three elements: individualism, universality and generality. Individualism means that the ultimate units of concern are human beings, or persons (as opposed to tribes, ethnic, cultural or religious communities, nations or states); universality means that the same status attaches to every living human being equally (not just a subset, such as aristocrats, whites, Muslims, etc.); and generality means that this status has global force so that 'persons are ultimate units of concern for everyone – not only for their compatriots, fellow religionists, or such like'.

Another way of navigating the various types of cosmopolitanism is to think of 'stronger' and 'weaker' versions (Delanty 2006). Rawls argues for a limited duty of assistance towards 'burdened states' – for example, if they could not govern them-selves (Rawls 1999: 5) – and this could be viewed as a weak form of cosmopolitanism. Scheffler (1997) is another weak cosmopolitan who accepts a duty towards others but only in the context of 'special obligations' for certain groups. The stronger form of cosmopolitanism would argue for distributive justice and the global application of egalitarian principles or democracy (Held 1995). Another example of a strong duty towards others is provided by O'Neill's (1975) famous argument about the right not to be killed (which must override all other rights), using the metaphor of the world as a lifeboat.

Given the general consensus around some of the key tenets of cosmopolitanism (e.g. the very notion of human rights), it could be argued that 'we are all cosmo-politans now'. However, as the strong/weak versions suggest, there are significant nuances and various positions along with a number of criticisms, even if there is widespread agreement on a very minimalist version. While here these critics have been described as 'weak cosmopolitans', they are also labelled variously as 'un-cosmopolitan', 'non-cosmopolitan' or 'communitarian'. The Marxist critique has already been mentioned, and there are also some 'communitarians' who see problems with the cosmopolitanism position. They argue, from within a realist perspective on international relations, that cosmopolitans overlook the value of national duties and responsibilities (e.g. MacIntyre 1995; Walzer 1983; for both sides of the debate, see Nussbaum and Cohen 2002). In contrast with this, postmodernist or poststructuralist critiques condemn the inherently modernist 'DNA' of cosmopolitanism. This includes, for example, a faith in reason, belief in historical progress, and confidence in universalism (all of which are seen as highly suspicious). For authors such as Foucault and Agamben, liberal discourse con-stituted by value-laden concepts such as 'freedom' actually works to control the individual and transmit the expanding disciplinary power of the state (Beardsworth 2011: 176–177).

From the perspective of the postmodern critique, any claim to 'universalism' will necessarily involve one person or group deciding what is universal, and then imposing that definition on everyone else. Harvey (2009: 84) puts it most bluntly by claiming that cosmopolitanism is a 'mask for hegemonic neo-liberal practices of class domination and financial and militaristic imperialism'. From this perspective, human rights become twisted into an ideology, used by politicians such as George W. Bush as part of a moralized mission of 'good' against 'evil' (Douzinas 2007: 3). However, it is precisely this Manichean narrative and the fear of a 'clash of civilizations' that led prominent academics such as Beck, Habermas and Derrida to call for a new cosmopolitanism (Kurasawa 2004: 233). For many of these writers, the importance of mediation and inter-subjective communication in contemporary society means that the field of communication and media studies is becoming ever more crucial in understanding the dynamics – and possibilities – of cosmopolitan ideas.

Mediated cosmopolitanism

Cosmopolitanism conceived as a 'project' requires action on a number of different fronts, and the ways in which this and ideas are 'mediated' become central. The focus for Kant was how to enable the creation of viable and effective global institutions and laws based on universal principles. But these constructions would work only if they were first perceived as legitimate, and then adopted and used. For this to happen, many have argued that there needs to be a redefinition of normative bonds beyond the national to inspire a mutual sense of global belonging. Crucially, this is then something that implies an important role for communications and media (Skrbiš and Woodward 2013: 75). How does a cosmopolitan culture come about, and how can the media play a role in this transformation?

Marshall McLuhan (1964: 5) was confident about the cosmopolitan impact of the development of technologies of 'mass media', famously arguing that 'the globe is no more than a village. Electric speed bringing all social and political functions together in a sudden implosion has heightened human awareness of responsibility to an intense degree.' While McLuhan's vision might now seem somewhat optimistic, others have developed the idea that media and communications are key to fostering a sense of global togetherness. This might be through the dissemination of information and human stories from afar bringing identification and a sense of responsibility for distant others (e.g. Silverstone 2007); by normalizing difference (Nava 2007: 13); by creating a global 'civil society' (Kaldor 2003); by making the global 'everyday' through the proliferation of commercial and non-commercial images and brands – 'from Coca-Cola to Greenpeace' (Szerszynski and Urry 2002: 464); through the influential actions of a particular group, such as journalists, who have embedded cosmopolitanism within their professional values and standards (e.g. Dahlgren 2013); or by creating a global public sphere (Lull 2007).

Much research has attempted to show how the media might play a role in creating the conditions for cosmopolitan culture – particularly with the massive audiences receiving news stories such as the release of Nelson Mandela, the death of Princess Diana, or the fall of the Berlin Wall. When it comes to the impact of global 24/7 television news in terms of building a cosmopolitan culture, there are optimists (Szerszynski and Urry 2006) and pessimists (Chouliaraki 2008), and between the two extremes those who try empirically to establish the complex ways in which messages are framed, sent and received (e.g. Cottle and Rai 2008; Robertson 2010).

The advent of new forms of internet-based communication technologies has predictably prompted an increase in research that examines the cosmopolitan possibilities of these new types of media. A special issue of *Journalism Studies* edited by Lilie Chouliaraki and Bolette Blaagaard draws on the examples of the Arab Spring and Occupy Wall Street in 2011, the Haiti earthquake of 2010, and the Iranian elections of 2009 as cases where the new media have changed 'the nature of journalism'. The editors pose the question of how this might be 'reconfiguring the cosmopolitanising potential of reporting' (Chouliaraki and Blaagaard 2013: 150), and the rest of the contributors consider this question in terms of whether new media are creating 'new solidarity' and 'new authenticity' (e.g. through citizen journalism).

A cosmopolitan deficit?

This still leaves the questions of how the media accomplishes these tasks and how it plays a role in creating a global citizenry and a sense of cosmopolitan solidarity. Despite the expectations that in today's increasingly globalized and interconnected world the cosmopolitan ethics of care and action will stretch to distant others, nationalism remains a strong identifying force. The national remains the lens and the interpretative framework through which most people make sense of global events, and in turn this makes commitment to humanity as a whole very difficult to sustain (Kyriakidou 2009). As Chouliaraki (2006: 6) concludes, 'despite the instantaneous and global reach of visibility that [media] technologies have achieved, the optimistic celebration of our planet as a global village or the [audience] as a new cosmopolitan should be held in check'. In a later work, Chouliaraki (2013: 2) detects changes in the communication of solidarity with vulnerable others and identifies the transformation of the West into an 'ironic spectator', understood as 'an impure or ambivalent figure that stands, at once, as skeptical towards any moral appeal of solidary action and, yet, open to doing something about those who suffer'. She argues that the move is

> from an objective representation of suffering as something separate from us that invites us to contemplate the condition of distant others towards a subjective representation of suffering as something inseparable from our own 'truths' that invites contemplation on our own condition … a move from an ethics of *pity* to an ethics of *irony*.

> *(Chouliaraki 2013: 3; emphasis in original)*

Thus, Chouliaraki is talking about the emergence of a new rationality and practice of solidarity different from previous ones and no longer based on an 'other-oriented morality', but rather focused on a 'self-oriented morality', where doing good to others is centred on how it makes us feel.

Clearly the effect of a globalizing media has multiple possible outcomes. One suggestion is that the increased access to images of suffering from across the world creates 'compassion fatigue' (Moeller 1999) or the 'distantiation from compassion' (Höijer 2004), rather than empathy. It is claimed that this can result from over-exposure to human rights violations and distant suffering through the media. Defined as 'becoming so used to the spectacle of dreadful events, misery or suffering that we stop noticing them … We are bored', it can lead 'to the conclusion that this is just the way things are and nothing can be done that will make a difference' (Tester 2001: 13).

Compassion fatigue is linked to the media's repetitive use of certain phrases and images. Moeller alludes to this when explaining the effects of the media's concern with what will 'sell' and media organizations' belief that what sold before will sell again:

> [Compassion fatigue] is a consequence of rote journalism, and looking-over-your-shoulder reporting. It is a consequence of sensationalism, formulaic coverage and perfunctory reference to American cultural icons … As a result, much of the media looks alike. The same news. The same pictures.
>
> *(Moeller 1999: 32)*

Those who despair at the growing levels of global inequality and the huge amount of human suffering that this generates are likely to point a finger at the global media and its reporting. These arguments are less about the hypothetical cosmopolitan potential of a global media and more about a perceived deficit: the distance between the ideal of a media that could and should help to develop shared global values and the far from ideal reality of a media driven by market dynamics and populism, appealing to the 'lowest common denominator'. This has obvious and less obvious effects. An example of the former is the media's avoidance of news that is 'difficult' or will not 'sell', or – from a more cynical perspective – does not align with the interests of the powerful (as explained in the previous chapter).

Framing cosmopolitanism

The notion of framing – a central theme of this book that was introduced in Chapter 2 – is essential to understanding the less obvious and more insidious ways in which these dynamics present themselves. This is because the way in which the media frames its stories is paramount to the way they are interpreted and understood by audiences. 'Empathy' and 'distance' framing – emphasizing or maintaining an emotional distance with suffering people – can have differential effects, for example, when it comes to foreign policies towards areas or states where human rights are under threat. The former is a 'narrative template of "proximity"'. It 'can be laid over humanitarian issues, which in turn emphasise[s] the geographic and societal closeness of war. The ordinary individual [is] highlighted, encouraging empathy and also clarity; the simple imperative of personal suffering' (Preston 1996: 112). In this case the focus is on the suffering of individuals who are identified as victims in need of 'outside' help, and only occasionally is the political dimension of the struggle highlighted (Robinson 2002: 29). The alternative framing – distance framing – creates an emotional distance between the audience and the people suffering in a conflict. This 'can be laid over the subject matter of diplomacy or politics; [use] dispassionate documentation as a reporting style; [have] a target audience of elites; and [emphasize] … the complicated or difficult' (Preston 1996: 112). It can also establish or maintain 'a degree of emotional, intellectual and practical closure to a situation, separating ourselves and maintaining our own ontological security' (Shaw 1996: 8). This kind of distance framing is often visible in the reporting of Africa as a 'dark continent' and a 'place of endemic and persistent pain and suffering' (Tester 2001: 7), implying that very little can and will change there. By using the language of 'criminals', 'looters', 'illegal immigrants' and so on, regardless of the accuracy of these terms, it is less likely that the media will provoke helpful activism (Borer 2012b). The framing of global crises 'in ways consonant to national interests and identities' (Cottle 2009: 509) also does not contribute to the creation of cosmopolitan citizenry.

Another type of framing relates to cosmopolitan/communitarian notions of global justice which are often present, but implicit, in the reporting of issues that involve serious dilemmas or conflicts between competing values. Most reporting of international events and political challenges have implications for notions of global justice, but there is rarely the time or the space (or the appetite) for a prolonged, sustained discussion of such issues in a 24/7 news environment. When states are faced with claims for admission, residence or assistance by those forced from their homes by environmental disasters, political conflicts or economic crises, they are inadvertently involved in decisions that relate directly to arguments based on global justice. The first case study in Chapter 6 demonstrates that the media is directly involved in these arguments by framing the policy debates in terms that denote a cosmopolitan or communitarian position on global justice.

Conclusions

The system of international human rights can be imagined as an attempt to transform governance, law and politics on the basis of universal values and principles. In this sense it is closely associated – but not synonymous – with cosmopolitanism. The ideal of universal human rights can be seen as one part of the cosmopolitan imagination which includes, inter alia, the notion of global civil society, peace among states and social solidarity (Fine 2009: 8). As with cosmopolitanism itself, the perfect conception of human rights brings to our attention the inadequacies of the actual system that has been progressively implemented since the end of the Second World War. It also highlights the lack of an enlightened global system of governance that can truly deliver and enforce common principles – a pressing problem in an era of globalization (Held 2003). This is why, for many, the human rights system remains a largely 'cosmopolitan promise' – providing real but limited impact in the present while holding out a tantalizing (or possibly utopian) vision of the future. The gap between the ideal and non-ideal (i.e. actual) versions of human rights creates what could be described as a 'cosmopolitan deficit'. One of the aims of this book is to develop a better and more nuanced understanding of the size and shape of this deficit – the areas and types of human rights in which it is more pronounced. Perceptions of this deficit, however, will be contingent upon the opinion that one adopts regarding human rights. In the context of cosmopolitan perspectives, there can be a division between 'strong' and 'weak' versions.

For strong cosmopolitans, the human rights system is a work in progress: it has a structure that must be improved and changed; its scope and coverage are incomplete; it incorporates numerous compromises and gaps; and it must be defended against the challenges of opposing forces. In brief, it is a necessary, but currently insufficient, part of the cosmopolitan project. It has done very little to tackle problems of global distributive justice, for example. For weak cosmopolitans (or communitarians), the current system is altogether more satisfactory because it provides minimum standards and values that can serve as a roadmap for national communities to develop their own systems of justice. They view the lack of a global enforcer with any real power as an advantage, not a disadvantage, because this greatly reduces the possibility of the creation of some kind of putative 'world government'.

The strong cosmopolitans maintain the more 'radical' position and as a result they have conceptual and practical concerns about the international human rights system that are more introspective. Some have argued that strong cosmopolitans should be wary of complacency over human rights: it is important that they do not become 'idealized' as a way of avoiding critical engagement with pressing contemporary problems of societal violence and inequality (Fine 2009). The growing popularity of human rights as an explanation of and solution to society's problems, based on a shallow understanding of the complexities of the actual human rights regime, also risks a deterioration of intellectual rigour and coherence as to what these rights currently are and what they should be (Føllesdal 2009: 77)

For the weak cosmopolitans, there are less conceptual difficulties over the meaning and significance of the international system of human rights, but they still have to perform a difficult balancing act. From their perspective, human rights are useful at times (when it suits) but limited in general terms because justice is ultimately bound up with questions of community. This does not entirely deny an ontology that includes human rights; rather it de-emphasizes, merges and integrates them within a hierarchy predicated on the importance of community. Weak cosmopolitanism is therefore complex, at times difficult, and also risks travelling in the direction of cultural relativism. While this might be significantly different from the strong cosmopolitan position, it is still 'modernist' and 'pro' human rights when compared with the more strident postmodern critique of human rights as 'quasi-imperialism' (e.g. Flikschuh 2011).

In addition to the strong/weak continuum of cosmopolitanism, there is an optimist/pessimist continuum regarding the role of the media in facilitating a cosmopolitan future. The optimists believe that the global media possesses transformative potential – from McLuhan's (1964) confidence in technology, to the power of banal cosmopolitanism to touch the 'everyday' (Ong 2009), to the belief in the transformative power of globalization (Held 2003). Needless to say, the pessimists acknowledge the presence of these forces but they draw very different conclusions. They look at the advent of new technologies, the increasing reach of social media and the ubiquity of global media channels and see ever more opportunities for authoritarians (Morozov 2011) or news oligopolies (Scott 2005) to use new communication technologies to consolidate or extend their power.

Figure 3.1 makes a suggestion about the relationship between different normative positions (along the x axis) and understandings of the role of the media with respect to the creation of shared universal values (along the y axis). Everyone will naturally fall somewhere within this space, depending on their particular combination of positions with respect to cosmopolitanism and the role of the media. The diagonal line represents a potential relationship between the two, suggesting that strong cosmopolitans will be more likely to see the media as a potentially transformative force, whereas weak cosmopolitans (or communitarians) will be less convinced of the media's ability to foster and forge shared universal values.

The construction of this simple two-dimensional relationship between different understandings of human rights and the media is intended as a heuristic device to provide a sort of conceptual 'map' that can link the main themes that will be explored in the rest of this book, and revisited in the concluding chapter. Part III moves from the abstract to the empirical by considering a range of human rights issues, with each chapter analysing a different aspect of the international human rights regime. Through the examination of case studies, each chapter seeks to develop a deeper understanding of the myriad roles that the media plays – or fails to play – in exposing the shifting size and shape of the cosmopolitan deficit.

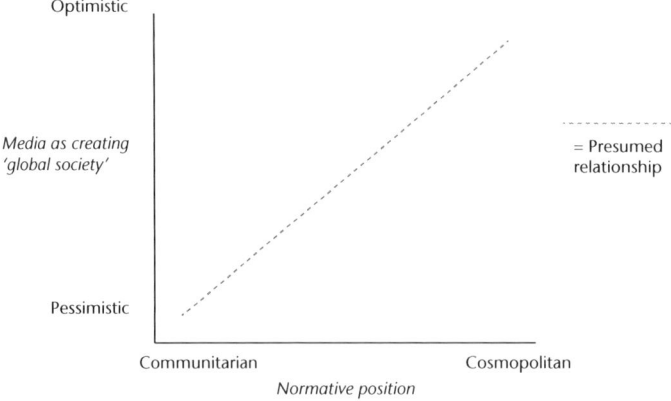

FIGURE 3.1 Media, cosmopolitanism and global society

Questions

- In what ways can the media create a more cosmopolitan future?
- Is the international system of human rights the same thing as cosmopolitanism?
- Will new communications technologies make us more or less aware of international human rights?
- What is the difference between stronger and weaker forms of cosmopolitanism?

Further reading

Beardsworth, R. 2011. *Cosmopolitanism and International Relations Theory*. Cambridge: Polity Press.

Beitz, C. 2009. *The Idea of Human Rights*. Oxford: Oxford University Press.

Brock, G. (ed.). 2013. *Cosmopolitanism versus Non-cosmopolitanism: Critiques, Defenses, Reconceptualizations*. Oxford: Oxford University Press.

Brown, G. W. and D. Held (eds). 2010. *The Cosmopolitanism Reader*. Cambridge: Polity Press.

Chouliaraki, L. 2006. *The Spectatorship of Suffering*. London: Sage.

Chouliaraki, L. 2013. *The Ironic Spectator: Solidarity in the Age of Post-humanitarianism*. Cambridge: Polity Press.

Douzinas, C. 2007. *Human Rights and Empire: The Political Philosophy of Cosmopolitanism*. London: Routledge-Cavendish.

Held, D. 2003. *Cosmopolitanism: A Defense*. Cambridge: Polity Press.

Moeller, S. 1999. *Compassion Fatigue: How the Media Sell Disease, Famine, War and Death*. New York: Routledge.

Robertson, A. 2010. *Mediated Cosmopolitanism: The World of Television News*. Cambridge: Polity Press.

Skrbiš, Z. and I. Woodward. 2013. *Cosmopolitanism: Uses of the Idea*. London: Sage.

PART III

4

HUMANITARIAN INTERVENTION

Introduction

Humanitarian intervention is a highly controversial phenomenon bringing together a range of political, ethical, legal, strategic, operational and economic tensions; it remains one of the most contested and divisive issues in the post-Cold war era. Simply describing an intervention as 'humanitarian' brings forth the problem of definition, since 'almost every aspect of humanitarian intervention is contested' (Bellamy 2006a: 202).[1] This relates to the status of the parties involved, the question of consent of the host country, the means of intervention, the motives and, quite importantly, the issue of legality – all of which are at the centre of debates about humanitarian interventions. This chapter uses the definition provided by Roberts (2000: 5) – a 'coercive action by one or more states involving the use of armed force in another state without the consent of its authorities, and with the purpose of preventing widespread suffering or death among the inhabitants'.

For those who support it, humanitarian intervention speaks directly to the cosmopolitan ethic because it is about universal principles guiding the global political community (Archibugi 2004; Kaldor 2010). It is about action undertaken to halt, prevent or punish systematic and severe human rights violations or in response to humanitarian crises, such as famines or massive refugee flows. It is fundamentally about helping people who live in a foreign country, or 'saving strangers' (Wheeler 2000). Those sceptical of these ideas doubt both the sincerity of those claiming a war can be humanitarian, and question the wisdom of applying cosmopolitan principles by means of force. In particular they point to the dangers of states using humanitarian justifications as a cover for military imperialism (Chomsky 1999).

This chapter explores how an international doctrine in this area has developed over time, and how it has been constantly challenged by these often irreconcilable perspectives. It also seeks to explore the extent to which the media has become an instrument for the main protagonists in violent conflict, and how it also provides a key battleground for ideas, arguments and decision-making about the legitimacy of war. The case studies used to demonstrate the key issues surrounding humanitarian interventions and the ways in which they play out in practice are the interventions in Kosovo in 1999 and Libya in 2011.

From the margins to the centre of the international policy agenda

The most obvious problem for proponents of humanitarian intervention is that the concept runs up against the principles of sovereignty that have been central to both the theory and practice of international relations since the 1648 Treaty of West-phalia. The contemporary international order is based on a society of states that possess exclusive jurisdiction over their territory and rights to non-interference and non-intervention. This is now also firmly established in the UN Charter, which links the principles of non-intervention and a state's right to sovereignty and makes intervention illegal. As already mentioned, Article 2(7) says: 'Nothing contained in the present Charter shall authorise the United Nations to intervene in matters which are essentially within the domestic jurisdiction of any state.' Similarly, Article 2(4) states: 'All Members shall refrain in their international relations from the threat or use of force against the territorial integrity or political independence of any state.'

These prohibitions, however, are tempered by two exceptions. First, the Charter preserves the 'inherent right of individual or collective self-defence' (Article 51). Second, if the Security Council determines that serious human rights violations are occurring or are likely to occur, and if it can establish that these constitute a threat to international peace and security, it can authorise enforcement action to halt or prevent the violations under Chapter VII. Thus, the UN Charter effectively allows humanitarian intervention under certain conditions and by specified means. The role of the Security Council in this regard, however, has been inconsistent, leading to 'ambiguous resolutions and conflicting interpretations [of Chapter VII]' and leaving the door open for both unauthorized actions by individual states and inaction by the international community (Chesterman 2001: 5). While interventions in northern Iraq and Somalia, for example, received Security Council authorization, NATO's use of force in Kosovo was neither expressly sanctioned nor condemned by the Council. In the case of Rwanda, the Council was reluctant to approve armed intervention, not on the grounds of violating the country's sovereignty, but because of a lack of political will to incur the costs involved. The Security Council has also generally refused to authorize forcible interventions into fully functioning sovereign states, with the conflict in Syria from 2011 (and still ongoing at the time of writing) the most recent example.

During the Cold War the deadlocked Security Council did not authorize a single humanitarian intervention. To use Weiss's (2010: 111) words, it 'was largely missing in action regarding humanitarian matters'. Since the 1990s, though, the practice of armed humanitarian intervention has gradually developed. Some have gone so far as to claim that the 1990s were 'undoubtedly the golden age of humanitarian diplomacy' (Falk 2003), while others have argued that 'the notion that human beings matter more than sovereignty radiated brightly, albeit briefly, across the international political horizon of the 1990s' (Weiss 2004: 136). The rise in the contemporary relevance of humanitarian intervention suggested a shift from pursuing clear national interests in foreign policy to focusing on human rights questions in areas where Western states claim little economic or geostrategic interest but have accepted the 'responsibility to act as a force for good in the world' (Blair, cited in Chandler 2002: 6).

Regardless of the motivations, the increase in the number of interventions was driven by a combination of four factors that collectively created a 'more permissive context' (Dannreuther 2013: 92). First was the new geopolitical environment, in which rivalry between superpowers no longer seemed to be an insurmountable obstacle to humanitarian action. Rather, the new structure of the world was seen as having potentially positive consequences for international justice and the promotion of human rights through enhanced prospects for great power cooperation and multilateral action via the Security Council (Shaw 1994; Weiss 2010). Second, many felt that the end of the Cold War signified a final victory for the combination of democracy and capitalism – as Francis Fukuyama (1992) argued in *The End of History and the Last Man*. The dramatic increase in democratization around the world (starting with Eastern and Central Europe) and the apparent unassailability of capitalism as the most legitimate form of economic and social organization (with China's belated embrace of it the most prominent example) offered support for this view. Since liberal democracies generally commit publicly to the importance of human rights in their foreign policies, the internal character of states became an international issue (Chandler 2002). As Hehir (2010: 3) argued, 'in the post-Cold War era ... the domestic dynamics within a state became, at least rhetorically, the seminal factor in determining its relationship with the West'. This resulted in increased tensions between liberal and 'illiberal' states, and occasionally led to the conclusion that certain human rights violations should be stopped by external military involvement – that is, 'humanitarian intervention'.

The third factor that contributed to the rise of such intervention on the international agenda was the unusually brutal character of the wars that were taking place at the time. These conflicts were happening *within* states, rather then between them; often in failing or failed states; they did not distinguish between civilians and soldiers, often intentionally targeting the former or even defining them as the enemy; and they were not financed from government tax revenues but from illicit activities, aid or plunder. Although labelled 'new wars' (Duffield 2001; Kaldor 2012; Münkler 2004), these conflicts were not really characterized by fully novel features; rather, 'elements thought extinct or tangential have come to the fore or been combined in ways that were heretofore unremarkable or largely unknown' (Weiss 2010: 63).

The fourth and final factor that accounts for the transformation of humanitarianism from the margins to the centre of the international policy agenda is the communication revolution (Gowing 1994; Neuman 1996; Carruthers 2011). In the 1990s instantaneity, immediacy and 'realism' became key characteristics in new forms of media coverage made possible by incredible advances in communication technology. Not only was more information now available, it was also accessible almost non-stop as part of the 'round-the-clock', 24-hour news day. While this led to a decline in investigative journalism and a lack of context and background in news reports, the proliferation of portable satellite dishes and editing equipment provided greater scope for journalists to cover distant events and draw upon unofficial sources (Robinson 2004; Thussu 2003). These developments, together with the rise of the internet, arguably resulted in a loosening of governments' control in the information environment; news media could, at least potentially, be more adversarial and 'off-message' (Deibert 2000; Nye 1999b; Robinson 2004). Part of this reduction in control was due to less dependence on government information sources defining and framing the news agenda, allowing more space for alternative viewpoints. Some of these new sources of information were non-governmental organizations (NGOs), whose number increased exponentially during the 1990s (Anheier *et al.* 2001). Many of the new NGOs were committed to highlighting human rights abuses, raising public awareness and creating domestic pressure for action within the Western states. Collectively, these communication developments contributed to the general public becoming more aware of the abuse of human rights in different parts of the world. They also led to the appearance of the term 'CNN effect' to describe the perceived new influence of media on public opinion and political elites in pushing governments (Robinson 2002).

The argument outlined above regarding the rise of humanitarian intervention to the top of the international political agenda has its critics. They argue that the increased focus on human rights and the willingness to intervene were motivated by something entirely different. 'The search for new ideals and common bonds in an era of failed ideologies' (Klug, cited in Chandler 2002: 63) turned the growing appreciation of human rights into an important resource of authority and credibility for Western political leaders. From this perspective, the new-found enthusiasm for humanitarian intervention was a legitimating ideology to justify the projection of US power that was necessary to maintain that country's economic hegemony. It allowed the US to legitimize its bloated arms industry in the absence of the communist threat and helped to create a conceptual distinction between the civilized and the barbarians (Chandler 2000; Chomsky 1999; Orford 2003).

In support of humanitarian intervention: the moral, legal and political dimensions

Once a humanitarian intervention is under way it is almost always contested, but the refusal to act also provokes tension. 'Doing nothing' can lead to accusations of moral indifference, just as 'doing something' prompts charges of interference in the internal affairs of a sovereign state. Nonetheless, the fate of populations caught up in conflict can generate considerable demands for 'something' to be done. The political, legal and ethical dimensions of an armed response have moved to the centre of public and intellectual debate.

The moral case in support of humanitarian intervention is usually the most obvious. Most contemporary moral and religious doctrines agree that the international community is duty bound to intervene to protect civilians from genocide and mass killing (Lepard 2002). When a state kills large numbers of its own population or proves incapable of protecting them from harm, it is failing in its duty and therefore forfeits its sovereign right to non-interference and non-intervention (Teson 2003). Various arguments have been put forward to support this view, such as the idea of common humanity (all individuals have basic human rights and duties to uphold the rights of others; Caney 1997) and the universal duty to offer charity to those in need (Ramsey 2002).

The biggest problem with this, according to Donnelly (2013a), is that the moral argument is usually applied only in cases of genocide. (This is one of the reasons why the international community is generally very reluctant to declare that genocide is taking place.) There is no evidence to suggest a pattern of humanitarian intervention spilling over into other, more common, human rights violations. In cases of torture or slavery, for example, the use of force has *never* been authorized by the Security Council, and such authorization is rarely even sought. Donnelly identifies a moral paradox: a willingness to respond to specific kinds of graphic and concentrated suffering clashes with a tolerance towards other types of suffering that might be substantial but remain diffuse or long term. He argues that if human rights are interdependent – that is, about a life of dignity and not just about survival – then the restriction of humanitarian intervention to genocide is problematic.

The legal case in support of humanitarian intervention is based on two arguments: the UN Charter's commitment to human rights protection and the existence of a right to humanitarian intervention in customary international law. For the first of these, the argument is that the UN Charter views human rights, peace and security as equally important, so the protection of human rights is one of the principal purposes of the UN (Article 1(3)). In this respect, Weiss (2010: 21) notes the 'seeming contradiction between the intervention-proscribing principle of state sovereignty (especially in Article 2) and the intervention-prescribing principle of human rights (especially in Articles 55–6)'. This has led to claims that the Security Council should have taken action during the Cold War against those states that committed genocide or mass killings (Reisman 1985).

The second argument relates to the fact that all civilized states have agreed certain minimum standards of behaviour. It could be said that there is a customary right of intervention in supreme humanitarian emergencies, such as genocide, mass killing and ethnic cleansing, albeit only when it is authorized by the Security Council (Bellamy and Wheeler 2008; Wheeler 2000). Thus, from this perspective, humanitarian intervention represents the collective will of international society. The interventions in northern Iraq, Bosnia, Somalia and Haiti are examples of actions following Security Council authorizations based on just such an expanded interpretation of international peace and security. Even China, a country that has consistently defended the principle of non-interference, has publicly acknowledged that massive humanitarian crises are a 'legitimate concern' for international society and that the Security Council is entitled to take action in such cases (Bellamy 2013: 113).

Turning to the political argument in support of humanitarian intervention, this was highly visible in the 1990s and became significant in the shift in policy in the field of human rights interventionism. In this respect, the positions of the political leaders of the US and Britain at the time were most important. The so-called 'Clinton Doctrine' (Daadler and O'Hanlon 1999; Daalder 1999) asserted that the United States would use its power to defend not only vital national interests in a specific region but human rights wherever and whenever they were violated. Alongside this, a 'Doctrine of the International Community' was proclaimed by British Prime Minister Tony Blair. This was based on the similar idea that 'we cannot turn our backs on conflicts and the violation of human rights within other countries if we want still to be secure' (Blair 1999a). Blair was effectively arguing that the integration and inter-connectedness of the modern globalized world meant that gross human rights violations in one region have an effect on every other region and thus create moral obligations. Thus, in the 1990s, Western political leaders demonstrated a greater readiness to define humanitarian crises arising out of internal wars as threats to international peace and security that required a collective response in accordance with the UN Charter (Minear *et al.* 1996).

Against humanitarian intervention: the moral, legal and political dimensions

Contemporary opposition to humanitarian intervention, in the words of Bellamy (2013: 113; emphasis in original), focuses on the question of '*who* can legitimately authorise intervention and *in what circumstances*'. These two key questions impact on all three dimensions – moral, legal and political. The moral challenge to humanitarian intervention comes from the lack of consensus about which principles should govern it, and a concern that the most powerful states impose their own culturally determined moral values (Bellamy and Wheeler 2008). An additional difficulty once a moral permit for intervention is granted is the possibility of potential abuse and for further wars to be justified on these grounds (Chomsky 2000). Other problems relate to deciding upon the scale of the humanitarian crisis necessary before force may be used, as well as the issue of whether force should be used in a pre-emptive way to prevent a humanitarian emergency from developing in the first place.

The legal argument against humanitarian intervention is based on the provisions of the UN Charter; international law does not recognize a responsibility/duty of humanitarian intervention, and the use of force is banned outside of the two exceptions set out in the Charter. This is because it is believed that unfettered humanitarian intervention could undermine international order and create disorder (Bellamy 2013). A right to intervention, it is argued, would not create more 'genuine' humanitarian interventions because the main barrier to intervention traditionally has been states' self-interest rather than international law (Chesterman 2001). With very few exceptions, when states have intervened, they have not invoked a norm of humanitarian intervention, but rather have used the language of self-defence or the 'implied authorization' of UN Security Council resolutions; or they have avoided making any legal arguments at all (Wheeler 2000). The historical record seems to demonstrate the lack of a strong consensus about the use of force to protect human rights. In the 1990s, Rwanda, East Timor, Darfur and Congo were all good examples of humanitarian emergencies not receiving the attention of the Security Council. Importantly, as Bellamy (2013) points out, it was only in relation to Libya in 2011, when the Security Council passed Resolution 1973, that the use of force was authorized against a fully functioning state for human rights reasons. Previously, the Security Council's involvement had been limited only to cases where the host state had collapsed or where the internationally recognized government was not the target of the intervention and supported it.

Political arguments against humanitarian intervention abound and also incorporate moral and legal claims to strengthen their position. The first concern relates to potential abuse. It is maintained that as long as there is no impartial mechanism for deciding when it is permissible to intervene, humanitarian motives can be used as pretexts to camouflage the pursuit of national self-interest (Chesterman 2001; Chomsky 1999). A good example is the intervention in Iraq in 2003, which the US and UK claimed was humanitarian only after the original reasons (weapons of mass destruction and links with al-Qaeda) were shown to be ill-founded (Bellamy 2004). Second, analysis of the evidence suggests that states do not tend to intervene for primarily humanitarian reasons (Power 2002). Behind every intervention there is a mixture of motives: realists, for example, point out the importance of national self-interest and maintain that genuine humanitarian interventions are unlikely. As a result, despite humanitarian pretensions, it is difficult to find cases of intervention that were undeniably undertaken primarily for humanitarian reasons. In addition, states are reluctant to risk the lives of their soldiers to save the lives of citizens of other countries, which explains the overwhelming reliance on air power – with its 'casualty-free' potential – during most interventions. In the words of Krauthammer (1999: 6), 'humanitarian war requires means that are inherently inadequate to its ends'. Robertson (2002: 402) goes further by pointing out the irreconcilable contradiction in killing for human rights and asks, 'When can it be right to unleash terror on terrorists, to bomb for human rights, to kill to stop crimes against humanity?' Humanitarian intervention seems to require a 'bloodless war' or a 'risk-transfer war' (Shaw 2003) that is more precise, where 'collateral damage' to civilians is 'accidental' and 'proportional' to the objective of ending or punishing aggression. In reality, the number of civilian deaths in military interventions tends to be high while military personnel deaths are limited. However, at a certain scale, civilian killings can threaten the media-formed legitimacy of the intervention, and even low casualty rates (in relative terms) can be magnified by the media, as will be discussed later in this chapter.

Another political argument employed against humanitarian intervention relates to the inconsistency and selectivity of its application. It is not surprising that questions have been raised about the practicality, longevity and even sincerity of the political doctrines announced by Clinton and Blair (Daalder 1999). Their application has remained highly selective and effectively they have not changed or even challenged the legal status quo in the field of humanitarian intervention. These doctrines proposed that national leaders should take into account their countries' national interests while also acting in accordance with the demands of law, morality and humanity. This means states are entitled, but not obliged, to intervene. Political interests may justify inaction, and material and political costs also have to be considered (Walzer 1992). Since states are driven by what they deem to be their national interests, the latter may dictate different responses to situations in which agreed moral principles are challenged. As a result, states are likely to treat similar cases differently – taking action over long-standing human rights violations in some areas of the world yet remaining completely passive over others. Similarly, when action is taken, it may be too late or consist merely of half-measures (Chandler 2006).

The responsibility to protect

The most ambitious and coherent attempt to promote a new and enhanced norm of intervention is based on the initiative of the UN to redefine 'sovereignty as responsibility'. Consecutive UN Secretary Generals – Javier Pérez de Cuéllar in 1991, Boutros Boutros-Ghali in 1992 and Kofi Annan in 1999 – argued for a reinterpretation of the UN Charter's principles on sovereignty and non-interference in domestic affairs. This was on the grounds that 'defence of the oppressed in the name of morality should prevail over frontiers and legal documents' (Pérez de Cuéllar, cited in Lyons and Mastanduno 1995: 2). In 1992 the Special UN Representative on Internally Displaced People Francis Deng claimed that sovereign states have a responsibility to protect their citizens, and if they are unable to fulfil this responsibility they are 'accountable not only to their national constituencies but ultimately to the international community' (Deng et al. 1996: 1). Kofi Annan (1999b) continued this agenda upon becoming a Secretary General by juxtaposing two versions of sovereignty:

> state sovereignty ... is being redefined ... States are now widely understood to be instruments at the service of their peoples, and not vice versa ... individual sovereignty – by which I mean the fundamental freedom of each individual, enshrined in the charter of the UN and subsequent international treaties – has been enhanced by a renewed and spreading consciousness of individual rights.

Together, these views challenged the traditional inviolability of national sovereignty by clearly suggesting that it is no longer sacrosanct when a large number of people are at risk; it can be overridden when governments fail to protect their own populations (Chopra and Weiss 1992). When combined with the UN Security Council's statements and several actions since the 1990s that have presented humanitarian emergencies as threats to international peace and security, as well as international political commitments, such as those expressed by Clinton and Blair, there is arguably evidence of an emerging commitment to and consensus on the promotion and protection of human rights.

The 'too little and too late' (Weiss 2010: 88) reaction of the Security Council to Rwanda in 1994 and its refusal to authorize NATO intervention in Kosovo in 1999 acted as triggers for the work of the International Commission on Intervention and State Sovereignty (ICISS). This organization had as its objective a framework to reconcile sovereignty and human rights. The outcome was *The Responsibility to Protect* (R2P), published in 2001. This report represents a major attempt to codify and systematize humanitarianism in international law and practice by calling on states to meet their responsibilities to their own citizens. It avoids the sovereignty versus intervention debate by concentrating not on what the interveners are entitled to do but on what is necessary to protect civilians, and thus shifts the focus from any state's right to intervene to every state's responsibility to protect. If domestic authorities fail to meet their responsibility to protect their citizens, they forfeit their sovereignty and the task of protecting should be assumed by the international community. Sovereignty is no longer seen as something states can take for granted, but rather as something they need to earn by protecting their people. R2P claims that an intervention is legitimate when 'major harm to civilians is occurring or imminently apprehended, and the state in question is unable or unwilling to end the harm, or is itself the perpetrator' (ICISS 2001: 16). In terms of means, the intervention is not only limited to the use of military force: non-violent measures such as diplomacy, sanctions, embargoes and referring crimes to the International Criminal Court are other appropriate responses to humanitarian emergencies.

The R2P has three dimensions. In addition to the responsibility to *act*, it includes the responsibility to *prevent*. States have a responsibility to ensure that domestic tensions do not escalate; failure by a state to take appropriate or effective measures results in this responsibility being transferred to the international community. Finally, there is the international community's responsibility to *rebuild* polities and societies in the aftermath of conflict (ICISS 2001). A key benefit of R2P is its replacement of the often divisive term 'humanitarian intervention'.

The ICISS (2001: 32–37, 47–55) proposed six criteria – 'principles for military intervention' – that must be met for an intervention to be legitimate on humanitarian grounds: *right authority, just cause, right intention, last resort, proportional means* and *reasonable prospects*. The latter four are drawn from the 'just war' doctrine and similar criteria have been suggested by Ignatieff (1997), Chesterman (2001), Wheeler (2000) and Teson (1997).

The *just cause* threshold outlines the harm that is deemed sufficient to trigger military intervention and justifies action in two sets of circumstances:

- large-scale loss of life, actual or apprehended, with genocidal intent or not, which is the product either of deliberate state action, or state neglect or inability to act, or a failed state situation; or

- large-scale 'ethnic cleansing', actual or apprehended, whether carried out by killing, forced expulsion, acts of terror or rape.

The criterion of *right intention* specifically refers to halting or averting human suffering as the primary purpose of intervention and asserts that this is most likely achieved through multilateral efforts. Military intervention can be justified only as a *last resort* – when every non-military option (e.g. diplomatic channels, appeals to the UN Security Council and General Assembly, economic sanctions) has been explored. International humanitarian law has to be adhered to and the military intervention has to be *proportional* – that is, the minimum necessary in terms of scale, duration and intensity to achieve the (humanitarian) aims. The intervention may also be undertaken only if there are *reasonable prospects* of success in halting or averting the suffering that justified the action in the first place. Similarly, interventions that have a high probability of escalating violence and conflict should be avoided.

The *right authority* is placed with the UN, specifically the Security Council, whose authorization is required prior to the launch of any humanitarian intervention. The Security Council determines not only if but when, where, how and by whom military intervention should take place. R2P, however, acknowledges the problems surrounding the Council's composition and competences and suggests alternatives if it does not act when a crisis passes the *just cause* threshold, such as involving the General Assembly or appropriate regional organizations. Thus, the ICISS, while not enthusiastic about unilateral humanitarian intervention, suggests a hierarchy of responsibility for such actions, starting with the host state, then the UN Security Council, the General Assembly, regional organizations, 'coalitions of the willing' and finally individual states. Therefore, if the Security Council fails to live up to its responsibilities, the door is opened for states to take the law into their own hands, leading to negative consequences for international order and justice:

> it is unrealistic to expect that concerned states will rule out other means and forms of action to meet the gravity and urgency of these situations … And there is a risk then that such interventions, without the discipline and constraints of UN authorisation, will not be conducted for the right reasons or with the right commitment to the necessary precautionary principles.

R2P also recognizes that if action is taken without the Security Council's approval, but proves successful, 'then this may have enduring serious consequences for the stature and credibility of the UN itself' (ICISS 2001: 55).

While representing a key statement on humanitarian intervention, R2P did not address the possibility that the agreement over criteria does not guarantee agreement on action in real cases, that the criteria might be manipulated by powerful states or that governments may not be persuaded to act (Bellamy 2006c; Bellamy and Wheeler 2008; Hehir 2010). The international reaction to the ICISS report was also mixed. Some states, such as Canada, Germany and the UK, were quite favourable; others, such as Australia, Argentina, Rwanda, Sweden, Colombia and Norway, offered qualified support; some, including the US, Russia and China, were very sceptical from the start. This was the context in which a compromise 'Outcome Document' was adopted at the 2005 UN World Summit. This committed all member states to the principle of responsibility to protect and thus represented an international agreement that institutionalized and incorporated this concept into international practice (Bellamy 2008). Assessments of this document, however, ranged from a 'revolution in consciousness in international affairs' (Joyner 2007: 720) to the rather more critical 'a step backward ... R2P lite' (Weiss 2010: 117). In order to achieve consensus, the final document contained concessions on some of the key aspects of R2P. In particular, the ICISS proposal to include criteria guiding the use of force was abandoned during the negotiations preceding the World Summit; but perhaps most importantly, it was agreed that the responsibility to protect required explicit Security Council authorization. This prevented the possibility of states acting legitimately outside of the Security Council, even when it was blocked by one of the five permanent members exercising its veto power. There was no agreement to remove the veto, just as there was no agreement from the permanent members to endorse an obligation to act whenever the just thresholds were crossed. If anything, the final document *restricted* the scope for intervention – limiting the criteria to genocide, war crimes, ethnic cleansing and crimes against humanity.

Despite these criticisms this was the first time that the international society had formally declared that sovereignty might sometimes give way to concerns over human rights. The term 'responsibility to protect' has now entered the international political vocabulary, and with debates about humanitarian intervention continuing the ICISS's report remains one of the key works on the issue (Hehir 2010: 126).

The role of the media

In the field of humanitarian intervention news media coverage of a given crisis has often been interpreted as a significant factor both in terms of affecting public opinion and in terms of influencing foreign policy decisions to deploy military power in support of humanitarian operations. At the centre of this thinking is the media's ability to communicate various crises around the world and to present and construct them as demanding recognition and response. The decision to create safe havens in northern Iraq following the 1991 Gulf War to protect the Kurds, the deployment of US troops in Somalia in 1992 to defend aid deliveries, and the international involvement in Bosnia between 1992 and 1995 in response to human rights violations are all cited as empirical examples of the so-called 'CNN effect' (Cohen 1994; Gowing 1994; Livingston and Eachus 1995; Robinson 2002; Shaw 1996). This is the idea that real-time news media coverage of human suffering from around the world not only creates a demand for 'something to be done' but prompts changes in foreign policy and can even influence governments to undertake military interventions on humanitarian grounds in 'other people's' wars (Carruthers 2011).

The arguments for the media's ability to exert influence on decision-makers can be traced back to the Vietnam War, when, for the first time, the media was seen as more independent and influential during a conflict. The belief that the graphic portrayal of the scale and destruction of the war in the mass media mobilized public opinion and forced US withdrawal from Vietnam gave rise to the so-called 'Vietnam syndrome'. While the argument for an oppositional media has largely been dismissed (particularly by Hallin's (1986) seminal work *The Uncensored War*), this has triggered substantial subsequent focus on the media's independent role. In the case of the post-Cold War period, this notion of the media's potential power in foreign policy was attributed to two key developments. First were the technological developments and the appearance of 24-hour news channels leading to increased delivery of news about previously unreported or underreported conflicts and the ability to bypass official channels and report directly from conflict areas (Robinson 2004). Second were changes in the world's geostrategic realities (Hoge 1994). With the end of the old bipolar order came the collapse of the old anti-communist consensus and the ideological bond between policy-makers and journalists. Released from the 'prism of the Cold War', journalists were, theoretically, freer not just to cover the stories they wanted to report but to criticize their governments' foreign policies. The constraints imposed by the Cold War ideology that kept journalists and policy-makers on the same page no longer applied in the post-Cold War world. As a result,

> news media had become less dependent upon government information sources in covering events and in defining the news agenda, more likely to include alternative and critical viewpoints, and therefore … the control of governments over the information environment [was weakened]
>
> *(Robinson 2012: 347–348)*

On the one hand, this transformative influence attributed to the media runs contrary to the critical view of the relationship between the media and political power that sees the former merely as a 'faithful servant' (Wolfsfeld 1997) of the latter. The tendency for state actors to have the upper hand in setting and framing the agenda when it comes to media reporting of international conflicts has been documented over a long period of time (GUMG 1985; Bennett and Paletz 1994; Hallin 1986; Knightley 2004; Wolfsfeld 1997). There are a number of explanations for this deferential media role and lack of autonomy and independence from government: reliance on official sources (Bennett 1990; Herman and Chomsky 1988; Wolfsfeld 1997); ideology (Hallin 1986; Herman and Chomsky 1988); media system type (Balabanova 2007, 2011); economic imperatives (Herman and Chomsky 1988); and patriotism (GUMG 1985; Bennett and Paletz 1994).

On the other hand, empirical verification for the existence of the CNN effect has remained rather limited and controversy around its validity and scope has flourished (Gilboa 2005). Those cases that seemingly provide support for the thesis of media-provoked humanitarian intervention have been questioned on the basis that the underlying reasons and driving factors were geopolitical interests and concerns. Shaw's study of the British media and policy towards the Kurdish crisis, for example, claimed that 'it was the British media and public opinion which forced governments' hands', making the crisis 'the only clear-cut case, of all the conflicts in the early 1990s, in which media coverage compelled intervention by the Western powers' (Shaw 1996: vii, 156). However, his conclusions – deduced from policy outcomes and based on a correlation with empathetic media coverage – have been criticized for not taking into consideration the policy-making process in relation to the conflict. Looking at the same case, Robinson (2002) identified a series of possible factors informing the decision to intervene, including the importance of geostrategic concerns in relation to Turkey in light of that country's membership of NATO, its loyalty to the US during the first Gulf War, and the Kurdish question within its own borders. At most, Robinson concluded that 'the critical and empathy-framed coverage would have had an enabling effect, helping to explain and justify the deployment of ground troops in Iraq to the US public, but the decision itself was most likely motivated by non-media related concerns' (Robinson 2002: 70–71).

Another example is provided by the case of the US intervention in Somalia. Cohen's (1994: 9–10) findings suggested that television 'has demonstrated its power to move governments … [as] TV mobilised the conscience of the nation's public institutions, compelling the government into a policy of intervention for humanitarian reasons'. Livingston and Eachus (1995: 413), however, concluded that the US decision to intervene militarily in Somalia 'was the result of diplomatic and bureaucratic operations, with news coverage coming in response to those decisions'. Wheeler (2000) and Robinson (2001) reached similar conclusions, whereas Gibbs (2000) offered an alternative explanation for the intervention: namely, the United States' strategic and economic interests in the area.

Recognition that initially enthusiastic accounts of media-inspired humanitarian action were simplistic and overstated (Gowing 1994; Robinson 2002) runs in parallel with evidence of the selective nature of humanitarian interventions themselves. The 1994 Rwandan genocide, examined in more detail in Chapter 5, illustrates this well. Rwanda demonstrated both the reluctance of the international community to get involved and the Western media's inaccurate reporting of the events as a supposed 'cease-fire breakdown' and/or simply another round of unstoppable tribal warfare (Livingston and Eachus 1999; Robinson 2002). Aside from Rwanda, other 'stealth' conflicts have scarcely been covered by the media, despite the massive human suffering associated with them (Hawkins 2008). This strongly suggests that media pressure alone cannot explain political decisions to undertake humanitarian interventions. At most, it might be viewed as one of a number of factors contributing to the final decision of when and where to intervene. Jakobsen (1996) looked at decisions to intervene in Kuwait, northern Iraq, Somalia, Rwanda and Haiti, and examined the significance of five factors: a clear humanitarian and/or legal case; national interest; chance of success; domestic support; and the CNN effect. His findings suggested that in humanitarian interventions the CNN effect 'does appear to be a necessary condition for humanitarian enforcement'; however, deciding to intervene or not 'was ultimately determined by the perceived chance of success' (Jakobsen 1996: 213). In a later study, Jakobsen (2000: 138) expanded on his list of factors:

> media generated pressure may make a difference to policy by putting military intervention on the agenda in situations when governments are reluctant to use force, interventions are unlikely to follow unless they can be conducted quickly with a low risk of casualties. Since this is rarely the case, media pressures on reluctant governments are most likely to result in minimalist policies aimed at defusing pressure for interventions on the ground.

Among the circumstances in which the media can become more or less influential, the role of elite disagreement or policy uncertainty is highlighted as particularly important (Gowing 1994; Strobel 1997; Robinson 2002; Seib 2002; Entman 2004). The news media has more potential to influence policy at times of uncertainty – when policy is weakly held, has little support, or is in flux. If policy-makers are unsure, they open the door for potential media influence. However, even in these cases, only tactical, rather than strategic, decisions tend to be affected. Alternatively, 'cosmetic' policy responses might be triggered, as arguably happened in Bosnia when limited air strikes were carried out and wounded children were air lifted to safety (Gowing 1994; Minear *et al.* 1996). Case study research has also found that the news media's impact upon policy is likely to lead to deployment of air power, rather than ground troops, in humanitarian actions (Bahador 2007; Robinson 2002).

Another factor affecting the potential for media influence over foreign policy is the type of policy in question, with the media likely to have a greater impact in some areas rather than others (Livingston 1997). For instance, media influence may be discerned when the policy is less costly in terms of financial or political risk, or when it deals with procedural-level issues, such as where to send humanitarian aid. By contrast, decisions to intervene militarily or to withdraw from an ongoing conflict are less likely to be swayed by the media because a number of other key factors – such as national interest, security concerns, international law and alliances – will be at play.

Notwithstanding the narrow opportunity for media influence to occur, the way in which a news report is framed is seen as crucial in terms of maximizing any impact. Preston (1996) identifies two distinct forms of media framing of disasters and humanitarian crises (see Chapter 3). First, critical/empathy framing encourages association with the suffering people, criticizes government inaction and effectively promotes a policy of intervention, and advances human rights-based approaches to solve the problem. The alternative is distance framing, where the style of coverage creates or maintains emotional distance between the audience and the people suffering in a conflict. Distance framing is also implicitly supportive of government policy that opposes military intervention and, as such, either consciously avoids or fails to promote a policy of intervention.

On a theoretical level, the empirical evidence for and against media power can be analysed and understood via the political contest model (Wolfsfeld 1997), the policy–media interaction model (Robinson 2002) and the cascading activation model (Entman 2004). All these models recognize elite dissensus as a key factor that allows greater media independence and potential to influence policy decisions in relation to humanitarian interventions. Wolfsfeld (1997), for example, identifies the conditions which allow non-elite groups to set the media agenda. At these times they are able to initiate events, control the information environment and gain support from at least part of the political elite. In this way non-elite groups can be successful at influencing the news media, as Palestinians were during the First Intifada (1987–1993). Robinson (2002) proposes that the media can influence government policy when there is policy uncertainty alongside critically framed media coverage. In this situation governments are unable to supply coherent, plausible and well-prepared lines to the media and therefore lose their power to set the agenda. Finally, Entman (2004) expects an independent and oppositional media when there is a dissensus among officials at the top level of government, but also when mid-level officials are promoting challenges to existing policy and exogenous events occur that are open to interpretation.

In addition to these conditioning variables, further scepticism over the media's power to influence decisions about humanitarian action comes from the 'compassion fatigue' thesis (Moeller 1999). While the CNN effect, in the words of Cottle (2008: 128; emphasis in the original), 'adopts a *morally benign* view of the humanitarian influence of global news media', the compassion fatigue argument 'discerns a *morally malign* impact in so far as our capacity for moral responses is undermined'. Indeed, the compassion fatigue thesis suggests that instead of triggering empathy with the suffering of distant strangers, the constant circulation of media reports about humanitarian crises overwhelms audiences, leading to them giving up hope of changing situations for the better. Another problem is that the media commodifies and objectifies the suffering to such an extent that the 'audience become passive spectators of distant death and pain without any moral commitment' (Höijer 2004: 527).

At the very core of this argument (as in the case of the CNN effect), however, is the understanding that media images alone cannot predict audience response. As Sontag (2003: 11–13) claims, 'Scenes of an atrocity may give rise to opposing responses. A call for peace. A cry for revenge. Or simply the bemused awareness, continually restocked by photographic information, that terrible things happen.' This highlights the centrality of the cosmopolitan values that underpin responses to human rights violations; it also adds to the significance of the type of media reporting that can invite or distance a sense of obligation to those who are suffering. In the language of the CNN effect literature, this can be through empathy versus distance framing. In the literature on compassion fatigue, it is conceptualized by Chouliaraki's (2006) three different 'regimes of pity' that position us as spectators. The first of these is 'adventure', where emotional content is restricted and scenes of suffering are presented in an objective and factual way. Second there is 'emergency', where the human element is emphasized and the past causes and future consequences of suffering are given greater space. Finally there is 'ecstatic', which is more intense and immersive, characteristic of live footage, and which invites identification with the suffering people (Chouliaraki 2006).

Both the different frames and the three 'regimes of pity' leave open the question of whether and how news resonates with actual audiences. Responses are likely to be quite differentiated and distinct from one another; focusing only on news media items as explanatory variables in isolation from the wider socio-political context of the audience may not be sufficient. According to Chouliaraki (2013: 173), we are currently in an age of 'feelgood' activism and 'ironic spectatorship' characterized by a 'shift in the moral agency of suffering from a disposition that is oriented towards the distant other, acknowledging human vulnerability as a cause for our action, to a disposition that is oriented towards the self, acknowledging consumerism as a key motivation for our humanitarian engagements'.

How audiences respond to news representations of distant suffering can be connected to the specific historical, social, economic and political context. Also crucial is the way in which universal human rights are perceived and embedded in domestic political dynamics and how cosmopolitan notions of solidarity have been supported or undermined previously. As Cottle (2008: 138) argues:

> As categories of the 'other' as alien become incrementally dismantled through processes of globalisation, democracy and the international regime of human rights (which is not to say that this is a one-way street) so the cultural and political environment which we inhabit also informs how and what we see and feel and, arguably, our sense of obligation to act.

The two case studies examined in the remainder of this chapter – Kosovo 1999 and Libya 2011 – are both examples of humanitarian interventions. They have been selected because they illustrate very well the tensions surrounding the nature, legality and practicalities of humanitarian intervention as well as the presumed media power in provoking and influencing political decisions to undertake military action on humanitarian grounds. In addition, they took place in distinct historical eras: the first during the 1990s and the second post-9/11 – one before and one after the advent of R2P. This makes it possible to consider the role of the global 'war on terror' in relation to both humanitarian intervention and the CNN effect and examine the impact of R2P in practice. Arguably, the war on terror pushed humanitarian concerns down the international agenda and humanitarian arguments became post-hoc justifications following interventions. Similarly, with regard to the debate over the CNN effect, the 1990s are now seen as an aberration (Robinson 2005), rather than the dominant pattern, with 'normal service' – characterized by a more deferential and constrained type of coverage with more limited opportunities for influencing policy – resuming since then (Entman 2004). While this view is not accepted by all (e.g. see Bahador 2011), the intervention in Libya was authorized as humanitarian and thus presents the ideal context in which to consider the media–policy dynamics in the age of R2P.

Case study: Kosovo 1999

The international military action against the Federal Republic of Yugoslavia (FRY) in 1999 'broke new ground' in that it was widely proclaimed as the first international military intervention against a sovereign state for purely human rights purposes (Ignatieff 2001b: 5). In the words of Tony Blair, this was a war fought 'not for territory, but for values' (Blair 1999b). Among the unique features of the 11-week bombing campaign conducted by the North Atlantic Treaty Organization (NATO) were that it was the first sustained use of armed force by the alliance since its establishment in 1949; the first major use of destructive armed force undertaken with the purpose of implementing UN Security Council resolutions, but without Security Council authorization; the first major bombing campaign to stop crimes against humanity committed by a state within its own borders; and, according to some commentators, the first bombing campaign to force a change of policy by the target government without the need to resort to subsequent sustained land operations (Roberts 1999: 102). Some also consider the Kosovo crisis as a prime example of how the CNN effect influenced Western governments (Nye 1999a; Livingston 2000). However, significant disagreements exist about NATO's 'true' motivation, the diplomacy that led to Operation Allied Force and the role of the media in relation to the decision to intervene.

Kosovo was a predominantly ethnically Albanian province of Serbia (in 1998 Serbs represented only 10 per cent of the province's population (Ilic 2001)) and as such it formally enjoyed a high degree of autonomy within the FRY until 1989. From the mid-1980s, however, conditions began to deteriorate for Kosovo Albanians: regional government was abolished; Serbo-Croatian was imposed as the official language; Albanian-language media and public education in Albanian were banned; and many ethnic Albanians were dismissed from their jobs (Donnelly 2013a: 192). In response to Serbia's revocation of autonomy in 1989, Kosovo Albanians declared independence and developed a parallel government, economy and welfare state. This moderate approach did not lead to any significant results and the Serbian state continued to erode Kosovans' rights with respect to property, employment, education and the exercise of basic freedoms. Despite high expectations, the 1995 Dayton Peace Accords, signed primarily to end the conflict in Bosnia, did not make any provisions relating to Kosovo. This signalled the end of passive resistance as a strategy and opened the door for the Kosovo Liberation Army (KLA), who stepped up their armed campaign (Hodge 2000; Judah 1999; O'Neill 2002). What followed was an escalating pattern of violence between the KLA and the Serbian police and military, leading to thousands of deaths, hundreds of thousands of internally displaced persons and thousands of refugees (Hehir 2010). The KLA's strategy of provoking excessive counter-attacks from the Serbians was aimed at both generating domestic support and provoking international condemnation of Slobodan Milošević's regime and ultimately intervention on the side of the Kosovo Albanians (IICK 2000; Gow 2003; Ignatieff 2001; Kuperman 2006; O'Neill 2002).

The initial international reaction to the developing crisis was limited and reactive, combining a concern for the victims with an unwillingness to get dragged further into the Balkan wars (Bellamy 2002). UN Resolutions 1160 and 1199 described the situation in Kosovo as a threat to peace and stability, but neither of them authorized the use of force. There was a level of disagreement over the scale of suffering, with some claiming that 'there was no humanitarian crisis in Kosovo in 1997, or in 1998, or in 1999 in any conventionally understood sense of the term' (Bardos 2003: 57), while others insisted that 'Anyone who was in Kosovo, as I was, in the winter of 1998–1999 could see that there was a humanitarian disaster' (Garton Ash 2000: 2). Following an increase in the number of internally displaced persons and refugees fleeing to neighbouring Albania and Macedonia (an estimated 300,000 people), international efforts intensified, including a negotiated but ultimately unsuccessful settlement in October 1998 and peace negotiations in Rambouillet, France, in February 1999. The specific trigger for the latter was the discovery of the bodies of 45 ethnic Albanians in the village of Racak on 15 January and the media's broadcast of images of this massacre around the world.

The Rambouillet negotiations broke down when the proposed agreement was signed by only the Kosovo Albanian delegation, thus effectively paving the way for the NATO air campaign against the FRY. Some controversy surrounds the fairness of the negotiations. On one hand, they are characterized as US Secretary of State Madeleine Albright's 'charade to get a bombing campaign' (Jatras 2000: 24; see also Judah 2000) by offering Belgrade an unacceptable deal. In particular, critics point to the provisions of Appendix B of the agreement, which gave NATO unrestricted access to FRY territory (Johnstone 2002: 244–247). On the other hand, some commentators view the talks as a genuine attempt to broker an agreement. From this perspective, Milošević had already decided that 'he would test NATO's resolve and go to war' (Bellamy 2002: 150).

Either way, the NATO air strikes began on 24 March and continued until 10 June 1999. The campaign was supposed to be 'short and sweet', with no plans for a subsequent land invasion and an expectation that the Yugoslav government would propose a cease-fire in order to renew negotiations at Rambouillet after only a few days (IICK 2000; Bacevich and Cohen 2001: ix; Ignatieff 2001; Roberts 1999). In the end, this proposal never materialized: the air campaign gradually intensified and expanded its targets to include military–industrial infrastructure, along with media installations and other targets in Serbia. The result was that the killings on both sides in the Kosovo conflict on the ground escalated, the number of refugees reached 600,000 people, and another 800,000 were displaced inside the country (Freedman 2000: 353). Still, there was an adherence to the original policy that there would be no deployment of ground troops or even low-level bombing. The air campaign finished on 10 June 1999 with the signing of a 'Military Technical Agreement' between the FRY army and NATO, subsequently endorsed by UN Security Council Resolution 1244. According to the Independent International Commission on Kosovo (IICK 2000: 96), 'the final agreement did contain some gains from the FRY point of view': for instance, there was no provision for

NATO presence in the FRY and the territorial integrity of the FRY was recognized, as was Belgrade's jurisdiction over Kosovo.

NATO's intervention in Kosovo has provoked a number of concerns that relate to the moral, legal and political considerations surrounding it. The moral argument was to the fore in these discussions. Operation Allied Force was described as 'the first war waged for ethical principles alone' (Robertson 2002: 451); it was about the West's '*moral responsibility* to stop the terrible atrocities taking place in Kosovo' (Wheeler 2000: 266; emphasis added). The moral claim was that NATO acted militarily not to defend any immediate, territorial national interest of one of its member states; rather, it was justified as a defence of human rights and the individual-level security of Kosovo Albanians (Solana 1999). These arguments seemed to herald the beginning of greater humanitarian activism incorporating increased coercive enforcement of human rights norms and the development of Western foreign policy based on universal values rather than national interests (Hehir 2010: 212). This was certainly the assessment of Human Rights Watch (2000), which referred to the 1999 Kosovo intervention as indicative of a new era for human rights when Western states would act to help the victims of atrocities.

Despite this dominant moral narrative advanced by NATO and supported by others (Guicherd 1999), the decision to launch air strikes proved to be quite controversial. Questions were raised about the humanitarian motives for the action, the methods used and the legality of the operation. The moral arguments were criticized as hypocritical, or as masking a desire for symbolism 'to demonstrate NATO's new mission in time for its fiftieth anniversary' (Johnstone 2000: 8). Other criticisms were that the action served the geostrategic interests of the US in Eurasia, and above all that it was designed to preserve NATO's credibility in the region. For some, the intervention was risky, setting a dangerous precedent that potentially could destabilize the whole international system (Chandler 2002; Chomsky 1999; Hammond and Herman 2000a; Mandelbaum 1999; Wood 2000).

Once an intervention is declared as humanitarian, it is not only the motives that come under added scrutiny but the way in which the action is carried out. Because the NATO intervention relied solely on high-attitude aerial bombardment, rather than the deployment of ground troops, it could be criticized for the imprecision of the bombs. These caused many civilian casualties, including the very Kosovo Albanians whom NATO had supposedly launched the campaign to protect. Limiting operations to the air also meant that NATO was unable to prevent attacks on the ground, and these arguably escalated after the start of the air strikes (McLaughlin 2002a; Roberts 1999). For these reasons, the NATO action was seen as a contradictory and even counter-productive means of protecting human rights. The priority of maintaining the illusion of a 'casualty-free' operation meant there was a gap between the language of ultimate commitment and the practicalities of conducting warfare of minimal risk (Ignatieff 2001: 111; Wheeler 2000).

Finally, there was the question of the legal status of the intervention. While NATO argued that its actions were consistent with Security Council Resolutions 1160, 1199 and, subsequently, 1203,[2] and as such in accordance with international law, the fact that none of these documents contained specific provisions authorizing the use of force effectively made the intervention illegal. Faced with Russian and Chinese opposition, NATO knew it was unlikely to obtain the agreement of all of the veto-bearing permanent members of the Security Council, which led to the decision to intervene without explicit authorization (Bellamy 2002; Booth 2001). Supporters of the intervention claimed that 'armed intervention was needed to prevent further humanitarian catastrophe' and referred to the overwhelming humanitarian necessity as a justification (Roberts 1999; Ronzitti 1999: 46). The IICK's (2000: 10) conclusion that Operation Allied Force was 'illegal but legitimate' highlights tensions that go beyond this specific instance and raises questions about the utility of international law and the vitality of the UN. The majority view was indeed that international law did not permit humanitarian intervention of the kind carried out by NATO. However, both critics and supporters of the intervention – although on different grounds – have used the case to question the legitimacy of the Security Council and highlight the need for amendments to international law and the UN Charter (Bellamy 2002; Daalder and O'Hanlon 2000; Guicherd 1999; Hehir 2008). R2P, discussed earlier in this chapter, was a direct response to the legal controversy triggered by this intervention and an effort to change the debate around humanitarian intervention to shift the focus on to states' responsibilities and away from the legal right to intervene.

Western media attention started to focus on the conflict in Kosovo in 1998; from then on, it arguably increased or decreased depending on the level of violence on the ground. Two opinions on the role of the media prior to and during the air campaign have been proposed: that it manufactured consent for Western policy and that media organizations acted as propaganda mouthpieces for NATO; and that it played an oppositional role by criticizing US and NATO policy (Robinson 2002). The argument that the media manufactured consent is based on the uncritical acceptance of the official policy by media organizations regarding the purpose and intent of the negotiations in Rambouillet and the lack of coverage of Appendix B and Serbia's attempts to reach a compromise (Chomsky 1999; Hammond 2000; Hammond and Herman 2000b). From this perspective, the media accepted wholesale the humanitarian justifications for the war and neglected to challenge the fundamental righteousness of the Western action (Hammond 2007; Thussu 2000). The media consistently reproduced the narrative that the Yugoslav government had caused a humanitarian emergency in Kosovo, which was interpreted as a threat to international peace and security (Solana 1999). NATO's action was uncritically reported as a humanitarian intervention – a last resort when all other channels had been exhausted (Hammond 2007). Questions relating to the legality of the bombing and its impact on national sovereignty were omitted from media debates. Milošević was demonized and compared with Saddam Hussein, whereas members of the KLA (which the US government had labelled a terrorist organization up to 1998) were presented as 'freedom fighters'. Furthermore, this assessment alleges that Serb atrocities – real or otherwise – were highlighted and exaggerated by US, UK and NATO military commanders and then reported uncritically by the media, unlike the atrocities committed by the KLA, which came to light only after the war was over (Hammond 2007; Herman and Peterson 2000; Thussu 2000). This happened because the coverage was dominated by information that came directly from NATO and other Western officials: the media reproduced NATO spin even when the journalists were aware that certain themes were being deliberately promoted by official spokesmen. In support of this argument, it later emerged that much of the information was inaccurate and of little direct relevance (Goff 1999; Hammond 2007; Thussu 2000). Regardless of the veracity of the reporting, however, an empathy frame prevailed in news media reports, encouraging empathy with Kosovo Albanians rather than emotional distance and thus effectively favouring a policy to intervene to prevent a humanitarian catastrophe (Balabanova 2007, 2010; Robinson 2002). As Hammond and Herman (2000b: 207) conclude, 'The mainstream media of the leading NATO powers supported the war against Yugoslavia with almost uniform and uncritical enthusiasm. They accepted without question the justice of the NATO cause.'

The alternative interpretation sees the media as highly critical of the NATO air campaign and functioning as a 'watchdog' of the official policy. It is argued that space given to critical voices – for example, those demanding ground troops – increased the pressure on the US administration in particular. Coverage of mistakes and 'collateral damage' caused by the air strikes (e.g. bombings of the Chinese Embassy in Belgrade, refugee columns and the Radio Television of Serbia headquarters) proved uncomfortable for NATO and Western governments (Robinson 2002). In the case of the British media, 'there was real media counterweight to NATO spin' in that sceptics were allowed to challenge the explanations offered by the Alliance for hitting the wrong targets (McLaughlin 2002b: 122). Bahador (2007) even argues that at some points the media had a galvanizing effect and led to policy shifts. He specifically refers to the massacres allegedly committed by the Serbs and reported by the Western media, with the Racak massacre in January 1999 being the starkest example.

However, critical coverage in the US really only focused on whether ground troops should be deployed, and appeared in the print media for only a brief period. This probably reflected the level of elite dissensus, and overall the media did not seem to influence decision-makers to change their policy from air bombardment to ground-troop intervention (Robinson 2002). Reporters in general agreed with the aims of NATO's action and accepted the underlying legitimacy of the operation. This suggests that Kosovo cannot be seen as an example of the CNN effect in action, of the media challenging government policy. Rather, it was a case of the media enabling and facilitating the execution of a firmly agreed policy of aerial intervention (Balabanova 2007; Robinson 2002).

Case study: Libya 2011

When, on 17 March 2011, the UN Security Council passed Resolution 1973, it effectively authorized the first military intervention against a functioning state for human protection purposes (Bellamy 2013). The subsequent operation in Libya has been hailed as a 'model intervention' (Daalder and Stavridis 2012: 2) and 'a text-book case of the R2P norm working exactly as it was supposed to' (Evans, cited in Hehir 2013b: 137). Still, questions have been asked about the net humanitarian impact of NATO's intervention, the true goals of the mission, and the implications for R2P (Kuperman 2013; Murray 2013). International media coverage was somewhat constrained by issues of access, which meant no Western journalists were present in some parts of the country (Kellner 2012). The majority of the reporting supported and encouraged the intervention, and very little attention was paid to the bigger questions relating to political considerations, financial implications and the responsibility to protect.

The events in Libya in early 2011 need to be seen in the context of the wider Arab Spring, the series of demonstrations that started in 2010 in protest against repressive regimes and their autocratic leaders in several North African and Middle Eastern countries. Unlike the non-violent uprisings in Tunisia and Egypt, the confrontation between the protesters and the Gaddafi regime in Libya followed the logic of a civil war (ICG 2011: i).

Ironically, in the years leading up to the start of the crisis, Muammar Gaddafi had been transformed from 'the most reviled international figure in the West' to an accepted international statesman who supported the 'war on terror' (Hehir 2013a: 2). During the 1980s, Gaddafi supported various international terrorist organizations, was directly involved in murderous attacks against the US, the UK, France and Germany, and tried to create a coalition in the Arab world that was hostile to Western interests. But after 2003 he disbanded his chemical weapons programme and started a process of reintegration with the West facilitated by a willingness to serve as a site for extraordinary rendition (AI 2012; Vandewalle 2006). Domestically, however, the nature of the regime did not change and it continued to be characterized by brutal and oppressive policies, no strong sense of national citizenship, and patterns of patronage and corruption. In a 2010 report, Amnesty International concluded:

> Libya's reintegration into the international community has not been accompanied by significant reforms or long-lasting improvements in the domestic human rights situation … members of the EU and the USA … are turning a blind eye to the human rights situation in order to further national interests.
>
> *(AI 2010: 9)*

On 15 February 2011 a wave of mass demonstrations erupted in Benghazi, government forces fired on the crowd, and the protests spread to the rest of the country. The international response – in contrast to many other similar, previous situations – was swift. It was also characterized by a high degree of policy consensus and certainty. The UN Security Council imposed sanctions, an arms embargo and an asset freeze on Libya; Gaddafi's crimes against humanity were referred to the International Criminal Court. The reaction of the Arab League was also significant in that it suspended Libya from its sessions and then called on the international community to impose a no-fly zone over the country (Bellamy and Williams 2011).

Despite this, the violence continued and on 17 March 2011 the Security Council passed Resolution 1973, which authorized the establishment of the no-fly zone. The resolution also condemned 'the gross and systematic violation of human rights ... committed by the Libyan authorities', and most importantly it authorized states to 'take all necessary measures ... to protect civilians and civilian populated areas under threat of attack'. The UK and France were the main drivers behind the resolution, which passed with five abstentions from Brazil, China, Germany, India and Russia. Military action began on 19 March and initially Operation Unified Protector was led by the US, France and the UK. Soon, however, NATO took over the control and command, and the US withdrew from direct combat. Instead, the latter played a central role in gathering and analysing intelligence, refuelling NATO and partner aircraft, and contributing high-end military capabilities (Barry 2011; Daalder and Stavridis 2012). The NATO-led mission in Libya had three goals: to police the arms embargo, to patrol the no-fly zone and to protect civilians (Daalder and Stavridis 2012). Gaddafi was captured and killed on 20 October 2011 and the NATO mission ended soon after (on 31 October), with a National Transitional Council coming to power.

NATO's military campaign in Libya was characterized by explicit UN backing, widespread regional and international support, restricted military involvement, avoidance of major ground operations, and minimal risk of large-scale casualties (Chivvis 2012; Clements 2013: 121–122; Morris 2013). Its two strongest advocates – Britain and France – insisted that action in Libya was 'necessary, legal and right' (Cameron, cited in *The Economist* 2011) in light of the Gaddafi government's 'brutal and bloody' repression (Araud, cited in Davidson 2013: 315). Two aspects of the intervention, however, became a focus of debate and controversy. First, the strategic aims of the military operation were surrounded in ambiguity. While the UN mandate called only for operations to defend civilians, the US, France and the UK had all called for regime change prior to the passing of Resolution 1973 (Chivvis 2012). Achieving the goal of protection of civilians, however, proved difficult since the rebel forces that NATO was backing were untrained, ill-equipped, disorganized and spread around the country in small groups that had difficulty communicating with each other. As Barry (2011) notes, without NATO's support, these rebels would not have been able to defend their positions. With the number of casualties and refugees increasing, stronger statements were made by leading Western governments in support of regime change; France unilaterally air-dropped weapons to the rebels; further arms were illegally smuggled to them from the UAE and Qatar; and military support was provided by Sudan (ICG 2011: i; Hehir 2013a). All of this, in the words of Hehir (2013a: 6), 'stretched the terms of Resolution 1973 beyond breaking point' and provoked strong criticism from Russia and China for what they saw as an illegitimate interpretation of the resolution (Barry 2011).

The second point of controversy relates to the R2P doctrine. Before the intervention into Libya, the concept had already received wide recognition, but its impact and application had remained patchy. The reaction to the genocide in Darfur, discussed in Chapter 5, demonstrated the selective approach to humanitarian crises and the continued predominance of national interests, despite the international acceptance of R2P. It confirmed Bellamy's (2008: 3) conclusion that responses to intra-state crises will continue to be 'made in an ad hoc fashion by political leaders balancing national interests, legal considerations, world opinion, perceived costs and humanitarian impulses – much as they were prior to the advent of R2P'. As a result, at the start of the military intervention in Libya, R2P faced challenges on three interconnected grounds:

> first, that evidence of its efficacy was lacking; second, that states held widely divergent understandings of its remit and this ambiguity diminished its putative status as a norm; and third, that it had catalyzed no actual legal reform and thus the very system it was established to change remained intact.
>
> *(Hehir 2013a: 8)*

When the intervention in Libya took place, opinions were divided as to whether this did indeed herald a new era in which the international community was going to abide by the principles of R2P. The UN Secretary General Ban Ki-Moon (cited in Hehir 2013b: 140) described the military action as a clear result of the Security Council's 'determination to fulfill its responsibility to protect civilians from violence perpetrated upon them by their own government'. The speed of the response, the significant (although not universal) international support and the assessment of the intervention as ultimately successful offer support for this view (Daalder and Stavridis 2012). Critics, on the other hand, dispute the clear and urgent humanitarian rationale for launching the intervention in the first place as well as the net humanitarian outcome (e.g. Kuperman 2013; Murray 2013). Instead of humanitarian concerns being the driving force for the intervention, these evaluations highlight geostrategic considerations as the primary factors: namely, the desire to prevent destabilization in an already unstable region. Some have also argued that it was in the West's economic and political interests to remove Gaddafi from power (Jewell 2011). In addition, the centrality of the R2P norm in the decision-making process has been questioned in light of the total absence of the term 'Responsibility to Protect' in Resolution 1973, the statements of the Security Council's member states when discussing Libya, and the rhetoric of the political leaders of the US and the UK (Hehir 2013b; Morris 2013).

If anything, Morris (2013) argues, Russia (explicitly) and China (implicitly) both used NATO's 'loose' interpretation of the UN mandate in Libya to discredit R2P in subsequent Security Council debates – for example, over action in the later Syrian crisis. This is cited as evidence for the norm not being 'as deeply internalized as is commonly suggested' (Morris 2013: 1280) and still 'contested by some members of the Security Council' (Welsh 2011: 255). It also renders the intervention in Libya as 'a unique constellation of necessarily temporal factors unrelated, or only tangentially related, to R2P' (Hehir 2013b: 140), rather than an illustration of the norm in action. Still, as Weiss (2011: 292) points out 'Libya suggests that we can say no more Holocausts, Cambodias, and Rwandas – and occasionally mean it.'

Unsurprisingly, then, the case of Libya did not resolve the debate surrounding humanitarian intervention. The questions of consistency, competing states' interests and decision-making within the Security Council all remain factors affecting the functioning of the Responsibility to Protect.

Western media coverage of the events in Libya was initially hindered by the ban on foreign journalists entering the country. Images appearing in the West were mainly uploaded via YouTube and then incorporated into the mainstream Western media's broadcasts. As a result, despite the absence of foreign correspondents on the ground, news and images of human rights abuses and of the developing humanitarian catastrophe did reach the outside world (Cottle 2011). On the back of these reports, calls were made in the news media for those responsible to be prosecuted and for a humanitarian intervention to be undertaken. Both Arab and Western media seemed convinced that the Gaddafi regime's days were numbered (Jewell 2011). Still, there were some marked differences in the coverage immediately before and during the military intervention between the UK, the US and France, all of whom supported Resolution 1973, and Germany, who abstained on the matter. To a large extent, this mirrored the differences in their political positions (Bucher *et al.* 2013). In the case of the US, media coverage of the bombing of Libya followed the same pattern and had the same characteristics as the media coverage of every other recent US military action – 'from a parade of officials to a narrow range of debate to an emphasis on the infallible precision of US weapons' (Hart 2011). The only limited criticism came from some Republican politicians and conservative commentators, which took the form of anti-Obama rhetoric or a call for swifter action and a broader military campaign. The US media also consistently maintained that the nation's way of fighting the war was safe, even when evidence of civilian casualties started to appear. This kind of coverage led Kellner (2012: 77) to conclude that CNN was 'pure US state and military propaganda during wartime'.

Similar to the US, the British print media was sold on the necessity of the intervention in Libya (Jewell 2011). This was achieved through presenting Gaddafi as a murderer of his own people, drawing parallels between him and Stalin or Saddam Hussein, and dehumanizing and even animalizing him by routinely referring to him as a 'mad dog'. This demonization, highlighting that Gaddafi was a tyrant who was capable of anything, was prominent on the pages of both tabloids and broadsheets, providing a narrative that was easy to understand. As Jewell (2011: 32) points out, as a result 'The moral authority of the west is reinforced once again and the righteousness of action against Gaddafi and his evil regime becomes axiomatic.' As far as the reasons for the war were concerned, the British media predominantly accepted the liberating nature of NATO's mission and its legitimacy, and high-lighted the protection of civilians. All this seems to suggest that 'by and large the mainstream press has faithfully reproduced the official line about intervention in Libya' (Jewell 2011: 35).

The French press also predominantly presented pro-intervention arguments, thus effectively adopting the same position as the French government on the events in Libya. There was only limited reporting of any counter-arguments; the main claims put forward related to the support of rebels, the Responsibility to Protect, human rights, the prevention of terrorism and economic factors (Bucher *et al.* 2013).

Taken together, the media coverage in these three countries clearly demonstrates the use of identical arguments by the media and those who draft foreign policy, with the reporting clearly in line with official government positions. While further research would be required to investigate any claims regarding causality along the lines of either the CNN effect or manufacturing consent, it can be argued that the coverage enabled and facilitated the execution of the military intervention in Libya. While time and space were given to the issues of a humanitarian response and the enforcement of a no-fly zone before the NATO mission began, the debate in the media did not engage with the norm of R2P and its implications for national sovereignty. Once the campaign started there was a pronounced advocacy for regime change and military support for rebels, but very little was said about the economic and political factors involved, or about the financial costs of involvement (Cottle 2011; Jewell 2011). Similarly one-sided, but from the opposite perspective, was the coverage presented by Russian television, which continuously broadcast anti-American propaganda and used the rubric 'Libya under fire' (Kellner 2012).

The German press followed a different pattern, starting with its initial limited coverage and few mentions of Libya (Bucher *et al.* 2013). Thereafter, unlike the British, American and French press, space was given to both sides of the argument – both in favour of and against the military intervention. On the whole, the debate was more comprehensive and a wider variety of anti-intervention arguments were presented, focusing on issues of legitimacy, national sovereignty and the need for a regional solution. Thus, the German press offered a more varied discussion of the issue, just as Hallin (1986) and Bennett (1990) would have predicted. It followed and reflected the more nuanced German political debate that was less confident of the merits of armed intervention and chose to abstain in the vote on Resolution 1973.

Finally, and notably, in Kellner's (2012: 77) assessment, the Al Jazeera TV network provided 'genuinely balanced reporting' and 'emerged as one of the most reliable sources of information on the war in Libya in the global media'.

Conclusions

When considering the extent of global suffering, it often appears that human rights are more honoured in the breach than in the observance. Debates around humanitarian intervention are therefore fascinating for exploring the international community's response to such situations; for examining the level of confidence which exists regarding the universal character of human rights and how these should be practically applied at times of emergency. Few would deny that there is a large gap between the cosmopolitan promise of developments such as R2P and the continuing array of human rights abuses that occurs across the world. The question this chapter asks is: what does this mean for international human rights and for the role of the media in that system? For writers such as Kaldor (2010) and Chomsky (1999), examination of humanitarian intervention highlights all of the disappointing features of international relations, the hypocrisy of the UN Security Council, and the powerful states that dominate global politics. For them, the way in which the media operates is part of the problem. From this perspective, the role of the media, in symbiosis with contemporary politics' 'short-termism', is partly to blame for the failure of humanitarian intervention which only 'raises public consciousness at particular times and particular places' (Kaldor 2010: 334–335).

However, for those cosmopolitans of a more optimistic disposition, the media is part of the solution, rather than the problem, performing a 'necessary and possibly influential role in alerting world opinion to repressive and potentially prosecutable acts of inhumanity such as those following in the wake of mass uprisings' and acting as 'a public forum for deliberating the moral dilemmas and practical difficulties involved in humanitarian militarized intervention' (Cottle 2011: 656).

Questions

- Is significant media coverage necessary for a humanitarian intervention to take place?
- Does the protection of human rights require states to go to war?
- Are all wars labelled 'humanitarian' by one side or another?
- What does global 24/7 news coverage of humanitarian disasters mean for the international system of human rights?

Notes

1 For a list of definitions of humanitarian intervention, see Hehir 2010: 17, Box 1.2.
2 Resolution 1203 was adopted on 24 October 1998. It demanded compliance with the previous resolutions (1160 and 1199) and cooperation with the NATO and OSCE (Organization for Security and Co-operation in Europe) verification missions in Kosovo.

Further reading

Bellamy, A. J. 2002. *Kosovo and International Society*. Basingstoke: Palgrave Macmillan.
Bellamy, A. J. 2008. *Responsibility to Protect*. Cambridge: Polity Press.
Chandler, D. 2006. *From Kosovo to Kabul and Beyond: Human Rights and International Intervention*, 2nd edn. London: Pluto Press.
Chomsky, N. 1999. *The New Military Humanism: Lessons from Kosovo*. London: Pluto Press.
Gilboa, E. 2005. 'The CNN effect: the search for a communication theory of international relations'. *Political Communication* 22(1): 27–44.
Hammond, P. and E. Herman. 2000. *Degraded Capability: The Media and the Kosovo Crisis*. London: Pluto Press.
Hehir, A. 2008. *Humanitarian Intervention after Kosovo: Iraq, Darfur and the Record of Global Civil Society*. Basingstoke: Palgrave Macmillan.
Hehir, A. 2010. *Humanitarian Intervention: An Introduction*. Basingstoke: Palgrave Macmillan.

Hilsum, L. 2012. *Sandstorm: Libya in the Time of Revolution*. London: Faber and Faber.
Holzgrefe, J. L. and R. Keohane (eds). 2005. *Humanitarian Intervention: Ethical, Legal, and Political Dilemmas*. Cambridge: Cambridge University Press.
International Commission on Intervention and State Sovereignty (ICISS). 2001. *The Responsibility to Protect*. Ottawa: International Development Research Centre.
Robinson, P. 2002. *The CNN Effect: The Myth of News, Foreign Policy and Intervention*. London: Routledge.
Weiss, T. G. 2010. *Humanitarian Intervention*. Cambridge: Polity Press.

Useful websites

www.responsibilitytoprotect.org (International Coalition for the Responsibility to Protect)
www.icty.org (International Criminal Tribunal for the former Yugoslavia)
www.globalhumanitarianassistance.org (Global Humanitarian Assistance)
www.pbs.org/wgbh/pages/frontline/shows/kosovo (War in Kosovo, PBS Frontline)
www.globalr2p.org (Global Centre for the Responsibility to Protect)

5

GENOCIDE

Introduction

The horrors of the Holocaust demonstrated that ideas about human rights were meaningless if states were able to deprive large portions of their populations of 'the right to have rights' (Arendt 1962: 299). The prohibition of genocide is considered by many to be the ultimate cosmopolitan norm – illustrated by the global revulsion over the crimes committed by the Nazis during the Second World War. But the fact that these atrocities happened proved Arendt's point that the existence of social norms was not enough. The international solution was for the norms to be formalized legally and backed up with the threat of force, because states could no longer be trusted to respect the human rights of their own citizens. However, the recurrence of genocide in the twentieth and twenty-first centuries, and the failure of the international community to prevent it, threatens many commentators' faith in, and the legitimacy of, the international human rights regime. As Mitchell (2014: 122) warns: 'what happened in the churches of Rwanda, the fields of Cambodia and the camps of the Second World War testifies to the dangers of developing an uncritical or idealized view of what cosmopolitanism can contribute to the creation of peaceable communities'.

This chapter examines the institutionalization of the norm of genocide, and the role of the media in both creating the connections with distant others and contributing towards accountability in the international community over the issue. The way the tensions surrounding the concept of genocide and the implementation of the international norm with regard to it play out in practice is analysed through the case studies of the genocide in Rwanda in 1994 and the conflict in Darfur, which was still ongoing at the time of writing.

The meaning of genocide

The legal codification of the norm of genocide was established by the Convention on the Prevention and Punishment of the Crime of Genocide in 1948 (known as the Genocide Convention), which designated it as an international crime 'whether committed in time of peace or in time of war'. This convention represents the most direct international response to the Holocaust and addresses 'the crime of all crimes'. It defines genocide and creates a genocide regime that has evolved and developed throughout the years. In the words of Shaw (2007: 27), the convention has 'remained the unamended basis of policy and law; it has also informed public debate and scholarly discussion in all disciplines'. However, it has been controversial in the US. It was signed by President Truman in 1948, but the US Senate did not ratify it until 1986 because of Southern states' concerns about its potential application to historic slavery practices (Power 2002: 69).

The term 'genocide' was first coined by Raphael Lemkin, a Polish–Jewish jurist, in 1944 to refer to a practice that had been perpetrated throughout the ages. The new term to describe this old crime combined the Greek *genos* (clan, race, tribe) with the Latin suffix *-cide* (to kill or murder) and was used by Lemkin to refer to any act or attempted act of destruction aimed primarily at a given racial, religious or social group. As Lemkin states, genocide is 'a coordinated plan of different actions aiming at the destruction of the essential foundations of the life of national groups, with the aim of annihilating the groups themselves' (Lemkin 1944: 79). A key dimension is that the intent of violence is to annihilate and eradicate groups of people, as Lemkin (1947: 147) describes: 'The acts are directed against groups, as such, and individuals are selected for destruction only because they belong to these groups.' Importantly, as LeBlanc (1991) observes, genocide was conceived in broader terms than simply killing individual members of a particular group. Instead, the destruction of a group could take place through a variety of means, including, but not limited to, the direct killing of its members.

Despite the apparent clarity of Lemkin's original definition, ever since 1944 'genocide' has been subject to ongoing debates trying to establish what constitutes the most precise and useful designation. The 1948 Genocide Convention offers the only universally accepted definition, yet it effectively started a process of narrowing Lemkin's core idea and produced a decidedly 'compromise definition' (Shaw 2007; Totten and Bartrop 2009: 5). Article 2 states that genocide involves any of the following acts committed with the intent to destroy, in whole or part, a national, ethnic, racial or religious group:

a) killing members of the group;
b) causing serious bodily or mental harm to members of the group;
c) deliberately inflicting on the group conditions of life calculated to bring about its physical destruction in whole or in part;
d) imposing measures intended to prevent births within the group; and
e) forcibly transferring children of the group to another group.

This definition has several key features and ambiguities that represent challenges when it comes to establishing what is and what is not genocide. First, it requires an *intent* to destroy a group. This means that, to confirm that genocide is taking (or has taken) place, a deliberate, usually planned campaign of violence with the express purpose of destroying a group must be demonstrated. However, the convention does not explain how this intent is to be proven. The degree of that specific intent is also not articulated explicitly. In the words of Kuper (1981: 33), this 'introduces a subjective element which would often prove difficult to establish'. Second, only national, ethnic, racial or religious groups are protected within the UN's definition of genocide. If other groups of people are persecuted – for example, members of political parties, disabled people, regional, gender or cultural groups – they are not explicitly protected by the convention. The exclusion of political and social groups as protected categories, in particular, was the result of objections from the Soviet Union, Poland and other countries, whereas the exclusion of cultural groups was due to US opposition (Cassese 1990). Third, genocide may involve 'whole' or 'partial' destruction of a group. What proportion of the whole constitutes a part, however, is not specified. While usually it has been interpreted as a 'substantial' part of the group, as Straus (2013: 275) notes, 'the standard for determining when "substantial" group destruction indicates intent to destroy a group is murky'. Finally, there is one area where the definition is actually broader than is commonly believed. Despite the popular view that genocide always involves killing, the convention lists a number of different forms, including activities in which lives are not necessarily taken.

As this discussion of the definition demonstrates, important ambiguities have been left unresolved in relation to the types of groups protected, the extent and means of violence that constitute genocide, and the demonstration of intent. As a result, there have been numerous attempts to redefine genocide and, importantly, there have been significant occasions when disagreements have arisen over whether it has actually occurred (Chalk and Jonassohn 1990; Charny 1988; Fein 1990; Shaw 2007; Smith 1987; Straus 2001). Furthermore, numerous alternative terms and concepts have been developed. It is particularly worth noting the idea of 'politicide', which refers to the systematic destruction of political groups – instances when 'governments respond … with violent tactics in an attempt to quell politically organized groups that actively seek to alter power relations within a nation state' (Harff and Gurr 1989: 24). The coining of this word marked an attempt to address the Genocide Convention's failure to grant protection to political and social groups, an omission that has been criticized by several prominent genocide scholars (see, e.g., Bartrop and Totten 2004; Charny 1988; Kuper 1985). Other suggested concepts describing forms of violence against civilians include 'ethnic cleansing', 'democide', 'ethnocide', 'cultural genocide', 'gendercide', 'classicide', 'urbicide' and 'auto-genocide'. They imply that genocide is only one form of violence directed at civilian groups, rather than a general framework for understanding such violence, which was in fact Lemkin's original proposition. He argued that 'Many authors, instead of using a generic term, use … terms connoting only some functional aspect of the main generic notion of genocide' and concluded that 'these terms are also inadequate because they do not convey the common elements of one generic notion' (Lemkin 1944: 80). This view has its supporters on the grounds that

> It is better to use genocide as the master concept, accepting that its meaning
> has expanded from the narrower meaning of genos as nation or ethnic
> group, to cover the destruction of any type of people or any group.
>
> *(Shaw 2007: 78)*

Overall, among all the definitions available, some are narrower, seeing genocide as
the extermination of racial, ethnic or religious groups (similar to the convention's
definition), while others are broader, seeing it as mass killing (understood as the
intentional killing of more than 50,000 civilians within a five-year period (Valentino
2004)). According to the narrow definition, there were only three cases of genocide
in the twentieth century – the Armenian genocide of 1915–1916, the Holocaust of
1941–1945 and the Rwandan genocide of 1994 (Midlarsky 2005). However, if the
broader definition is accepted and politicide is included, between 1955 and the end
of the twentieth century there were 37 cases, including Serbia (1998–1999), Bosnia
(1992–1995), Sri Lanka (1989–1990), Somalia (1988–1991), Iraq (1988–1991),
Cambodia (1975–1979) and Burma (1978) (Harff 2003).

In addition to offering a definition, the Genocide Convention obliges its signatories
'to prevent and to punish' genocide. Historically, the punishment provisions have
been more effective than those relating to prevention. As Schabas (2000) notes, from
the very outset the meaning of 'undertaking to prevent' has been left unclear, with
not much attention devoted to the issue in the drafting process. The only specific
text is contained in Article 8, which suggests that parties 'may call upon competent
organs' of the UN to take action under the Charter to prevent and suppress genocide.
This provision has been interpreted by some as opening the door for states to
intervene pre-emptively in the territory of another state to stop genocide. Still, 'the
treaty language is fairly vague and weak as to specific mechanisms, policies and
procedures that states must take to prevent genocide' (Straus 2013: 276).

These weaknesses of the normative regime against genocide have been criticized
as the main reason why it is so difficult to stop genocide and why the international
community has failed to do so consistently. The bar for intervention is set too high,
requiring evidence of clear intent to destroy a national, ethnic, racial or religious
group. According to Pape (2012: 42), this means that by the time it is clear that a
genocide is occurring, it is often too late to stop the killing. He adds:

> by leaving the acceptable costs of intervention undefined, the norm does not
> resolve the inevitable trade-off between the obligation to save lives of a foreign
> population and the obligation of potential interveners to defend and protect
> the welfare of their own populations.
>
> *(Pape 2012: 42)*

This lack of a clear and specific enforcement mechanism that could initiate collective
action to stop genocide is arguably contrasted by the better-developed and more
effective mechanisms of punishment. The Genocide Convention lists specific
charges and conditions for extradition; it states that individuals may be punished

irrespective of whether they are public officials; it insists that contracting parties must enact legislation outlawing genocide and that persons charged with genocide must be tried by either a domestic or an international court. In line with the convention, international and hybrid domestic–international courts have been set up for crimes committed in Former Yugoslavia, Rwanda, Cambodia and Sierra Leone. Two ad hoc international criminal tribunals – the International Criminal Tribunal for the Former Yugoslavia and the International Criminal Tribunal for Rwanda – have been particularly prominent and 'moderately successful' (Bartrop and Totten 2004: 48). The creation of the International Criminal Court on 1 July 2002 further strengthened the international judicial mechanisms for punishing mass violations of human rights by establishing the court's jurisdiction over the most serious crimes of international concern, which include genocide as well as crimes against humanity and war crimes.

Concerns over implementation during and after the Cold War

After the Second World War and during the Cold War period the international community did not really act consistently to stop genocide, even though 'the trend over the course of the past century has been towards greater killing, greater targeting of civilians, and a greater likelihood than ever before that groups are being singled out for destruction' (Bartrop and Totten 2004: 48). Genocide arguably took place in Burundi, Cambodia, East Pakistan (Bangladesh), Uganda and East Timor in this period. These atrocities were met with verbal expressions of concern by the inter-national community but little in the way of concrete action. Exceptions include cases where neighbouring states, such as India and Vietnam, had clear reasons to intervene. Their interventions, as Donnelly (2013a: 205) points out, were not accepted as legal by the international community; and, more importantly, they were not even presented as primarily humanitarian by the interveners themselves. On the whole, during the Cold War, both communist and capitalist states saw internal conflicts as opportunities to gain an advantage over their rivals by either action or inaction. Effectively, at times, this meant aiding and abetting the perpetrators of genocide (Bartrop and Totten 2004). Thus, the rhetorical international commitment to prevention and the promise of 'never again' with respect to genocide were not realized during the Cold War and remained aspirational, despite the international recognition of individuals' human rights through the UDHR generally and the Genocide Convention specifically.

After the end of the Cold War – as discussed in the previous chapter – a practice (of sorts) of multilateral armed intervention against genocide has developed. This has challenged and even transformed the traditional notion of sovereignty, suggesting that committing genocide or other serious human rights violations against one's own population is no longer an internal matter, and states engaging in such activities might well face international intervention. The new concept of R2P stipulates that a government is responsible for protecting its own citizens against major human rights violations, and if it fails to do so then the international community has the 'responsibility to protect' individuals within that state. In this sense, R2P addresses some of the weaknesses of the Genocide Convention by removing the need to prove intent and extending protection to civilians who are targeted for reasons other than ethnicity, nationality, religion or race (Grzyb 2009b).

Nonetheless, despite the existence of international legal and institutional processes against genocide, it still happens and responses to it remain selective and inconsistent. Bartrop and Totten (2004: 47) claim it is wrong to suggest that a 'sea change' has taken place when realities on the ground are considered, '[b]ecause the international community [has] failed, time and again, to halt various genocides in a timely and effective manner'. The evidence indicates a certain willingness to respond after genocide has occurred, but a reluctance to respond to prevent genocide from happening in the first place. This paradox is illustrated in the case studies that are examined later in this chapter.

The role of the media

In many ways this chapter continues Chapter 4's discussion of humanitarian intervention as the identification of genocide is supposedly one of the few justifications for humanitarian intervention. The arguments with regard to the CNN effect and compassion fatigue therefore all apply when it comes to understanding the role of the media in influencing public opinion through its coverage of genocide. However, it is worth dwelling briefly on the importance of the media role from a different perspective: namely, its instrumental role. This concerns both those who wish to encourage the cosmopolitan promise of developing empathetic ties towards the 'other' and those who try to use the media for the purposes of manipulation and to dehumanize 'enemies of the state'. If the media is understood as a platform, it can be used by state and non-state actors either to perpetuate or to challenge human rights abuses; to incite violence or to promote peace. As will be seen in the case study on Rwanda, the use of radio to inflame violence and the failure of foreign media to raise awareness of the massacres reflect badly on both local and global media (Mitchell 2014).

The view of the media as 'complicit' in manipulating public opinion dates back to the first studies of propaganda (Lasswell 1971) and to observations about the First World War, when whole societies were mobilized for violent purposes. A combination of factors, including 'democratic suffrage, a new appreciation of public opinion in the era of "total war", [and] the growth of mass media', meant that 'a new political form: the modern media democracy' (Ross 2006: 184) developed at the end of that war. The best-known example of the media providing support for genocide is, of course, Nazi Germany, where propaganda against the Jewish minority and others was used to devastating effect. The story of an 'innocent Germany besieged by international Jewry intent on its "extermination"' served as both the public announcement of and justification for the Final Solution' (Herf 2006: vii). As Ross (2006: 187–188) points out, propaganda became an important instrument of power in Germany partly because the political class in that country believed that they lost the First World War because of a failure to control the media and thus public opinion. The first steps to rectify this began as soon as the Nazis gained control in 1933. The new government removed thousands of journalists from their posts, bought media companies and institutionalized the propaganda machine (Herf 2006: 18–20). However, historians have questioned the notion that the Nazis had complete control of Germany's media – domination of the press was counterbalanced by looser control of film, for example (Zimmerman 2006) – and their propaganda built upon existing prejudices rather than created them (Welch 2013).

Turning to the positive instrumental role of the media, some have pointed out that the media has a potentially significant role to play in preventing genocide from taking place. The previous chapter examined the different ways in which the media–political relationship can influence decisions to intervene in foreign crises, under certain circumstances. Staub (2013: 186–187) also argues that the media, along with all other influential members of society, can engage in symbolic actions that help to develop a more positive orientation to the 'other' by humanizing devalued groups. The role of the media is central to the creation of a cosmopolitan connection with the distant other, which is the first step towards 'do something' demands and subsequent humanitarian interventions in response to gross human rights violations. As Silverstone (2007: 7) has argued,

> the world's media are an increasingly significant site for the construction of a moral order, one which would be, and arguably needs to be, commensurate with the scope of global interdependence. Insofar as they provide the symbolic connection and disconnection that we have to the other, the other who is the distant other, distant geographically, historically, sociologically, then the media are becoming the crucial environments in which a morality appropriate to the increasingly interrelated but still horrendously divided and conflictful world might be found, and indeed expected.

The two case studies explored below consider the moral and legal obligations of the international community, the UN and individual Western states to respond to violence, their actual reactions and the media coverage of two cases of genocide – Rwanda and Darfur.

Case study: Rwanda 1994

The events in Rwanda in 1994 – when up to a million Rwandan Tutsis and Hutus were killed by Hutu extremists, the Interahamwe – are widely acknowledged as an unambiguous case of genocide and 'the great, and horribly tragic, failure' of the 1990s (Donnelly 2013a: 198). The UN failed to intervene during the genocide, provoking questions about its competence and, more importantly, its potency as an international peacekeeping force. Likewise, the international media failed to report on the evolving genocide as it was happening; instead, it told the story of the refugee crisis after the atrocities. This raises questions about the media's ability to alert far-off audiences and generate pressure for state action. Moreover, local media was implicated in the atrocities. The radio station RTLM incited people to commit mass killings, and media channels were used as a 'tool of genocide' (Destexhe 1995: 29). The overall international response is generally viewed as too little, too late. It did nothing to stop what many felt was a 'preventable genocide', given the early signs of escalation, the presence of a peacekeeping force (UNAMIR) in the country, the rudimentary weapons used and the lack of ambiguity about the genocide itself (Straus 2013).

The genocide took place in a state that was moving away from the one-party rule that was established after the withdrawal of the colonial power – Belgium – in 1962. Rwanda was going through a civil war between the Hutu-led government and the RPF (Rwanda Patriotic Front), largely composed of Tutsi refugees whose families had fled to Uganda following Hutu violence against them. As a result of international pressure, a cease-fire was brokered in 1993 and a roadmap to implement the Arusha Accords was supposed to lead to the creation of a Hutu/RPF power-sharing government. However, the shooting down of a plane carrying the presidents of Rwanda and Burundi – Juvénal Habyarimana and Cyprien Ntaryamira – acted as a trigger for the start of a planned campaign of genocide on 6 April 1994. Both Tutsis and moderate Hutus were targeted in a brutal series of massacres carried out mainly with machetes.

The role of the media in facilitating these atrocities is particularly striking as the state-controlled Radio-Télévision Libre des Milles Collines (RTLM) 'became the principal weapon in the anti-RPF and anti-compromise propaganda war, used effectively to indoctrinate the population and coordinate the genocidal militias' (McNulty 1999: 275). RTLM was used by the minority Hutu elite to mobilize Hutu citizens against the majority Tutsi population, with the result that around a million people were murdered in the space of only 100 days. A racist anti-Tutsi ideology was propagated, drawing on historical myths and stereotypes of the Tutsi and appealing for Hutu unity. The broadcasts referred to the killing as 'work' and labelled the Tutsis 'cockroaches', spreading a sense of terror and panic across the country and exploiting the Hutus' fears and suspicions. Tutsis were depicted as the cause of the political instability in Rwanda and the source of all economic hardship and the privations of the Hutu population (Apodaca 2007). As Kimani (2007: 111) puts it, 'The media defined who the enemy was, and why. Later on, they would also explain what was to be done to this enemy.' The authorities used RTLM to spur and direct killings, first inciting and mobilizing the armed gangs and then giving them specific directions for where and when to launch their next attacks (Des Forges 2007).

In contrast to the direct involvement of RTLM was the shortage of Western journalists on the ground. This added to incomplete, and perhaps ineffective, reporting of the atrocities and may even have resulted in the unintentional sanctioning of government propaganda (Schimmel 2009). The Western media depicted the catastrophe as a tribal conflict, a civil war that erupted suddenly and spontaneously, thus the reality of a pre-planned and deliberate policy of genocide remained hidden from view:

There is a general tendency to portray Africa as chaotic, the Dark Continent, and so on. Sometimes indeed, it is very dark. It was in Rwanda in 1994. But Rwanda was not, after a while, chaotic or impenetrable. It was, as we now know, a very well planned political and ethnic genocide. That didn't really fit the media image of chaotic Africa and various things flowed from that.

(Doyle 2007: 154)

Thus, what happened in Rwanda in 1994 serves as a powerful example of how the media itself can become an actor in the context of worsening human rights violations and the important role it can play in supporting official propaganda by failing to hold governments to account.

The international reaction to the gross violation of human rights in Rwanda is of particular interest here in light of both existing legal mechanisms and arguments about the extent of media power since the end of the Cold War. When the massacres started, the UN was present in Rwanda, having deployed a small peacekeeping force (UNAMIR) as part of the peace agreement. Despite early warnings from General Dallaire about the unfolding major atrocity and requests for reinforcements to protect Rwandan civilians, the international response from the UN, European states and the US was to avoid direct confrontation (Dallaire with Beardsley 2003). This, in effect, allowed the genocide to continue despite the provisions of the Genocide Convention.

On a political level, several factors explain (but hardly excuse) the decision not to organize an adequate humanitarian response. First, there was the specific timing of the case. The Rwandan genocide took place in the aftermath of US involvement in Somalia in 1993, when 18 US troops were killed in the capital, Mogadishu. Following this perceived failure and embarrassment, neither the US nor the UN was keen to undertake a risky intervention in another African country (Barnett 2002; Gourevitch 1998; Power 2002; Wheeler 2000). This reluctance was further strengthened by Presidential Decision Directive (PDD) 25, invoked in 1994 in the US, which imposed stricter conditions with regard to US military involvement in multilateral interventions. The new stipulations included the need for a clear statement of US interests, the approval of Congress, a fixed date for withdrawal and an agreed command and control structure. Thus, the overall context was one where a high degree of policy certainty was required, and this led to extreme caution whenever addressing potential intervention (Robinson 2002).

Second, the geography of Rwanda was important. It is a small, landlocked, francophone country in Central Africa with an economy based on coffee and tea exporting. In 1994 it enjoyed little name recognition in the anglophone world and the Northern powers felt it had negligible geostrategic value (Hilsum 1995; Straus 2013). This probably contributed to the policy certainty against intervention in this instance. After the killing of Belgian peacekeepers in Rwanda, the Security Council unanimously agreed to cut the UNAMIR force to 270 people, despite estimates that by then around 100,000 civilians had already been massacred.

Third, the non-intervention of the international community was characterized by a culture of denial that led to a refusal to label the events in Rwanda correctly. Initially, the violence was described as a breakdown of the fragile cease-fire and the term 'genocide' was conspicuously avoided. Subsequently, both the US and the UN Security Council admitted only that 'acts of genocide' had been committed, thus effectively sidestepping obligations under the Genocide Convention requiring action to be taken to prevent massacres in cases of genocide (Melvern 2006).

Accusations have been levelled at the international media for failing to report the Rwandan catastrophe in an accurate and timely manner. Instead, it was said to have 'obscured, distorted and denied current events and thus undermined the public's ability to understand the context, causes, and consequences of the genocide' (Schimmel 2011: 1125). Indeed, prior to April 1994, there was almost no coverage of Rwanda in the Western anglophone media, despite repeated human rights abuses by the RPF and the Rwandan military. This reflects a common pattern of news avoidance of African issues (Livingston and Eachus 1995). Once the genocide started, only a few journalists reported on the mass slaughter as it was happening. Television crews arrived only after most of the violence was over and huge numbers of refugees were pouring into neighbouring countries (Chaon 2007; Doyle 2007). Considering that conditions within Rwanda during the genocide were far more dangerous for journalists than during the subsequent refugee crisis, and that even the UN withdrew its minimal presence at the start of the genocide, Carruthers' (2011: 165) observation seems quite accurate: 'Initially … Rwanda seemed a case of media attention calibrated not to the magnitude of the killing but to the level of (un)interest it was arousing in distant capitals.'

The lack of media attention can be attributed to a number of factors, including the inadequate resources devoted to African reporting, the use of parachute journalism rather than fixed-base correspondents, the perceived lack of audience interest in news from Africa, and a good news story happening simultaneously in South Africa (Nelson Mandela's inauguration as that country's first black president). The latter meant not only that most resources and available crews were sent to South Africa but that two African stories were competing for attention in the Western media at the same time. The broadcasters calculated that the Western audience was incapable of dealing with both a good and a bad news story from Africa simultaneously. Moreover, the continent is generally associated with bad news – natural disasters or acts of 'ancient tribal hatred' (Alozie 2007) – so 'African news is generally only big news when it involves *lots* of dead bodies' (Keane 1996: 7; emphasis added). Consequently, Rwanda made its way to the top of the Western news agenda only when the true scale of the catastrophe became apparent later. The crisis also took place at a time when the O. J. Simpson trial was dominating bulletins in the US due to its irresistible combination of sport, glamour and violence, and the conflict in the Former Yugoslavia was providing no end of newsworthy material for European broadcasters and newspapers. Furthermore, there were challenges for the Rwanda story relating to the commercial imperatives for news that was graphically compelling. Because there were very few journalists and photographers on the ground in Rwanda, there were few accompanying images with which to tell a story that would arouse audience interest. Later, at the time of the refugee crisis, there was a clear spike in coverage because newspapers and TV bulletins were able to present sensationalist graphic images of human suffering and tell a story that was uncomplicated and simple. The aftermath of the massacres also allowed the media to demonstrate and celebrate Western humanitarian generosity by reporting the flying in of food and medicine, for example. As Fair and Parks (2001: 47) point out, 'Covering genocide meant having to understand politics to assess both domestic and international accountability. By comparison, covering refugees was easy.'

The nature of the media coverage is also worth exploring, as it is significant in terms of its potential to influence Western foreign policy decisions relating to intervention. Initially, the reporting was dominated by a framing that highlighted an ethnic and tribal understanding of the causes of the violence. The killings were seen as unplanned and spontaneous – acts of primordial hatred – rather than the result of a pre-planned and politically motivated campaign of genocide (Fair and Parks 2001; Livingston and Eachus 1999; Melvern 2007; Schimmel 2011; Wall 2007). This effectively helped to facilitate the banal distancing coverage at the start of the genocide and reduced the media's potential for impact over Western poicy with regard to intervention (Robinson 2002). On a domestic level, 'journalists contributed to the behaviour of the perpetrators of the genocide – who were encouraged by the world's apathy and acted with impunity' (Thompson 2007: 3).

The above analysis underlines that there was a complete failure of prevention when it came to the genocide in Rwanda. Since the killing ended, significantly more effort has been directed towards punishing the perpetrators of the genocide, demonstrating that the punishment provisions of the Genocide Convention are more effective than those aimed at prevention. At the international level, in 1994 the International Criminal Tribunal for Rwanda was established by the UN to prosecute the major architects and planners of the genocide. Among those brought before the court were Ferdinand Nahimana and Jean-Bosco Barayagwiza, the directors of RTLM, and Hassan Ngeze, the editor of the extremist newspaper *Kangura*. All three were found guilty of 'genocide, direct and public incitement to commit genocide, conspiracy to commit genocide and crimes against humanity (persecution and extermination)' (Thompson 2007: 9) in recognition of the role played by the local media in galvanizing and actively instructing the Interahamwe why they must kill, when to do so, and whom to attack (Des Forges 2007). At the local level within Rwanda, ordinary Rwandans organized grass-roots tribunals called *gacaca* that judged perpetrators in open-air sessions. Both of these mechanisms have their problems and both have been criticized as 'victor's justice' (Lemarchand 2009; Peskin 2008; Waldorf 2006).

Case study: Darfur 2003–present

If Rwanda was one of the worst genocides of the twentieth century, Darfur, in western Sudan, is arguably the first genocide of the twenty-first. The ongoing conflict there began in 2003 and has been described by UN Secretary General Ban Ki-Moon (cited in Carey *et al.* 2010: 180) as the world's first 'global warming conflict'. This refers to the fact that the war is being fought over resources that are diminishing year by year as a result of environmental devastation in the region. The international response to Darfur bears some similarities to the one to Rwanda, particularly in terms of the tension between sovereignty and international action and the slow and inadequate response of the UN Security Council to an African crisis. Also similar is the presence in the region of an under-staffed and under-funded peace mission, this time under the auspices of the African Union (AU) – the African Union Mission in Sudan (AMIS) – and then the deployment of a hybrid UN/AU force (UNAMID) of nearly 20,000 uniformed peacekeepers (whose number has since grown). Furthermore, the Western media has largely failed to adequately report the scale and brutality of the ongoing human rights abuses and their underlying causes in Darfur, resulting in a lack of information about the crisis and a very low level of media pressure for the international community to intervene (Melvern 2006).

Sudan has experienced almost uninterrupted warfare since 1956 (Straus 2005). A civil war between the northern and southern regions of the country ended in the creation of an independent state of South Sudan in 2011. Since 2003, the western region of Sudan Darfur has been another centre of violence and mass human rights violations, with the worst of the fighting taking place between 2003 and 2006, but low-level conflict continuing to this day. Two main rebel groups – the Sudan Liberation Army (SLA) and the Justice and Equality Movement (JEM) – are ranged against the Sudanese government, backed by its militia, the Janjaweed. It is seen as a conflict between Arab and African farmers in a context of increased drought and desertification, which has led to sharper competition for the most important resources in the region – water and arable land. Government forces and militias have carried out joint attacks against non-Arab civilian populations. The pattern of violence has included government aircraft bombing villages, followed by looting of those villages, arson attacks against homes and other buildings, poisoning wells, killing stragglers and sexual violence by the militias (Daly 2007; Flint and de Waal 2008; Grzyb 2009b; Prunier 2005). According to the UN, an estimated 300,000 people had been killed in the Darfur conflict by the end of 2013, and nearly two million had been displaced, although the Sudanese government disputes these figures (Gladstone 2014).

The international reaction during the first year of the conflict was limited, but attention grew from 2004 onwards. The experience of Rwanda certainly informed the response to Darfur, at least to an extent. International efforts were 'in many ways rapid and robust', but they were still 'somewhat timid and noticeably unsuccessful' in stopping the genocidal violence in the country (Donnelly 2013a: 207; Lu 2006). In the words of Slim (2004: 811), 'The international community has not denied, but it has delayed and dithered. Once engaged, it also fumbled and took far too long to achieve a united and sufficiently assertive response.' A number of Security Council resolutions have been issued and sanctions have been imposed on Sudan. AU (and later UN/AU) peacekeepers have been deployed on the ground, and numerous initiatives aimed at brokering cease-fires and some sort of final resolution have been undertaken by both bilateral and multilateral actors from inside and outside the region (Hehir 2010; Totten 2009; Totten and Markusen 2006). Significantly, charges have been brought in the International Criminal Court against some of the leaders in the conflict, including President Omar al-Bashir. His indictment in 2009 was the first time a sitting president had been subjected to such a process. However, the act was mainly symbolic and al-Bashir's response was to remove from the country most of the international relief agencies, thus further worsening the humanitarian situation. At the time of writing, the most recent peace agreement was that signed by the Sudanese government and the JEM in Doha in 2011. However, little progress has been made since then and violence in the region has continued.

Undeniably, one of the obstacles to effective international intervention has been the lack of agreement on whether the violence in Darfur amounts to genocide and what the appropriate political response should be. However, the conflict demonstrates that even when major political actors accept that genocide is the correct label, it remains extremely difficult to secure agreement at the UN level over who, if anyone, will take action. On this occasion, the US was the first to use the term 'genocide': both Congress and the administration of President George W. Bush described the situation in Darfur as such and thus effectively invoked the Genocide Convention (Straus 2005). However, following legal advice, the administration was confident that using the word 'would not obligate the US to anything beyond – in the words of the Genocide Convention – calling upon the competent organs of the United Nations to take such action' (Mayroz 2008: 367).

In 2005 the UN commissioned an independent report which concluded that crimes against humanity, not genocide, had been perpetrated in Darfur. This conclusion was based on the absence of sufficient indicators of intent to destroy an ethnic group and on the lack of distinction between those who were the targets of attacks and those who were carrying them out (International Commission of Inquiry on Darfur 2005).

This episode showed that one country's assertion that genocide has taken place is insufficient justification for effective action to be launched, since 'the finding of genocide will only be meaningful if it's backed up by more assertive action at the UN Security Council' (Prendergast, cited in Reeves 2004). It 'made it clear that "genocide" is not a magic word that triggers intervention ... [and] showed that the Genocide Convention does not provide nearly the impetus that many thought it would' (Straus 2005: 132). Given the contrasting conclusions of the Bush administration and the UN report, the case of Darfur also showed how different categorizations of human rights abuses can impede the task of protecting civilians. It highlighted the need for 'genocide to be considered less in narrowly legal terms, and more as a general socio-political phenomenon' (Shaw 2007: 171).

Among the factors that contributed to the speed and nature of the international response were the competing political priorities. Within Sudan, peace talks for resolving the country's southern war were taking place as the conflict in Darfur was beginning (Evans 2008). Given its military commitments in Iraq and Afghanistan, the US was not in a position – or was unwilling – to lead a mission to Darfur

(Weiss 2010). The UN Security Council was also divided on the issue, with Russia and China opposing military intervention. Both countries traditionally oppose the use of military force in the name of human rights, but in this instance China's economic (oil) interests in Sudan and Russia's arms trade with the Sudanese government also no doubt contributed to their reluctance (Slim 2004; Straus 2013). The size of Sudan – it is the largest state in Africa – and its poor infrastructure, which makes troop movement logistically difficult, alongside the fear that an intervention could disrupt aid supplies to those already suffering in Darfur, further explain the lack of military intervention (Evans 2008; Mayroz 2008). There also seemed to have been a determination, supported by the major powers, for the AU to lead a regional process shaping an African solution to Darfur, despite that organization's lack of moral authority in Sudan and a shortage of the resources necessary to deliver positive results (Slim 2004). The Sudanese government, for its part, carried out what Mayroz (2008: 365) has called a 'defensive campaign against external intervention'. Taken together, all of these considerations suggest a lack of political will in the Western world to undertake a humanitarian intervention facilitated by the decision-making mechanisms within the Security Council.

Significantly, the international community's reaction to the crisis in Darfur casts considerable doubt over the relatively new norm of R2P. The idea of responsibility for the welfare of people belonging to their host state but transferring to the international community if and when this fails was directly relevant. Just such a failure occurred in Darfur yet it did not lead to military intervention by the international community, despite assessments that the scale of the tragedy passed the 'just cause threshold' and warranted external intervention (Bellamy 2006a; Slim 2004). As Hehir (2010: 252) points out, Darfur demonstrates that even if agreement on the criteria justifying humanitarian intervention exists through R2P, disagreement over whether such criteria have been met is eminently possible and this will affect the overall effectiveness of the norm.

The nature of the atrocities in Darfur, and the fact that they were committed slowly and sporadically over a long period of time, had implications for effective media coverage. While no doubt there was more information about the ongoing crisis in Darfur than there was about Rwanda at the time of the genocide there, there was a lack of continuous exposure, some inconsistent reporting and 'confusing, inadequate, insufficient and not timely' coverage, sometimes creating an inaccurate impression that the conflict had either eased or stopped completed (Grzyb 2009a; Waisbord 2008: 75). The media was alerted to the systematic nature of the violence in Darfur by a number of NGOs, such as Justice Africa, the International Crisis Group, Amnesty International and Human Rights Watch. However, in parallel with the political response, significant media attention began only in 2004, when a 'workable angle' was established – 'Darfur was a genocide and the Arabs were killing the Blacks' (Prunier 2005: 127). The spark for this was an interview with UN Human Rights Coordinator for Sudan Mukesh Kapila, who declared that Darfur was 'the world's greatest humanitarian crisis' and that 'the only difference between Rwanda and Darfur is now the numbers involved' (cited in Prunier 2005: 127).

While the violence in Darfur has since received more coverage, sustaining media interest has generally proved difficult. The increased reporting has coincided with discussions around international military interventions involving Western troops. In this coverage human rights abuses have been explored in the context of the possibility of international troop deployment in the area (Heinze and Freedman 2010). NGOs, aid agencies and even individual activists[1] have often been responsible for bringing Darfur back to the public's attention, leading to media stories focusing on humanitarian aid to the region (Grzyb 2009a). Overall, there has been more publicity of the crisis in the US than in Europe (Heinze and Freedman 2010), and more stories in the print media than on television (Eke 2008).

The nature of the media coverage of Darfur evolved from an initial simplistic tribal representation (Campbell 2007; Mamdani 2007; Parks 2009; Prunier 2005; Waisbord 2008) to less reliance on stereotypes of African warfare (Gruley and Duvall 2012). The tribal framing of the conflict, similar to that used with respect to Rwanda, served to deflect attention and marginalize the political roots of the violence by relying on traditional, stereotypical interpretations of African warfare. This was done to make the conflict intelligible to Western audiences, but simplifying Darfur's cultural and political complexity effectively played into the hands of the Sudanese government, which has repeatedly labelled the conflict 'entirely tribal' in order to deny its own involvement and discourage third-party intervention (Prunier 2005: 212). Later, while still consistently framing the violence as originating across an African–Arab cultural divide, the media developed a secondary narrative in which the conflict was portrayed as more complex and political. In the assessment of Gruley and Duvall (2012: 42–43) this secondary narrative remained historically shallow, but it arose from recognition that the warring parties could not be categorized simply as 'Arab' or 'African', and that various actors had stated political motivations. Still, most of the reporting remained descriptive and graphic, rather than analytical; it failed to raise important questions or offer accurate explanations for what was happening in Darfur (Tatum 2010).

Any potential that the media coverage might have had in terms of raising awareness about Darfur and/or generating public pressure on policy-makers to intervene was undermined by its slow start and subsequent inconsistency. Tatum (2010: 179) concludes that 'Rather than sleeping through the news about genocide as they had in the past, the American people tried to stop it. Neither the American media nor the American people abandoned Darfur; the American government did.' Once again, then, when it comes to making decisions about armed intervention, the media's role is at best one of many factors, and not necessarily the decisive one, even when it reveals an instance of genocide to the global public.

Conclusions

Genocide is the ultimate crime against humanity. The desire to stop it happening has been foundational to the international legal order that has been constructed since the end of the Second World War. However, while the agreements and institutions to achieve this are largely in place, the failure of this regime and its guardians when it came to stopping the atrocities in Rwanda and Darfur is often cited as evidence of the uselessness of the international human rights system.

This chapter has explored some of the reasons for this. It has shown how difficult it is to reach agreement on definitions and international legal frameworks even when the vilest of crimes have been perpetrated. It has also explored the perceived failings of the global media. The evidence from Rwanda and Darfur has demonstrated that the media is central to raising awareness and building consensus over decisions about intervention, but it is not the only or even the most important factor. As we saw in the previous chapter on humanitarian intervention, factors connected to national interests and the realities of geopolitics are often more significant in determining states' decisions to intervene – or not – to stop genocide taking place. Interestingly, these same factors also govern which crises are covered by the media: those in African states are often overlooked by a global media that is Euro- and US-centric in terms of its primary focus.

Questions

- Why should we expect the media to play a role in stopping genocide from taking place?
- What were the main reasons that explain the failure of the international community to intervene in Rwanda?
- Which groups should be included in the definition of genocide?
- What does the international community have to do to create a system that prevents genocide from happening again?

Note

1 Celebrities such as George Clooney, Mia Farrow, Oprah Winfrey and others have been extremely active in bringing attention to Darfur.

Further reading

Dallaire, R. with B. Beardsley. 2003. *Shake Hands with the Devil: The Failure of Humanity in Rwanda*. Toronto: Random House Canada.

Flint, J. and A. de Waal. 2008. *Darfur: A New History of a Long War*. London: Zed Books.

Gourevitch, P. 1998. *We Wish to Inform You that Tomorrow We Will Be Killed with Our Families*. New York: Picador.

Grzyb, A. 2009. 'Media coverage, activism, and creating public will for intervention in Rwanda and Darfur'. In *The World and Darfur: International Response to Crimes Against Humanity in Western Sudan*, A. Grzyb (ed.). Montreal: McGill-Queen's University Press.

International Commission of Inquiry on Darfur. 2005. *Report of the International Commission of Inquiry on Darfur to the United Nations Secretary-General*. Geneva: UN.

Power, S. 2002. *'A Problem from Hell': America and the Age of Genocide*. London: Flamingo.

Thompson, A. 2007. *The Media and the Rwanda Genocide*. London: Pluto Press.

Totten, S. and P. R. Bartrop (eds). 2009. *The Genocide Studies Reader*. London: Routledge.

Wheeler, N. J. 2000. *Saving Strangers: Humanitarian Intervention in International Society*. Oxford: Oxford University Press.

Useful websites

www.ictr.org (International Criminal Tribunal for Rwanda)
http://endgenocide.org (United to End Genocide)
http://genocidearchiverwanda.org.rw (Genocide Archive Rwanda)
http://voicesofrwanda.org (Voices of Rwanda)
http://combatgenocide.org (The Combat Genocide Association)
www.icc-cpi.int (International Criminal Court)

6

ASYLUM AND IMMIGRATION

Introduction

The topics of immigration and asylum garner an enormous level of media coverage across the world. They are areas that provide a battleground for ideas and political forces both within and outside the state. They are also emotionally charged due to connections with historical memory – for example, in Europe with the bleak past of intolerance and genocide towards excluded groups (Agamben 2005), or in the US with the importance of immigration in state-building (Motomura 2006). Sometimes states have sought to maintain human rights for their own citizens while simultaneously attempting to avoid such responsibilities with respect to outsiders, which has led some commentators to describe immigration policies as the liberal 'grand bargain' (Hollifield 1992).

While it is common for politicians to argue for ever-stricter immigration controls, some theorists have challenged the right of any state to control borders and immigration (e.g. Carens 1987; Cole 2000). Completely open borders may seem a distant possibility, but nevertheless immigration always seems to be a 'productive' question in liberal democratic states, creating multiple policy dilemmas. One of the reasons for this is that the topic represents a central tension between the values of individualism and community. Or, to put it another way, immigration can define the conflict between a desire for greater equality within the state and the necessary sacrifices that are required to achieve it (Dauvergne 1999).

This means that immigration and asylum are policy issues that are often high on the political agenda at all levels of the political system; in many countries, immigration is also one of the top issues mentioned by voters when asked to list the most important challenges facing the government. Yet there is often a large gap between perceptions and reality when it comes to migratory patterns. As in many other aspects of the political debate, the quality of media coverage is frequently blamed for this discrepancy (Duffy and Frere-Smith 2014).

This chapter introduces the key relevant human rights agreements and explores how discourses around immigration illustrate the inherent tensions in the human rights regime. It examines how these tensions operate through the media by exploring the role of language in representation, and the way in which the issue can be framed. The case studies demonstrate the issues of representation and framing through analysis of UK press coverage of Eastern European immigration and the UNHCR's annual World Refugee Day campaign.

Immigration and asylum as 'hot topics'

In 2013 in Australia images of boats filled with asylum-seekers became central to the outcome of that country's general election, and not for the first time – the topic had been crucial in previous elections, too. For the last two decades in the US the question of irregular migration has haunted the political debate, particularly since George W. Bush increased border enforcement after 9/11 (Alden 2009). But this is not just a post-9/11 phenomenon. Since the 1990s, popular magazine covers in the US have been using highly charged images that depict a 'war on immigration' that has helped to shape the national discourse (Chavez 2001). Immigration has likewise been a political 'hot potato' for British politicians since the 1960s, and it has been cited as a cause of electoral defeat ever since the 1970s (Crossman 1977).

What role does the media play in these public debates? Research has found that it is significant in shaping public perceptions of the issue (Boomgaarden and Vliegenthart 2009; Schemer 2012; Soderlund 2007), but also that its coverage is preconditioned by specific local economic and geographical factors (Branton and Dunaway 2009; Fryberg *et al.* 2012). While human rights issues appear in the debates over immigration and asylum, they are often implied rather than explicit, with cosmopolitan and communitarian justifications underlying the ethical arguments in the media (Balabanova and Balch 2010). What is clear from a number of studies is that the media tends to employ a discriminatory discourse that separates 'us' from 'them' (Wodak 2008), using stereotypes and metaphors (Cisneros 2008) to stigmatize migrant groups (Philo *et al.* 2013). The media also tends to simplify a complex issue by drawing from a narrow range of 'expert' sources (which can be quite politicized) and aggregating statistics to generate sensational headlines (Balch and Balabanova 2011).

Research into media coverage of immigration issues has typically been conducted in countries that have experienced migration for a relatively long period of time, particularly Western Europe and the US. However, it is not only in the traditional 'receiving states' where the issue is politically divisive. Countries in the south and east of Europe, for example, which until recently have been 'sending states', are now experiencing inflows of refugees and economic migrants from the Middle East and the global South, and nationalist political parties such as 'Golden Dawn' (Greece), 'Ataka' (Bulgaria) and the 'Northern League' (Italy) are seeking to exploit the subject to increase their support. The media is important in this process, as it often provides far-right parties with the oxygen of publicity and a platform from which they can deliver their message of fear regarding newcomers (Ellinas 2010). The effect of this coverage can be quite significant in the political system, albeit in an indirect way. While the extreme right rarely gains overall parliamentary power in Europe, its attitudes towards immigration and immigrants have certainly influenced the policies of mainstream parties (Carvalho 2013). The potential political gains are at the national level not without risk, however, as the issue can cause reputational damage at the regional and global levels. For instance, France's treatment of Roma communities in 2010 led to widespread international condemnation of what seemed to be a racist and discriminatory policy (Balch *et al.* 2014). An investigation by the UK's *Guardian* newspaper in 2013 which focused on the plight of migrant Nepalese guestworkers in Qatar prompted an international outcry: human rights NGOs lobbied FIFA to strip the country of its right to hold the 2022 Football World Cup (Booth 2013; Booth *et al.* 2013). UK Prime Minister David Cameron has been widely criticized for his 'chauvinist' approach to intra-EU migration and for using 'scaremongering' and 'stereotypes' following the end of transitional controls on Romanians and Bulgarians on 31 December 2013 (Barroso 2014).

No borders?

One way of thinking about the range of ideas relating to migration is to imagine the various arguments across a cosmopolitan–communitarian spectrum. At one end are the cosmopolitans, who believe in 'global citizenship' and would therefore probably argue that borders should be removed, or at least lowered significantly, on the basis of universal human rights principles. By contrast, communitarian liberals would counter that it is impossible to achieve successful and cohesive societies without retaining the ability to decide who is allowed inside and who is kept outside our communities.

On the 'no borders' side of the argument, authors such as Teresa Hayter see borders and immigration controls as a form of 'international apartheid' that inherently undermines a number of human rights (Hayter 2003: 10). Excluding so many people from the advantages of membership in the rich part of the world is inherently unfair. For Carens (1987: 252), 'Citizenship in Western liberal democracies is the modern equivalent of feudal privilege – an inherited status that greatly enhances one's life chances. Like feudal birthright privileges, restrictive citizenship is hard to justify when one thinks about it closely.' The cosmopolitans' basic argument is one of equality: 'there is no logical or moral reason why non-nationals of a state should not have the same opportunities and freedoms as nationals in that state' (Bagaric and Morss 2005: 27). But there are also those who believe that borders are effectively doomed in any case, because of the inevitable march of human development. This argument sees open borders as 'an inevitable long-term consequence of globalisation, as well as a policy option for addressing North–South inequalities and a moral touchstone for the global extension of human rights' (Casey 2010: 14).

Those who are critical of immigration controls often point out that they have not existed for very long – most of them are relatively new and they were often instigated for racist reasons – so we should not accept them as permanent 'fact'.

They also argue that there will not be the disastrous consequences that many predict if everyone has the right to live wherever they want; indeed, there would most likely be economic benefits from greater mobility. The 'no borders' activists focus on the injustice of the current arrangements, concluding that 'there appear to be very few reasons to not move towards implementing looser border controls' (Gill 2009: 112). However, the current orthodoxy is that fully open borders are impractical. Even NGOs working on behalf of migrants' rights tend to shy away from demanding the removal of all controls (Casey 2010).

Ranged against the 'no borders' argument is the seemingly common-sense proposition that borders and migration controls are here to stay because no country would unilaterally renounce rights that provide the state with significant powers. Liberal theorists have also provided supporting ethical arguments by pointing out that some sort of closed system is essential for the state to function properly and deliver all the public goods which accrue to citizenship (e.g. Rawls 1985: 233). From this perspective, migration controls and borders help to create stable, flourishing communities (e.g. Dworkin 1986: 208). The most famous expression of this idea is perhaps Michael Walzer's (1983) argument that closed borders are a necessary precondition for justice.

We shall return to this cosmopolitan–communitarian debate over immigration in one of the case studies later, but first it is key to explore the human rights regime. How can it 'square the circle' with migration? How can we simultaneously concede that a state has the right to decide who enters and resides in its territory, while also maintaining a genuine sense of 'universality' when it comes to human rights?

The human rights dimension: the human rights of non-citizens

The human rights situation for migrants and refugees is often very complicated. The Convention Relating to the Status of Refugees (1951), to which all liberal states are signatories, defines what is meant by 'refugee'. It stipulates that refugees are individuals who due to 'well founded fear of prosecution' for reasons of political opinion, race, religion, nationality or membership of a particular social group are outside their country of nationality and are unable or unwilling to return to it (Article 2). Thus, this definition emphasizes three primary features of refugee status:

- first, a refugee is someone who is outside his or her country of nationality;
- second, a refugee has fled and cannot return home because he or she faces the reality or the risk of persecution; and
- third, the persecution in question is due to the refugee's political opinions, race, religion, nationality or membership of a specific social group.

The very conception of a refugee enshrined in the Refugee Convention reflects the framing of the issue in the context of the early Cold War years. Western states viewed refugees – not least for ideological reasons – as products of oppressive, totalitarian regimes, such as those of Nazi Germany and later the communist states of Central and Eastern Europe.

It could be argued that the right to move, the need to flee danger, poverty or persecution, and others' corresponding obligation to welcome and provide hospitality for those in need are fundamental to the human condition. However, the specifics of the formal system of human rights in this area are quite intricate. Article 13(1) of the UDHR states that 'Everyone has the right to freedom of movement and residence within the borders of each state', while 13(2) establishes 'the right of everyone to leave any country, including his own and to return to his country'. Article 14(1) states that 'everyone has the right to seek and to enjoy in other countries asylum from persecution'. However, these rights of movement are not absolute, and there is no general right for individuals to migrate to a foreign country: such a right is not explicitly recognized in the main human rights conventions, and no such principle is enshrined in the constitution of any receiving country (Hines 2010). On the contrary, the ability and right to control the entry and residence of non-citizens have traditionally been considered key aspects of state sovereignty.

Ironically, the general principles of universality within international human rights law make this right to control movement all the more essential for states. The idea that all people – by virtue of their humanity – enjoy human rights implies an obligation to treat citizens and non-citizens in exactly the same way. Therefore, if an individual arrives in a liberal state's territory, it is difficult for that state to deny their human rights, especially if they have an immediate or potential claim to citizenship. This is one of the many reasons why states are so sensitive about the issue of immigration and so keen to emphasize their right to control and restrict movement into their territory. The right to enter, for example, was a massive issue in the debate over immigration in the UK in the 1960s, when all citizens of the British Commonwealth (theoretically, as it turned out) had the right to live in Britain (Hansen 2000; Higgins 1973).

However, the international human rights system does include some obligations that mean states' powers in this area are limited in important ways. Outside of totalitarian regimes, the borders of states must be porous, at least to a certain extent. Obviously it is in liberal states' economic interests to allow a degree of international movement, but certain rights enshrined in the UDHR (Article 3 on personal liberty; Article 4 against slavery; Article 8 on the right to effective remedy; and Article 12 on fair trials) could also be seen as bolstering a broader right to free movement (Higgins 1973: 342–343). Overall, there is a tension between a state's right to control population movement and an individual's right to human rights and equal treatment. This is demonstrated clearly in the International Covenant on Civil and Political Rights, for example, which declares that 'everyone shall be free to leave any country, including their own' (Article 12), but offers no corresponding right to *enter* any country. It also excludes non-citizens from political rights pertaining to citizenship (such as voting) and allows states to deny freedom of movement if individuals are not properly documented (Weissbrodt 2008: 35).

This situation means that policies governing the international movement of people have a peculiar ability to reveal certain aspects of nation-states, in particular the nature of exclusion and inclusion within those states. State responses have been relentless in limiting access to citizenship and creating complex stratifications of rights based on immigration status (Morris 2002). But human rights institutions (such as the European Court of Human Rights) often find that national systems governing migrants and their movement do not comply with basic human rights. The problem is that it is notoriously difficult (lengthy and expensive) for non-citizens to challenge national governments. While over the last 50 or 60 years human rights have acquired an increasingly international dimension, they are still interpreted, protected and enforced at the national level. This is why it is often possible to find the edges and limits of this protection by exploring how governments treat non-citizens, such as immigrants.

In practice, every nation-state (liberal or otherwise) differentiates in important ways between citizens, residents and aliens in its allocation of rights. Citizens have rights to all the benefits of membership in the state: rights to residence; rights to welfare and income benefits; rights to healthcare and education; rights to democratic participation. Persons given the status of legal residents may be granted some or all of these rights, although certain benefits, such as state pensions, usually remain out of their reach. In the case of the EU – where a process of widening or sharing of citizenship has been under way for several decades – citizens of other member states may enjoy most or all of the rights of the citizens of the countries where they reside. However, citizens of countries outside the EU do not enjoy those rights. Finally, irregular or undocumented migrants enjoy none of the rights that states grant to their own citizens and legal residents. Irregular migrants enjoy only those rights that are recognized as fundamental, universal human rights, applicable to every human being regardless of status. Even these rights have to be interpreted, however, and the emphasis on security and exclusion in legislation and policy means that they tend to be interpreted as narrowly as possible.

The rights to life and to protection from torture and inhuman or degrading treatment – contained in the UDHR and the ECHR – are at the centre of the universal human rights regime. Articles 2 and 3 of the ECHR state that 'Everyone's right to life shall be protected by law. No one shall be deprived of his life intentionally save in the execution of a sentence of a court following his conviction of a crime for which this penalty is provided by law', and 'no one shall be subjected to torture or to inhuman or degrading treatment or punishment'. These articles seem to provide strong protection to various categories of migrants; however, they still leave some issues open to interpretation and states do take advantage of that. What constitutes 'degrading and inhuman treatment', for example? Does this comprise only direct persecution or should the deliberate withholding or even the unavailability of welfare or health provisions be included, too? Returning people to countries where they might be tortured should be prohibited with no exceptions, but some countries have tried to reach agreements with states suspected of using torture. Much of the UK's recent immigration and asylum legislation, for example, has attempted to speed up the removal of failed asylum-seekers and illegal immigrants, and reduce their opportunities to appeal. These changes have often been attributed to public pressure on the issue, which in turn is often based on inaccurate or misleading reporting in the media (Philo *et al.* 2013). Procedures for the detention and removal of migrants are politically contentious, and the ECtHR has examined the legality of deportations with respect to Article 5 (the right to liberty and security of the person), Article 8 (the right to respect for private and family life) and Article 12 (the right to marry and form a family).

Even though there is a provision for fair trials, this depends on the legal system of each country – which might, for example, distinguish between criminal and immigration law (with the latter exempt from the fair trials provisions). Again, there is a link here with the role of the media. The way in which journalists report (and often simplify) complex statistics and official estimates relating to immigration can place great pressure on governments to 'get a firm grip' on the numbers (Balch and Balabanova 2011). This provides an obvious incentive for the manipulation of, for example, appeals systems, the interpretation of rights, interrogation processes by border officials and general decision-making in relation to migration. The dynamic of securitization is also important to note in this regard (see below). Anti-terror legislation, anti-trafficking policies and the criminalization of irregular migration have all served to increase the power of the state over the individual when it comes to excluding, detaining, deporting and suspending the rights of non-citizens. By contrast, there has been very little public or political pressure for any extension of the rights of migrants, whether legal or illegal.

Human rights versus sovereignty?

One of the key arguments used by governments and often echoed in media coverage is the notion that both immigration and international human rights norms present 'threats' to state sovereignty. This distils a complex issue into a simple oppositional one, mainly through a rather anachronistic reading of the concept of state sovereignty.[1] The underlying assumption is that sovereignty is in some way absolute, unchangeable and inherently national. These ideas can be traced back to the Treaty of Westphalia (1648), in which it was agreed that states were independent, sovereign actors and the major European powers promised to abide by the principle of territorial integrity. For those at the extreme of the 'state-sovereignty' debate, these agreements set in stone the configuration of states in the world, so the UDHR in 1948 – with its espousal of universal principles – and international migration – with its disorienting effects on (supposedly) territorially aligned and homogeneous populations – posed enormous challenges to the integrity and power of the nation-state (Joppke 1998). Yasmin Soysal (1994) looked at post-war immigration to Europe and suggested that it would be immigrations itself that would finally unravel the Westphalian system of nation-states and kick-start a post-national era of belonging in which international human rights would trump state sovereignty.

Twenty years on and Soysal's prediction looks increasingly inaccurate. A more realistic assessment of the modern system of government in most of Europe would suggest that it is far removed from the largely monarchical and feudal systems that Westphalia protected. Human rights are, to a large extent, embedded in – rather than a challenge to – sovereignty, usually in the form of constitutions (written or otherwise), and often reflect national lawmakers' intention to protect people from the abuse of power. In addition, most states do not think of the international movement of people as a threat to their existence; on the contrary, they depend heavily on it for their survival and construct their policies accordingly. The problem is that certain ideas, even those that are inaccurate or anachronistic, have a tendency to survive – particularly when they can portray a clear oppositional dynamic of 'immigration versus the state'. The simplicity of this narrative dissolves when one considers the increasing number of policies that are designed to encourage tourism and highly-skilled or 'managed' programmes trying to attract workers in particular sectors.

Indeed, in the European Union, whole categories of people enjoy the right to work in other member states thanks to the integration process, and the European Commission (EC) has attempted to reframe immigration as 'mobility'. Free movement has expanded because the member states have supported it, despite their (sometimes unconvincing) protests, because of a fairly widespread consensus over the economic benefits of a more mobile European workforce (CEC 2003), and agreement on the aggregate economic impacts of migration more generally at the beginning of the twenty-first century (Balch 2010). However, the politics of intra-EU migration remain difficult. The increase in flows of Central and Eastern European migrants to the UK following enlargement in 2004 and 2007, for example, has been portrayed by right-wing politicians as a challenge to the sovereignty of the nation-state and its ability to control who enters (Balabanova and Balch 2010). Indeed, there has been a growth in anti-immigration and 'Eurosceptic' political parties across Europe since the start of the financial crisis in 2007 (see, e.g., *The Economist* 2014).

Despite this, the facilitation of cross-border movement alongside a parallel politicization of certain forms of international migration suggests that modern politics are transforming traditional concepts of sovereignty. The notion that states have absolute sovereign control over their borders in peacetime has become both an anachronism (in the context of increasing globalization) and a rhetorical device for politicians attempting to build support on the basis of traditional concepts of belonging and nationalism.

Human rights versus security?

One of the key reasons why the subject of immigration has become so divisive and contentious within public debates is that it relates both directly and indirectly to deep tensions in the architecture of international human rights – for example, between international agreements and national implementation; or between universal notions of personhood and national models of citizenship. The net result is a potent political mix because, as the examples given at the start of this chapter demonstrate, the subject often becomes highly 'politicized' or even 'securitized'

(Buzan *et al.* 1998), with the rewards for politicians who speak out on the matter potentially significant. According to the Copenhagen School's theory of 'securitization', political actors can use the topic of immigration to manipulate public debate and extend their powers – for example, by increasing enforcement capacity. Using their terminology, issues can be securitized when they are 'presented as posing an existential threat to a designated referent object … justifying the use of extraordinary measures' (Buzan *et al.* 1998: 21).

There are similarities between the theory of securitization and that of media framing, as they both hinge upon the importance of language in delivering arguments about cause-and-effect and power relations. Securitization highlights the unique ability of politicians – due to the offices they hold and their access to authority – to communicate ideas about threats and potentially convince audiences of the need for more security measures. This, in turn, might allow politicians to improve their own, or their party's, electoral prospects. However, there are even more powerful – structural – forces at work here, because such actions inevitably lead to expansion in the power of the state. What does this mean for human rights?

The theory of securitization explains that the impulse to 'act tough' on immigration and asylum can be very seductive, but it also presents a direct challenge for any approach to the subject that is based on human rights. This is demonstrated by various backlashes against increased security measures – from opposition politicians, the migrants themselves, or more often NGOs and individuals that seek to protect human rights – which frequently use the language of human rights as a counter-argument. A good example of this was the reaction to France's expulsion of Roma in 2010 (Balch *et al.* 2014).

It might be expected that certain international responses are more likely to draw on the language of human rights, for example from the home countries of those migrants who have been subjected to poor treatment, and those that have signed up to the UN Convention on the Protection of the Rights of All Migrant Workers and Members of Their Families (1990). However, it is interesting to note that very occasionally the plight of migrant workers becomes a human rights story worthy of consideration outside both the sending and the receiving state. A good example here is the European Parliament's resolution condemning the Qatari government following reports of deaths of migrant workers working on the country's construction sites (European Parliament 2013).

To summarize, for all sides and for all countries involved in the international movement of people, the subjects of immigration and asylum can be a significant vote-winner (or vote-loser), making it an area in which the media has the potential to play a powerful role. Analysis of that role is the subject of the next section.

The media and asylum and immigration

Language and concepts

A starting point in any analysis of how the media–human rights nexus operates for immigration and asylum should be to think about language, concepts and definitions.

In this way some of the assumptions and misconceptions that structure debates can be exposed. Language is important. The terms 'illegal alien' and 'illegal asylum-seeker' are commonly used, for example, but these are very 'loaded' terms that imply a pre-existing position in the debate (Lakoff and Ferguson 2006). Many would argue that a person can never be 'illegal': they might have contravened immigration regulations, but they are still a legal entity; to suggest otherwise would seem to go against the general understanding of human rights. The term 'irregular migrant' is therefore often preferred. Another point is that it is theoretically impossible to be an 'illegal asylum-seeker' because everyone has the right to claim asylum on the basis of the accepted international definition of 'refugee' as outlined in the Geneva Convention. In the UK, the oxymoronic nature of the term is highlighted and discussed in the National Union of Journalists' guidelines for reporters, which identify its potential to contribute to audience misunderstanding and to bolster racial prejudice (NUJ 2005). Of course, difficulties arise because it is still left to nation-states to determine who is, and who is not, granted refugee status through the process of asylum. Everyone might have a right to claim asylum, but states retain the right to decide who is a genuine refugee and who is not. It could be argued that by choosing the term 'asylum-seeker' over 'refugee', we raise a question regarding the authenticity of that individual's claim against the state, thus (re)asserting or privileging the state's role as the ultimate arbiter over the individual's status.

Following on from this preliminary observation about language, terminology is important because it can contain hidden logic about the causes and effects of migration. One might assume, for example, that migration patterns themselves have a quite straightforward impact on public debates and how the media deals with the subject, but this is not necessarily the case. The terms 'sending state' and 'receiving state' to categorize countries according to whether they primarily send people to other nations or are mainly recipients of migrants have already been used. The notion of 'old' and 'new' countries of immigration or emigration, depending on the particular era when they began to be net importers or exporters of migrants could be added to this typology (see, e.g., Freeman 1995 for a well-known typology). Another category might be that of 'transit' countries, which have a mixture of immigrants and emigrants. On the one hand, the position of any particular country within this spectrum of immigration experiences will have significant consequences for the type of debate which is likely to arise in its pubic sphere. A familiar issue for receiving countries, for example, is the notion of the 'unwanted migrant' – someone who is an economic migrant, an asylum-seeker, or irregular and undocumented; someone who is suspected of trying to 'play the system'. However, we should be careful when attempting to make a direct correlation between migration patterns and debates about migration. Evidence strongly suggests that perceived (rather than the actual) migratory patterns are most important in determining how the debate develops. The role of the media, as a key site where politicization and securitization occurs, and where information about the subject is transmitted, discussed and reinterpreted, therefore becomes central. As any examination of United Nations High Commissioner for Refugees (UNHCR) statistics will confirm, the numbers of refugees in countries where asylum is high on the political agenda are minuscule when compared with those countries near disaster zones or areas of armed conflict. Evidence from surveys in the UK consistently show a significant gap between actual numbers of migrants and perceptions of those numbers among the general public (Duffy and Frere-Smith 2014).

Framing immigration and asylum

These points about language and the importance of 'perception–reality gaps' have led to a large and growing body of work that is highly critical of the way in which the media frames issues of migrants, minorities, asylum-seekers, refugees and so on (Buchanan *et al.* 2003; Cohen 2011; Finney 2003; Greenberg and Hier 2001; King and Wood 2001; Philo *et al.* 2013). These studies demonstrate quite clearly that there is a tendency in media reporting of these topics for a framing that discriminates against these groups and presents representations that are heavily dependent on stereotypes. An intriguing aspect of this is that the explicit language of human rights is not usually present in the debates. Discussions often purport to be about practical issues such as implementation, particular pressures and migratory flows, with the discriminatory dimension always hidden in the way that the migrants are framed – as 'criminals', 'scroungers', 'parasites', 'asylum cheats', 'unskilled' and so forth (see, e.g., Buchanan *et al.* 2003). A number of myths are constantly used to discuss refugees: the ineligibility myth (stressing that they are not genuine); the cost myth (presenting them as a financial burden); the social cost myth (highlighting the cultural harm they pose to the 'national way of life'); and the criminality myth (casting them as criminals or even terrorists) (Alia and Bull 2005: 27–28). However, while analysis of the way in which these topics are framed in the media can be useful in identifying latent discrimination and prejudice, the same methodology can also be used to discover how ideas relating to human rights underpin discussions of immigration.

The most obvious frame in the debate over immigration relates to the distinction that is made between 'wanted' and 'unwanted' newcomers. While there might be a warm welcome in Germany for highly skilled IT workers from the US or India, the red carpet vanishes if the new arrival is an economic migrant from a country where there is no agreement over recognition of qualifications, if they are low-skilled, or if they are an asylum-seeker from Africa or the Middle East. Where migrants come from, and how their country of origin is classified by those who receive them, has never been more important than it is today. Again, it is perception, rather than reality, which is crucial here. Categories of wanted and unwanted migrants constructed as an attempt to manage migration in the interests of nation-states suggest there is a real difference in the motivations and circumstances of migrants. Empirically, however, these distinctions are much harder to maintain. The differences between those who flee wars or persecution and 'economic migrants' are much less clear cut than legislation and policy suggest: most people move for a combination of reasons, and economic privation itself is often a result of bad governance or discrimination against a particular ethnic or religious group. The fact that political context is omitted when refugees and asylum-seekers are discussed in the media further aggravates this problem and helps mislead the public about the causes behind asylum-seeking. As the Institute for Public Policy Research (IPPR) noted in an audience reception study it carried out in 2005, 'virtually no participant mentioned events such as the wars in Iraq and Afghanistan as potential drivers for asylum' (cited in Philo *et al*. 2013: 4).

Research into the media's portrayal of refugees and asylum-seekers in London conducted by the Information Centre about Asylum and Refugees in the UK concluded:

> Newspapers often present images of asylum seekers and refugees that contain language, graphics and photographs likely to give rise to feelings of fear and hostility towards asylum seekers and refugees among their readers. This effect is compounded by inaccurate and unbalanced reporting.
>
> *(ICAR 2004: 41)*

The freedom of speech advocacy group Article 19 (Buchanan *et al*. 2003) also conducted research into the media's role in informing the public policy debate on asylum and immigration in Britain. Its research confirmed the overwhelmingly negative and hostile nature of the coverage. The main findings were: inaccuracy, provocation, incorrect use of definitions, an obsession with exaggerated numbers, a lack of contextualization, and a reliance on a narrow range of sources. As a result of this coverage, the researchers found that asylum-seekers felt alienated and sometimes threatened, wary of 'hidden agendas', unable to complain and isolated. A study carried out ten years later confirmed the persistence of the earlier identified patterns: an overwhelmingly hostile national press, confusion over terminology, a paucity of refugees' voices and inaccurate and partial reporting continued to characterize media coverage of immigration (Philo *et al*. 2013). The effects of this coverage and the policies it encourages were reiterated, too – it further isolates and stigmatizes the refugees, but also has negative consequences for the stability of existing communities.

The notion of framing corresponds to the need for reporters and editors to make choices. The inclusion or exclusion of contextual information, the emphasis on one aspect of a situation over another, and the selection of sources all determine the angle taken on a particular story and, ultimately, the impression it makes on the reader/viewer. This framing of stories is carried out on the basis of those issues that – rightly or wrongly – have become central to the asylum and immigration debate in the UK: the number of asylum-seekers and the manner in which they arrive to Britain; the alleged loss of control of Britain's borders; the treatment of asylum-seekers and refugees in comparison to British citizens; and the charge that the asylum system is an open door for uncontrolled, illegal immigration (Buchanan *et al*. 2003). In addition, the moral panic about terrorism that was created post-9/11 has resulted in a fusion of prejudices about asylum-seekers, Muslims and migrants to create the concept of an 'enemy within' the West, particularly in multicultural Europe (Leiken 2005).

Case study: Mobility in the EU

The first case study focuses on economic migration and human rights in Europe. It involves a specific use of framing in order to explore the nature and extent of cosmopolitanism in public debates over migration. As the previous discussion explained (see also Chapter 2), the use of framing allows us to analyse media coverage systematically – in this case, coverage of migration policies and policy decisions. When this is combined with the previously discussed cosmopolitan and communitarian arguments over migration, it is possible to expose the structure of ideas that underpin the debates. This approach also allows us to demonstrate how media coverage (which on the surface might seem to have little to do with human rights) is fundamentally based on ethical arguments about the rights of individuals.

Balabanova and Balch (2010) looked at media coverage of intra-EU migration in the UK and Bulgaria in the year leading up to the latter's accession to the EU on 1 January 2007. There was a fairly clear policy question: should the UK maintain closed borders or open them up? The role of the media was very important here because politicians are always cautious about making decisions relating to migration if they are likely to prove unpopular. There was, however, an opportunity for all of those in the debate to put forward both communitarian and cosmopolitan arguments for and against the removal of transitional arrangements. The assumption was that the Bulgarian media would be much more pro-migration and adopt a more cosmopolitan 'open borders' approach, while the UK's media would be more restrictive and communitarian in its thinking. The researchers aimed to find out if this was indeed the case by asking: which kinds of communitarian and cosmopolitan frames emerged in the public debate over European mobility in the UK and Bulgaria, who put these arguments forward, how were they used, and how did they differ across the two countries? In order to answer these questions, Balabanova and Balch (2010) went through a number of stages.

Before any analysis can take place, there needs to be a 'corpus' of material, which is usually collected by conducting an online word-search to identify articles that discuss the subject that is the focus of the research. Once that is done, these articles need to be filtered to remove any that are not relevant and then organized in terms of the different 'topics' where this subject appears. This is the first part of the framing analysis; in it, topics for each article are identified and recorded. This is also where the overall perspective (positive, neutral, critical and so on) of the article with respect to intra-EU migration, the sources and the actors involved are recorded. The topic is the main subject of the article or the main issue that it addresses. However, as there are often multiple topics or subjects, it is often necessary to record two topics, with the first the most important and the second of lesser importance. This first-level framing analysis is also where the final screening of articles takes place. The article might have extremely low, or even zero, relevance to discussions about intra-EU migration, in which case it could be ignored.

The second-level framing analysis is the most important, and also the most difficult. The question here relates to the communitarian and cosmopolitan arguments that underpin discussions of immigration controls. In other words, on what basis is the existence of border controls justified? What is the key or dominant ethical argument that is deployed in order to justify them? The main point here is to strip away the surface-level framing of the topic (the topic that has been identified) and distil the article down to its core arguments in relation to immigration controls themselves.

A preliminary list of possible arguments from the political theory literature was assembled to provide a set of 'ethical frames' that could then be applied to the media texts. Bader (2005) provides a useful summary of the communitarian arguments that are used to maintain or increase controls over international movement. He claims that these arguments can be boiled down to five main ideas (each of which appears in stronger or weaker versions). The first is duty towards the national community, which means that governments argue that they have special obligations towards fellow citizens, so if there are scarce resources (which there usually are), then compatriots should be considered first. Consequently, newcomers should be kept to a minimum because the more people there are, the less there is to go around, and the less likely it will be that the existing citizenry will enjoy the full benefits. The second argument is known as 'cultural protectionism'. Here the justification for migration controls lies in protecting national identity, which could be threatened by the arrival of newcomers who have different cultures or identities. The third argument is described as 'liberal constitutionalism'. This revolves around the liberal and democratic institutions of the state, and the need for an engaged and stable community of citizens for this to function properly. Large numbers of migrants (who might not have the right to vote) could therefore threaten the democratic system. The fourth argument, 'domestic social justice', includes a range of points that connect with the first (about prioritizing compatriots). Here the focus is on who deserves and who does not deserve help through the welfare system, and the effects that migration will have on the economic health of the state. The final argument relates to security, and the fear that large numbers of migrants might threaten the state's ability to maintain public order (Bader 2005: 345–352). It should be noted that not all of these communitarian arguments necessarily demand completely closed borders. Indeed, some of them could be used to argue for *greater* immigration (for example, when the newcomers are richer or more democratic than the local population), but generally they are employed in defence of strong migration controls.

Turning to cosmopolitan perspectives, there are a number of arguments for the 'open borders' position, which were mentioned earlier in the chapter. These can be put into three main categories. The first, and most obvious, is based on the universal nature of human rights – everyone is the same, so any discrimination or differential treatment of someone due to their migration status is wrong. The second is based on a more consequentialist logic, where free movement is either a solution to global inequalities or contributes in a slightly less defined way to better human relations – peace and harmony or enhanced intercultural/multicultural social cohesion (Tomlinson 1999). The different kinds of cosmopolitanism are connected by an appreciation of the individual and of the 'other' as equal to the 'self'.

The third type of cosmopolitanism relates to identity formation and the everyday – quotidian – accommodation or appreciation of the 'other'. This concept is of interest to those who are searching for an emerging European identity (Cram 2009). To summarize, the universalist position might be called 'ecstatic', the consequentialist position 'instrumental' and the quotidian position 'banal' (Ong 2009).

However, as with the communitarian positions, each of these arguments can be twisted to a different purpose. For example, consequentialist arguments are based on assumptions regarding the positive economic consequences of immigration. If there is consensus over economic benefits, there could be overlap between a communitarian 'economic nationalist' and a cosmopolitan 'utilitarian' (Higgins 2008). They might agree on the economic benefits of lowering barriers to migration, but they would do so for different reasons – the former because of the advantages that will accrue to the nation-state; the latter because of increased welfare at the global level.

How did the frames fit the evidence? Balabanova and Balch (2010) found that in their sample of articles, the vast majority did employ an ethical frame from the above list: 95 per cent in the UK sample (88 out of 93) and 81 per cent in the Bulgarian sample (75 out of 93). See Table 6.1 for a full list of frames, descriptions and examples.

In both cases, the majority of frames employed by the media were found to be communitarian. There was not the expected difference between the two countries, although slightly more (statistically insignificant) communitarian arguments were employed in the UK sample (76 per cent, compared to 72 per cent for Bulgaria). The main differences were not between the two main categories, but within them: arguments relating to public security were more common in the UK, for example. In Bulgaria, within the cosmopolitan frames, there was a greater emphasis on universalism (17 out of 28), compared to the more consequentialist tone of the UK coverage (17 out of 26). Analysis of the differences between newspapers revealed a clear left–right split. Those generally considered on the left were keen to counter the arguments of right-leaning publications, but both sides were reluctant to employ outright universalist arguments, preferring to resort to instrumental linkages between migration and economic output.

The results of the analysis showed that the media generally framed intra-EU migration with nationalist, communitarian arguments, and that these were very similar across cases. One of the more interesting findings was that frames could not be logically linked to the presumed interests of the country in question: the communitarianism in the Bulgarian press was 'by proxy' – imported (mainly from the UK). Ironically, while Bulgaria was sending migrants it was simultaneously receiving ideas about restricting migration from one of the countries those migrants were travelling to. Thus, the roles of sending and receiving country were reversed.

Case study: The UNHCR and World Refugee Day

Considering the general problems with the media when it comes to the issues of immigration and asylum that the rest of this chapter has described, and given the

TABLE 6.1 Communitarian and cosmopolitan frames over intra-EU migration

Frames	Description	Example
Communitarian		
Domestic social justice	Immigration should be controlled to deliver the best possible economic, social and welfare conditions for citizens	'Immigration has increased unemployment ... Schools, hospitals and GPs also come under pressure' (*Daily Mail*, 2 May 2006)
Cultural protectionist	Ethno-national arguments for controls to maintain a 'national culture'	Immigration threatened 'the very essence of our society' (*Dnevnik*, 15 August 2006), 'the white population will decline' (*Daily Telegraph*, 27 January 2006)
Public security	Uncontrolled immigration poses a threat to public order and social stability	'immigrants who can't get jobs will survive on the streets by begging and stealing' (*Sun*, 31 July 2006)
Liberal constitutionalist	Restrictions are needed to maintain the democratic functioning of the state	'migrant workers are exploited in a number of sectors. Unions need to step up their recruitment and government must do more to enforce legal standards' (*Independent*, 1 May 2006)
Priority for compatriots	Special ties or obligations related to the nation-state, e.g. civic practices or historical (national) conflicts/struggles	Uncontrolled immigration 'is putting Britons out of work' (*Daily Telegraph*, 18 August 2006)
Cosmopolitan		
Universalist (ecstatic)	Freedom of movement as part of universalist conceptions of human rights	'If you want to achieve a united Europe, to build social conditions and standards, you cannot impose restrictions' (*Dnevnik*, 13 September 2006)
Consequential (instrumental)	Immigration as a means to maximize total welfare	Positive: 'mutual interest dictates our welcome' (*Independent*, 21 August 2006) Negative: 'the consequences are not only negative for the British people but also for the immigrants themselves who leave themselves open to exploitation' (*Daily Mail*, 14 November 2006)
Quotidian (banal)	Linkages between immigration and post-national forms of identity formation	'Polish delis are sprouting up across the country' (*Independent*, 11 June 2006)

media's tendency to adopt a non-cosmopolitan position, how is it possible to communicate a human rights 'message' about refugees? While one might be forgiven for thinking that this would be a fruitless task, those who actually look after refugees have no choice in the matter. They desperately need to get a human rights message across to the rest of society, because public support (in both financial and non-financial terms) is vital for every agency or organization that works in this area.

This second case study looks at one such organization – the UNHCR – and examines how it has developed a key tool in its battle to communicate a human rights message about refugees. This is the World Refugee Day (WRD), a high-profile global communications event that emerged from a smaller regional event – African Refugee Day – which was established in 1975 through the Organization of African Unity's adoption of Resolution 398. The success of this annual African event led to it becoming one of the key elements for the UNHCR in its deliberations over how to celebrate the fiftieth anniversary of the Geneva Convention in 2001. The UN General Assembly adopted Resolution 55/76, which established, with the agreement of the OAU, an international refugee day to coincide with African Refugee Day. According to the UNHCR itself, this is a day 'to recognize and applaud the contribution of forcibly displaced people throughout the world'.[2]

The rest of this case study examines the evolution of the WRD and focuses on a particular year (the Dilemmas campaign of 2012) to examine its core message and to consider the main challenges faced by the UNHCR in successfully using campaigns to spread a message about refugees that emphasizes human rights.

The evolution of WRD: towards a single message?

The very existence of WRD reflects the global scale and importance of refugee issues and the ambition of the UNHCR to be a truly global 'brand', but the strategy has evolved considerably since its inception in 2001. The history of WRD demonstrates the opportunities and difficulties that arise when organizing a single global media 'event' which has resonance at the local level, but also shows how a small UN agency can have a significant impact without enjoying the resources or capacity available to multinational corporations.

Over the years there has been notable centralization of WRD, but this is not just because communication technologies have enabled greater control and oversight from the centre. It has grown in importance to become a key tool for the UNHCR and is now the organization's most important focal point in terms of its regular communication activities relating to refugees. At first, local agencies were free to use WRD however they saw fit in their own countries and regions, and a certain degree of flexibility remains. The specific goals, objectives and issues to be addressed have naturally varied among different countries and over the years, but in essence they have all aimed to raise awareness about refugee issues, WRD and the UNHCR; to support refugee activities; to encourage greater understanding; to commemorate refugees' cultural identities but also to facilitate local integration; and to counter xenophobic attitudes, negative public perceptions and negative media coverage in host countries.

Each year a specific theme/topic has been at the centre of WRD: in 2002 the focus was on refugee women; in 2003 on youth; in 2004 on repatriation; in 2005 on courage. The organizing idea was simply to create a consensual and globally pertinent theme behind which all could rally, but which was generic enough to allow interpretative flexibility that was culturally and geographically appropriate. According to Leigh Foster (2013), Head of Events, Campaigns and Goodwill Ambassadors at the UNHCR, the approach in the first few years was 'basic' – offices across the world engaged with WRD without any guidance or coordination from the headquarters in Geneva. The most marked shift took place nearly ten years after the first WRD when a more strategic approach was adopted as part of a general rebranding exercise for the organization.

Since this watershed moment much more thought has been put into the way in which WRD is approached, how it is executed, and what the message is for specific audiences. This is because WRD is now seen as an important opportunity to raise brand awareness and establish the UNHCR as an authority on forced displacement around the world (Foster 2013). The first formal campaign with a branded message was launched in 2011 – the '1' concept. It was to be used by all of the UNHCR's 120 global offices at the local level, but local audiences were to be reached with specific messaging. With the new approach and the commitment of (albeit still limited) resources at the centre came an associated demand to measure and evaluate WRD's effectiveness.

So, in 2011, the first new WRD with a piloted global/local strategy and a new set of benchmarks to try to establish how well the exercise was working was launched. The immediate advocacy priorities were still decided at local level, with advice from UNHCR headquarters, but regardless of the nature of the local-level goals and objectives there was now a requirement for greater levels of professionalism. Advocates needed to speak consistently about the issues in the same way in all of their publicity material and outreach projects (traditional or digital media) (UNHCR 2012b).

The 2012 Dilemmas campaign: communicating cosmopolitanism?

The 2012 Dilemmas campaign featured the use of celebrities as 'ambassadors' (most notably a public service announcement by Angelina Jolie), extensive use of social/digital media and a mobile application (app) with the title 'My Life as a Refugee'. Given the limited human and financial resources of the Strategic Communications Team of the UNHCR, online tools proved to be a useful way to keep costs down. Since 2012, materials have had the same look and feel, thus guaranteeing consistency and coherence with respect to WRD and avoiding mixed messages about the UNHCR and specific issues. In this respect, according to Foster (2013), the 2012 Dilemmas campaign achieved significantly more engagement and understanding among the local and regional offices compared to the pilot project in 2011.

Interestingly, and in parallel with the centralization of the WRD campaign, the message in 2012 favoured an explicitly cosmopolitan set of ideas. The Dilemmas campaign continued the trend started by the UNHCR a few years earlier to focus on individuals in terms of the stories being told and by asking individuals to consider what they personally would do in a similar situation and following from that what difference they might make to the bigger picture (UNHCR 2012a). In light of the possible combination of 'compassion fatigue' (Moeller 1999), the distance framing of human suffering (Robinson 2002) and the generally anti-asylum and anti-refugee discourses within national contexts in most Western countries (Balabanova and Balch 2010; Philo *et al.* 2013), this cosmopolitan framing of the message aims to appeal to our common humanity, to interact at a personal level and as a result provoke reactions from broad audiences. A campaign that is built on more generic, inclusive ideas and cross-cutting issues, rather than one that tries to appeal to a single group, has greater potential to attract wide audiences and achieve its communication objectives. Similarly, the interactive component – asking people to do something (engage, follow, choose an option and so on), rather than merely watch and/or read – theoretically has the potential to increase impact. But how might this impact be measured or 'captured'?

Evaluating human rights campaigns

The 2012 Dilemmas campaign was recognized in professional terms (it received an EACA Care Award (EACA 2013)), but how well did it achieve what it had set out to do? This is a very difficult question to answer: the aims and objectives of WRD mentioned at the start of this case study were quite broad and vague. However, it is increasingly important for organizations in all sectors of society to demonstrate impact, so how did the UNHCR go about doing this? The key performance indicators it used consisted mainly of numerical indices that could prove a certain kind of impact: the number of stations that aired the Angelina Jolie piece; the audience numbers for those channels; the number of visits to (and time spent on) the campaign website; the growth in Facebook 'likes'; the extent of media coverage; and so on (UNHCR 2012c). On most of these indicators the campaign was successful (UNHCR 2012d), but how might one prove that the WRD campaign also changes attitudes, or changes the way that people think about refugees? The UNHCR conducted public opinion surveys in eleven countries after the campaign but it has decided not to make the results publicly available. This might be a sensible precaution for a number of reasons: it is easy to measure the number of 'hits' on a website, but changes in perceptions and attitudes are unlikely to take place overnight, and they may well be subtle and nuanced; also, the techniques required to measure this kind of impact rest on complex qualitative analysis, such as sustained engagement with a wide range of audiences over a period of time. This, of course, demands resources – for both data collection and analysis. Indeed, it is questionable whether sufficient or satisfactory techniques are even available to capture the impact of the personal encounters that were a feature of the 2012 campaign.

The challenge for an organization such as the UNHCR is considerable, given the number of countries that filtered the campaign through a variety of combinations of arts and culture, used different means of reaching opinion leaders, employed different mainstream partners, and so on. The KPIs applied to evaluate the 2012 campaign are strong indicators of how many people were reached (UNHCR 2012c, 2012d), but without a qualitative assessment of that reach they cannot serve as definitive evidence of positive engagement. As with all other human rights campaigns, the UNHCR is unable to identify specifically which audiences are reached by WRD, or how they are affected by the message.

This question is further complicated when the proliferation of new types of communication is taken into consideration. Whether social media is more or less capable of changing people's perceptions remains open to debate, as relatively little research has been undertaken in this area (Okazaki and Taylor 2013). Digital campaigns may well speak primarily to the already converted – to those who are convinced before they hear or see the campaign's message. What does a Facebook 'like' really signify? For some, a shift in perceptions from one end of the spectrum to the other is not very likely, but a series of incremental shifts from one position to another, resulting in a more substantial change over the long term, is perhaps a more realistic possibility.

Conclusions

The international movement of people causes considerable challenges for states when it comes to human rights. First of all there is immigration policy: should newcomers have all of the same rights as those who are already members of the community; and, if not, which rights should they enjoy? Then there is the issue of refugees: states were keen to sign up to conventions following the horrors of the Second World War, but many are now very concerned about the costs of providing shelter to the ever more number of displaced people that exist around the world. This chapter has demonstrated how the position that one takes on these issues can be linked to cosmopolitan values because they all relate to questions of global justice.

The case studies revealed two contrasting ways in which human rights and the media interact when it comes to migration and refugees. The first showed that human rights are largely absent from public debates over policy but universal values are central to those debates because policies need to be justified on the basis of *something*. The overwhelmingly communitarian framing of immigration policy in the UK press reflects the quite restrictive approach which that country has followed since the collapse of its colonial system. The second case study showed that international organizations such as the UNHCR have cosmopolitanism embedded in their very structure, and naturally rely on these ideas when attempting to influence the global debate and legitimize their work. The findings indicate the scale of the challenge of creating a message that is truly global. When taken together, the gap between the cosmopolitan promise of international human rights and the reality of resolutely communitarian national media systems is clearly visible.

Questions

- What are the main problems in the way that the media treats the subject of asylum?
- How do ideas about global justice affect the way in which immigration policy is discussed?
- Should there be a human right to migrate?
- Can a global human rights campaign change the way that people think about refugees?

Notes

1 http://mysite.du.edu/~jdonnell/papers/hrsov%20v4a.htm. There are other, more legalistic, criticisms, however: www.law.harvard.edu/students/orgs/hrj/iss15/kennedy.shtml.
2 'World Refugee Day' at www.unhcr.org.

Further reading

Alden, E. 2009. *The Closing of the American Border: Terrorism, Immigration, and Security since 9/11*. New York: Harper Perennial.

Castles, S., H. de Haas and M. J. Miller. 2013. *The Age of Migration: International Population Movements in the Modern World*. 5th edn. Basingstoke: Palgrave Macmillan.

Freeman, G. 1995. 'Modes of immigration politics in liberal democratic states'. *International Migration Review* 29(4): 881–902.

Hayter, T. 2003. 'No borders: the case against immigration controls'. *Feminist Review* 73(1): 6–18.

Hollifield, J. F. 1992. *Immigrants, Markets, and States: The Political Economy of Postwar Europe*. London: Harvard University Press.

Philo, G., E. Briant and P. Donald. 2013. *Bad News for Refugees*. London: Pluto Press.

Walzer, M. 1983. *Spheres of Justice: A Defense of Pluralism and Equality*. New York: Basic Books.

Useful websites

www.unhcr.org (UN Refugee Agency)

www.europa.eu/index_en.htm (Official website of the European Union)

www.migreurop.org/?lang=en (Network of activists and scholars)

www.migrantsrights.org.uk (UK Migrants' Rights Network)

www.iom.int (International Organization for Migration)

www.compas.ox.ac.uk (UK Centre on Migration, Policy and Society)

www.statewatch.org (Statewatch)

7

FREEDOM OF SPEECH

Introduction

Interdependency, or the links between different human rights, is a theme of this book, but this is especially pronounced when it comes to freedom of expression. This is because it is a 'framework' right based on freedom of opinion that incorporates several elements that are intricately linked to the whole democratic process. This is not just about the right to speak freely; it is about the right to seek and receive ideas regardless of borders, and about a free press which acts as an important check on governments and the exercise of authority and power. Smolla (1992) summarizes the key functions of freedom of expression that are essential for democratic self-governance as: a means of participation; to serve the pursuit of political truth; to facilitate majority rule; to provide restraint on tyranny and corruption by keeping government in check; and, finally, to help ensure stability by allowing minority voices to be heard.

A central issue is the possibility that freedom of expression conflicts with other human rights, something which theorists accept is possible (Freeman 2011). The UDHR's Article 29(2) acknowledges the same:

> In the exercise of his rights and freedoms, everyone shall be subject only to such limitations as are determined by law solely for the purpose of securing due recognition and respect for the rights and freedoms of others and of meeting the just requirements of morality, public order and the general welfare in a democratic society.

Thus the human rights of some people can conflict with the human rights of others and/or one right may conflict with another right for the same person.

How does this fit with the different cosmopolitan positions and perspectives on the role of the media? For strong cosmopolitans, freedom of expression should be protected against relativistic claims for special group exceptions, such as those who are religious and seek to prohibit the publication of critical materials (Cohen 2013). For those who are optimistic about the power of the media to transform governance, the capacity and ability of authoritarian regimes to maintain restrictions on freedom of expression has been increasingly compromised. This is because the forces of globalization have resulted in a combination of new communications technologies, global migration and a growth in civil society which is forcing many previously closed countries to enlarge freedom of expression. By contrast, pessimists point out that authoritarian states are strongly motivated to resist this globalizing dynamic and that such developments have merely fuelled governmental efforts to restrict expression (HRW 2007).

New media optimists argue that new communication technologies have greatly increased individuals' opportunities to exercise their right of freedom of expression. More than this, they also 'bring new issues to the fore and reorganize traditional political allegiances' (Neuman 2001: 317). For strong cosmopolitans, freedom of expression is central to the human rights system because it is seen as a right that is essential for the enjoyment of other rights. This is often said about the freedom of the press, too. In 1999 UN Secretary General Kofi Annan described the latter as 'a cornerstone of human rights. It holds governments responsible for their acts, and serves a warning to all that impunity is an illusion' (Annan 1999a). However, communitarians argue that it is legitimate to impose certain restrictions on these rights – for example, for reasons of national security, or to preserve public order and societal cohesion.

This chapter examines how these different positions play out when freedom of speech is set against other rights, such as freedom from discrimination, and when it is accused of endangering other societal values, such as national security. The case studies have been selected to exemplify these tensions. The first focuses on the publication of cartoons featuring the Prophet Mohammed in Denmark in September 2005, that raised questions about the right of free speech and the right to be free from discrimination. The second examines the practice of 'whistle-blowing through the example of Edward Snowden's revelations in order to demonstrate the potential for conflict between freedom of speech and security. First, though, the roots of the right to freedom of expression need to be explored.

Freedom of expression as a human right

The roots of contemporary debates about freedom of speech can be traced right back through the liberal political tradition – for example, to the views of John Locke, who favoured minimal state intervention, or to John Stuart Mill, who advocated the concept of a 'marketplace of ideas'. In his seminal work *On Liberty*, Mill (1987 [1859]) defended freedom of speech on the following four grounds:

- a suppressed opinion might turn out to be true;
- even if an opinion is false, it may still contain some truth and the only way we can get closer to the 'total' truth is by listening to other accounts;

- even if a true account is already a 'total' truth, it should still be criticized or challenged in order to understand why it is true, rather than uncritically accept it as such; and
- only by challenging an established truth it is possible to maintain the vital link between theory and action.

Regardless of the strength of these arguments, it is accepted that freedom of speech is not an unlimited right, and no country guarantees it in absolute terms. In that sense it is different from the right to life, the right to freedom from slavery and the right to freedom from torture, all of which are seen as absolute in that they do not allow for limitations, exceptions, qualifications or any kind of balancing against other rights. No country is supposed to override these absolute rights under any circumstances, and the ideas behind them are thought to transcend each and every political and/or theological concept. Freedom of speech, on the other hand, can be limited through legal restrictions designed to protect a defined legitimate objective. The perhaps clichéd (but very effective) example is that of shouting 'fire' in a crowded theatre – an act that can be (and is in fact) punished because of its potential consequences in endangering others. Similarly, while in general the freedom to receive and impart information is beyond doubt, some restrictions are usually considered legitimate – for example, in the passing on of commercial or military secrets. Conceding that certain types of expression are dangerous to society, however, raises questions about how to determine which types of speech are dangerous, who should have the power to make the ultimate decision, who should implement the restriction, and how.

In its very first session, in 1946, the UN General Assembly adopted Resolution 59(I), which states: 'Freedom of information is a fundamental human right and ... the touchstone of all the freedoms to which the United Nations is consecrated.' The European Court of Human Rights has also recognized the crucial role of freedom of expression in the underpinning of democracy: 'Freedom of expression constitutes one of the essential foundations of [a democratic] society, one of the basic conditions for its progress and for the development of every man' (cited in Article 19 2008: 2).

Freedom of expression is firmly established as part of the modern human rights regime. Article 19 of the UDHR guarantees the right to freedom of expression by saying

> Everyone has the right to freedom of opinion and expression; this right includes the right to hold opinions without interference and to seek, receive and impart information and ideas through any media regardless of frontiers.

The 1966 International Covenant on Civil and Political Rights, which imposes formal legal obligations on state parties to respect the human rights set out in the UDHR, guarantees the right to freedom of opinion and expression in terms very similar to those found in Article 19. The same goes for the three major regional human rights systems: the European Convention for the Protection of Human Rights and Fundamental Freedoms; the American Convention on Human Rights; and the African Charter on Human and Peoples' Rights. The right is recognized as multifaceted, including not only the right to express, or disseminate, information and ideas. As seen in Article 19, it has at least three distinct aspects: the right to *seek* information and ideas; the right to *receive* information and ideas; and the right to *impart* information and ideas. The right to freedom of expression can also be exercised in a variety of means ('through any media') and without concern for local, national or regional boundaries ('regardless of frontiers'). This means that international law protects the means of expression as well as the content. This is particularly important for the media as it plays a special role as the bearer of the general right to freedom of expression for everybody else.

All of the above-mentioned international conventions recognize that freedom of expression is subject to limitations with respect to the rights of the 'other' and wider society. However, this in turn prompts the need to ensure that state authorities do not abuse their power to enforce such limitations. Freedom of expression is necessary to democracy, but as with other human rights there is a circularity – limits must be placed on democratic governments in order to preserve democracy itself. So guarantees of freedom of expression could be described as imposing 'limitations on limitations'. As a result, the imposition of limitations on freedom of expression is only permitted by law. In general, such limitations are allowed only on the grounds of protecting the rights and reputations of others, national security, public order, public health or morals. In addition, the authorities are expected to establish that the limitations they impose are necessary and proportionate, meaning that a limitation must not be imposed in an arbitrary manner even if it is enshrined by law and is based on one of the prescribed grounds. Article 19(3) of the ICCPR is definitive on this point:

> The exercise of the rights provided for in paragraph 2 of this article [the right to freedom of expression] carries with it special duties and responsibilities. It may therefore be subject to certain restrictions, but these shall only be such as are provided by law and are necessary:
>
> (a) For respect of the rights or reputations of others;
> (b) For the protection of national security or of public order, or of public health or morals.

The UDHR, the European Convention, the American Convention and the African Charter, while using different wording, all contain similar 'tests' to determine the legitimacy of restrictions on freedom of expression. Thus, it is internationally agreed that restrictions on freedom of expression may be imposed in support of human rights and democracy only when they are narrowly drawn and independently policed, and when the criteria of legitimacy, legality, proportionality and democratic necessity are met.

Freedom of expression and freedom of the press

The importance of the media as central to freedom of expression can be demonstrated by the correlation with other freedoms. For Freedom House, the link between freedom of expression and freedom of the press is straightforward. Freedom House defines itself as 'an independent watchdog organization dedicated to the expansion of freedom around the world'[1] and it does this partly by measuring the extent of press freedom which exists in various counties. This information then informs its yearly reports, which classify countries as 'free', 'partly free' or 'not free'. As the organization explains, the

> free press plays a key role in sustaining and monitoring a healthy democracy, as well as in contributing to greater accountability, good government, and economic development ... Most importantly, restrictions on media are often an early indicator that governments intend to assault other democratic institutions.
>
> *(Freedom House 2013)*

Freedom House considers three specific dimensions as important for press freedom:

- the legal environment (i.e. the laws and regulations influencing the media);
- the political environment (i.e. the degree of political control over the content of the media); and
- the economic environment (i.e. issues of ownership, subsidies and corruption).

According to the Freedom House's 2013 Freedom of the Press Index, only 14.5 per cent of the world's population live in countries that enjoy a free press. In that year, 63 countries (32 per cent) were categorized as free, 70 (36 per cent) as partly free, and 64 (32 per cent) as not free. Interestingly, this was the lowest percentage of free countries since the report was first produced in 1980, indicating a global pattern of decline in the number of people enjoying a free media environment. The region with the worst standard of press freedom was the Middle East and North Africa, where no country was categorized as free, whereas the worst individual offenders against freedom of the press were North Korea, Turkmenistan, Uzbekistan, Eritrea, Belarus, Iran and Cuba (Freedom House 2013).

Considering the function of freedom of expression in liberal democracies, it is no surprise that authoritarian governments across the world seek to restrict and control both freedom of expression and freedom of the press. In Russia, for example, journalists are often the targets of secret service harassment (Harding 2012). Unfortunately, individual journalists sometimes pay the ultimate price. Attacks on media freedoms in Russia in the early 2000s (IPI 2008) continued following Vladimir Putin's return for a third term as President in 2012. For instance, a law was passed in July 2013 prohibiting the distribution of information about homosexuality to minors, and making it illegal to 'equate' gay relationships with straight ones. Although this did not make it illegal to be homosexual in Russia (as it is in much of Africa, for example), it effectively banned the distribution of material that was pro-gay rights (Elder 2013). Another law, on blasphemy, which was passed the following month, was drafted in response to protests by the punk band Pussy Riot inside a Moscow cathedral in February 2012. This followed other Russian legislation against 'extremism', which has been used to target artists and journalists but enforced selectively and with mixed results. As largely symbolic legislation (it is usually very vaguely worded), it manages to threaten freedom of expression while simultaneously failing to achieve its stated objectives (Verkhovsky 2013).

China is another state that has famously fought long and hard to maintain government control over its citizens' internet access through various methods of blocking, filtering, corporate complicity and censorship (MacKinnon 2009). This means that while there is massive online activity and social media has enabled certain forms of political participation to expand (Zhang and Lin 2014), the public sphere in China is still dominated by pro-state, pro-status quo material (Lagerkvist 2012).

However, it is not just in authoritarian regimes that fights are taking place both inside and outside the courts over the appropriate legal framework for freedom of expression. In liberal states there has been a rise in hate speech and the laws to prevent it (Bleich 2011). There are also transnational campaigns demanding laws to criminalize 'homophobic hate speech' (Bob 2014).

Freedom of speech versus freedom from discrimination

Both freedom of speech and freedom from discrimination are fundamental rights in a democracy. They relate to the crucial need for people to be able to express their views freely, and thereby act as a check on government power, while also fully enjoying political equality and thus political participation. Article 19 of the UDHR says that everyone has the right to freedom of expression, whereas Article 7 proclaims equality before the law and includes the right to equal protection against incitement to discrimination. This is where the potential conflict lies. A particular tension relates to so-called 'hate speech' and questions over how it can be defined and prohibited while maintaining the right to freedom of expression. As Jones (1994: 199–201) points out, there would be no conflict if some forms of abuse were explicitly excluded from the right to freedom of speech. In the absence of such an exclusion there needs to be some kind of restriction in the range of at least one of the two rights at stake. Different countries have adopted various approaches in response to this tension, but in general freedom of speech has not been seen as an absolute barrier to state regulation of harmful expression. National and international laws have been introduced targeting hate speech and punishing speech that incites imminent violence or is offensive in recognition of the variety of psychological, sociological and political harms that can be caused by 'words that wound' (Matsuda et al. 1993; Vick 2004). Most countries prohibit expression that promotes discrimination or hatred, or even that which causes anger and resentment, without requiring evidence that it will lead to a breach of peace. However, the debate over whether the expression of extremist views should be tolerated is ongoing, and it is particularly relevant in relation to far-right movements and parties that preach racial intolerance.

It is important to remember that prohibitions have been used to silence political opponents as well. In 1988 the UK Parliament passed a broadcasting ban which made it illegal for television companies to broadcast the speech of any 'known terrorist group'. This ban was aimed at the Irish republican party, Sinn Féin, with the intention of denying them the 'oxygen of publicity'. The subsequent aban-donment of this approach in the mid-1990s and its replacement with 'megaphone diplomacy' confirmed that depriving the republicans of coverage had serious negative consequences, including hindering discussion of one of the most serious issues facing British society at the time. Thought-provoking news programmes were discouraged from covering Northern Ireland and as a result important ques-tions about the tactics of the police and the military were relatively undercovered. This arguably led to abuses of power and further erosion of the possibility of reconciliation between the two sides in the conflict (Oates 2008).

A similarly contentious issue for the UK has been the question of whether the media should provide a platform for the British National Party (BNP). O'Byrne (2003: 117) reviews the debate that took place in the pages of the *Guardian* in 1994 between Seamus Milne and Polly Toynbee. Milne argued against, on the grounds that the BNP violated the rights of a large proportion of the population and by doing so surrendered its right to freedom of speech. He was concerned that the spread of racism would be encouraged if the party was allowed to express its views freely. Toynbee, on the other hand, claimed that banning the BNP would set a dangerous precedent whereby in future any group (on the left or the right) that did not conform to a specified norm might be similarly silenced. She advo-cated allowing the broadcast and publication of dislikeable opinions and trusting in human rationality to see them for what they are, rather than censoring them and thus potentially sending them underground, where they might continue unchecked. Her argument was that proscription and censorship are often counter-productive, which makes engaging with and challenging those who express extreme views a better approach than trying to eliminate them through suppression.

Fifteen years later, in October 2009, the BBC's decision to invite Nick Griffin, the leader of the BNP, on to *Question Time* sparked considerable public and political debate in the UK, illustrating how difficult it is to overcome these tensions. The corporation justified its action by declaring that the public had the

> right to hear the full range of political perspectives, to hear other members of the public putting those perspectives to the test, and then to form their own conclusions. Excluding any party with demonstrable popular support from taking part in the programme would be to curtail this public right.
>
> *(Thompson 2009)*

Hate speech

The term 'hate speech' is an American expression that has gained international prominence. It

> describes a problematic category of speech and related freedoms, such as freedom of assembly and association, that involves the advocacy of hatred and discrimination against groups on basis of their race, colour, ethnicity, religious beliefs, sexual orientation, or other status.
>
> *(Boyle 2001: 489)*

An example of hate speech, in this case genocidal speech, occurred in Rwanda in 1994 when broadcasters on the RTLM radio station urged Hutus to kill their Tutsi neighbours (see Chapter 5).

At the international level, Article 20 of the ICCPR defines 'hate speech' and prohibits it (although it does not categorize it as a crime):

1 Any propaganda for war shall be prohibited by law.
2 Any advocacy of national, racial or religious hatred that constitutes incitement to discrimination, hostility or violence shall be prohibited by law.

More recently, the First Additional Protocol to the Council of Europe's Convention on Cybercrime (2003) required states to adopt measures prohibiting the transmission of racist or xenophobic messages through computer systems.

The principle of freedom of speech became a crucial part of the Cold War when there were significant differences between the positions of the US, the USSR and Europe. The US has often presented itself not only as a defender of free expression but as the country with the strongest legal protection for free speech, due to the fact that this is enshrined in the First Amendment of the US Constitution. The USSR took the opposite position, while Europe occupied what could be described as the middle ground. Post-Cold War, the US has continued to follow a path that sets it apart from the rest of the world. It has been criticized internationally for favouring the rights of speakers rather than protecting those who are the targets of hate speech (Vick 2004). However, the US disagrees with other countries not so much over whether hate speech should be controlled and limited, but rather over the best way to respond to such speech. To what extent should it be suppressed by law and governmental regulation, and what is an acceptable cost in terms of limiting freedom of expression (Boyle 2001)?

The US position is that prohibiting speech because of its content harms those whose speech is prohibited. Such prohibition is also seen as state support for (or active opposition to) particular viewpoints or ideologies (Donnelly 2013a). In accordance with this, in 1992, when the US ratified the ICCPR – whose Article 20(2) calls for national laws against 'advocacy of national, racial, or religious hatred that constitutes incitement to discrimination, hostility or violence' – it attached a reservation: 'Article 20 does not authorize or require legislation or other action by the US that would restrict the right of free speech and association protected by the Constitution and the laws of the US.' Therefore, the US rejected any legislative restriction on abusive speech that is not content-neutral.

The US has also displayed reservations with regard to another international convention dealing with hate speech: the International Covenant on the Elimination of All Forms of Racial Discrimination (the Race Convention), 1969. This convention requires parties not only to prohibit violence and incitement to violence but to 'declare an offence punishable by law all dissemination of ideas based on racial superiority or hatred' (Article 4(a)). It also requires states to prohibit racist organizations, declare them illegal and make it an offence to join one. In effect, Article 4 attempts to assert that in any conflict between freedom of speech and freedom from discrimination, the latter should be given priority over the former when it comes to race. The compromise in the US is therefore that incitement to violence is legally prohibited, but hate speech is still tolerated. This arrangement reflects the important place that freedom of speech has historically occupied among human and constitutional rights in the US, as well as the long legal history of allowing hate speech in the country.

Of course, some critics continue to argue that certain ideas – such as assertions that one race or sex is genetically inferior to another – are inherently and undeniably bad and should be prohibited. Others add that hate speech requires attention from the state because it can cause great psychological harm; that protecting racist, sexist or homophobic declarations should not come at the expense of maintaining an equal society (i.e. the Fourteenth Amendment of the US Constitution); that any gains in protecting the principle of freedom of speech (for those who choose to use hate speech) are outweighed by the damage caused by hate speech on its victims; and that protecting politically extremist and often anti-democratic messages does not serve any useful purpose in preserving and promoting democracy (Delgado and Stefancic 1997; Fraleigh and Tuman 2011: 161–163; Vick 2004). However, in response to these points, other commentators argue that the US position is sustainable because, while targets of hate speech may be harmed, they are legally protected against violence (Donnelly 2013a).

In Europe, the most prominent example of restricting hate speech is the criminalization of certain forms of historical 'revisionism' through the introduction of laws dealing with Holocaust denial. These laws were drafted amid concerns over ongoing anti-Semitism and in response to the horrors of the Second World War. Belgium, Germany, France, Spain, Switzerland and Austria have all adopted legislation that in essence makes it a criminal offence to trivialize or deny the historical facts of the Holocaust or to justify the Nazi genocide. The proliferation of these laws in the 1990s, as Human Rights Watch (2007: 73) highlights, was more of a political statement against anti-Semitism than a response to any genuine prospect of incitement to genocide in Western Europe. The increasing marginalization of those who deny the Holocaust might even have eased the passage of such laws. However, their continuing relevance is demonstrated by prominent cases, such as those brought against the French comedian Dieudonné M'Bala M'Bala, who has a number of convictions for hate speech and inciting violence through his anti-Semitic comments. For example, on 26 June 2008, he was fined for describing Holocaust commemorations as 'memorial pornography'.

It is worth noting that the initial hate speech provisions of the ICCPR were negotiated in a context where memories of the Holocaust were quite fresh. The intention was to establish that hate speech, even if not representing direct incitement, was often a crucial factor in facilitating violence and state discrimination against minorities. As memories of the Nazi regime have faded, this rationale has been progressively sidelined, particularly in Europe, with increasing priority given to social equality:

> Laws and prosecutions for hate speech often seemed focused on limiting certain content no matter the context, and seemed unmoored from hard analysis of whether the speech in question, however repugnant, had any potential actually to incite violence or any other criminal action by third parties.
>
> *(HRW 2007: 70)*

The first case study examined in this chapter – the Danish cartoons controversy – sharply highlights the tensions between these two interpretations: hate speech as a catalyst for criminal acts; and hate speech as a threat to dignity.

Freedom of speech versus survival/security

Demands for states to limit freedom of expression are perhaps greatest when there is considered to be a threat to national security. National security is a societal value of the highest order, upon which the protection of all human rights, indeed the whole way of life, depends. It is thus generally accepted that certain restrictions on freedom of expression are warranted to protect national security interests. Withholding military information from the press, increasing surveillance of suspected persons, and limiting criticism of war efforts are all practised by governments and justified on the grounds that they protect national security (Fraleigh and Tuman 2011). In the US, the Sedition Act of 1798 is seen as the first major government effort to limit free speech on national security grounds. This was followed by the Lincoln administration's limiting of expression during the Civil War (1861–1865) and the Wilson administration's introduction of the Espionage Act and the Sedition Act in 1918, which had a similar effect. During both the First and Second World Wars restrictions were imposed on freedom of speech – through legislation and direct guidance to reporters about the limits of safe reporting, on one hand, and through voluntary media cooperation or self-censorship, on the other. This happened in Britain, Germany and other countries in addition to the US (Carruthers 2011; Graber 2003a). Free speech was regularly under threat during the Cold War in countries on both sides of the ideological divide, and there have been further challenges since the 9/11 attacks.

Historically, around the world, 'the interests of national security' have been invoked repeatedly to justify unwarranted restrictions on freedom of expression and information, and this practice continues to this day. Countries' attempts to balance individual human rights and national security can veer towards eroding the fundamental principles of a liberal democratic society, thereby weakening the very principles that were being protected in the first place (Jones and Howard-Hassmann 2005). Many states impose criminal restrictions on the making of statements which purportedly undermine national security. Cases based on such restrictions are relatively rare in liberal democratic countries and are usually high profile and contentious. However, those restrictions tend to be much more common in repressive countries, where they may be used to suppress political opposition and critical reporting. And in almost all countries where freedom of information is guaranteed by law, that right is limited in relation to national security, often in very broad terms (Mendel 2003: 5). This can sometimes be fairly clear cut because the information obviously relates to national security and its secrecy is uncontroversial – for instance, operational details of the D-Day landings during the Second World War. Mostly, however, what constitutes 'national security' is poorly defined and may be subject to very wide interpretation by governments, to the extent that it becomes not much more than an 'ambiguous symbol' (Wolfers 1962) or an 'amorphous concept' (Fraleigh and Tuman 2011: 96).

In the words of Buzan (1983: 4), national security remains a 'weakly conceptualised, ambiguously defined, but politically powerful concept' because

> for the practitioners of state policy, compelling reasons exist for maintaining its symbolic ambiguity ... An undefined notion of national security offers scope for power-maximising strategies to political and military elites, because of the considerable leverage over domestic affairs which can be obtained by invoking it.
>
> *(Buzan 1983: 9)*

None of the international bodies charged with interpreting and applying the various human rights treaties has been able to provide an acceptable definition of 'national security', which further exacerbates the problem. This means that there is little meaningful guidance that might have limited the scope of the term's application, and consequently numerous national interpretations have developed (Coliver 1998).

Given these difficulties, how can we assess the legitimacy of restrictions on freedom of speech on the basis of national security? A lack of information, as well as the inability of non-experts (such as judges) to objectively measure – or even understand – the level of threat to national security, make it difficult to construct effective oversight mechanisms. The sheer range of threats and their sources adds to this challenge: there is a great difference between independently assessing claims that a demonstration will pose a public order risk and assessing the risk posed to national security by another state, such as Iraq, for example (Mendel 2003; Article 19 n.d.). Also, unlike most areas of restriction on freedom of expression, the very nature of the legitimate interest at stake (i.e. 'the state') is by nature political, making it difficult to separate politics from assessment of a threat.

These difficulties can lead to a situation where spurious claims about security are used to limit free speech for ulterior motives. The (sometimes legitimate) shroud of secrecy that surrounds national security matters only increases this risk. This means that courts, human rights organizations and others are often forced to rely on circumstantial or tangential evidence (Article 19 n.d.). For example, the US and UK authorities claimed they had evidence which proved that Iraq possessed weapons of mass destruction, but they refused to make this evidence public, even to the UN weapons inspectors, on the grounds of national security.

Evidence of the profound tension that exists between freedom of expression and national security can be found in the rationale for Article 19's 1995 initiative (the Global Campaign for Free Expression). This brought together 37 international experts in Johannesburg to draft a set of principles with the aim of adequately safeguarding freedom of expression while simultaneously protecting governments' prerogative to limit this right when necessary for legitimate national security interests. The resulting Johannesburg Principles on National Security, Freedom of Expression and Access to Information (1995) have been accepted as the definitive standards for the protection of freedom of expression in the context of national security laws. They narrowly define as 'legitimate' only those laws introduced 'in the interests of national security' that have genuine purpose and demonstrable effect to protect a country's existence or its territorial integrity against the use or threat of force, or its capacity to respond to the use or threat of force.

The Johannesburg Principles (Article 19 1995) highlight four central points:

- governments and officials must tolerate peaceful criticism and advocacy of constitutional change;
- they must allow access to information about the operation of the government in the public interest;
- they must permit the media to report on armed conflicts; and
- governments which restrict due process rights on national security grounds must be able to show not only that any restrictions are necessary but also that they do not violate fundamental due process obligations.

Thus, the principles sought to clarify the point that censorship must not be used to protect the state against embarrassment, industrial unrest, exposure of wrongdoing, ideological deviance or 'muckraking'.

Post 9/11 – a new era for free speech?

The events of 9/11 had a significant impact on freedom of expression around the world, with the subsequent increase in restrictions justified on the grounds of national security. These responses to the terrorist attacks combined with dynamics that pre-dated 9/11 to produce a new wave of threats to free expression. New anti-terror laws were introduced in many countries, including Australia, Morocco, Algeria, Tunisia, Thailand, Malaysia, the Philippines, the UK, the US, Turkey, Russia, Jordan and Egypt, among others. In general, they tended to extend the coverage of counter-terrorism regulations to a wider range of groups and activities, including forms of protest that would normally be covered by public order laws. As Klang (2004: 136) points out, 'The political discourse on terrorism has shifted the focus from the methodology of violent action to the descriptive term for those who would oppose the established order.' Thus, while counter-terrorism was the motive for new speech-restrictive laws, it also became a pretext for repression of political dissent. In Uzbekistan, China, Nigeria, Jordan, Ethiopia and Nepal, in particular, 'anti-terror' laws were used to clamp down on peaceful protesters, political dissidents and/or the media (Callamard 2007; HRW 2007).

The new anti-terror legislation in some countries criminalized statements that glorified terrorism or provoked and/or indirectly incited terrorist acts, raising concerns about excessive interference with freedom of expression. In 2006, a Council of Europe Convention on the Prevention of Terrorism was drafted and opened for signatures and ratification. It required states to criminalize 'provocation' of terrorism – a crime that could include indirect incitement – and thus opened the door for domestic legislation. The UK, Denmark, France and Spain are just some of the countries that have laws criminalizing the 'justification' or glorification of terrorism. Whether this additional legislation is necessary or beneficial is questionable, considering that the right to freedom of speech does not shield or protect incitement to terrorism (Callamard 2007). However, as historical examples prove, the emergence of a threat and the response to that threat are often very poorly balanced. This is because, as Ignatieff (2004: 58) explains, 'the political costs of underreaction are always going to be higher than the costs of overreaction'.

Probably the most famous example of anti-terror legislation post-9/11 is the United States' Patriot Act, introduced 'to deter and punish terrorist acts in the United States and around the world, to enhance law enforcement investigatory tools, and for other purposes'. It was overwhelmingly approved by the US Congress and signed into law by President George W. Bush in October 2001. Provisions include the 'authority to intercept wire, oral, and electronic communications relating to terrorism'. According to Chang (2002), this Act places the First Amendment rights to freedom of speech and political association in jeopardy; decreases government accountability and citizen access to government information; adversely impacts on political activists who are critical of the government; and creates a climate of suspicion and self-censorship. Suspicions that the Act might be made permanent (Jones and Howard-Hassmann 2005) were justified in 2011, when President Barack Obama signed the Patriot Sunset Extension Act 2011, which maintained three key provisions of the Act for another four years: roving wire-taps; searches of business records; and conducting surveillance on 'lone wolves'.

In addition to specific anti-terror legislation in the post-9/11 era, extensive use has been made of Official Secrets Acts. In the case of the US-led intervention in Afghanistan in 2001 there were numerous examples of official secrecy: refusals to discuss war-related matters with reporters; withholding of information about people detained by the government; briefings about military activities in Afghanistan only from the Secretary of Defense and a few generals; and a failure to publish records of what the government knew prior to 9/11 that might have forestalled it (Steinhauer 2002). The subsequent invasion of Iraq in 2003 was also clouded by secrecy over the information used to justify the decision to go to war. Analyses by the Central Intelligence Agency (CIA) and the Defense Intelligence Agency suggesting that Iraqis would not greet US troops as liberators and that Saddam Hussein did not have any links with al-Qaeda or possess any weapons of mass destruction were not made public (Fraleigh and Tuman 2011).

Furthermore, the US Justice Department argued that press enquiries about detainees following 9/11 could be denied on national security grounds because 'public disclosure would undermine counter-terrorism efforts and put the detainees at risk of attack from angry Americans as well as terrorists' (Sachs 2002). The clear argument was that national security interests outweighed any public right to know who was detained, for what reasons and for how long. All high-level government officials were instructed to be 'extraordinarily, probably excessively, tight-lipped' (Graber 2003a: 35). The US government clamped down on access to video footage, which caused considerable problems for the country's television news journalists. As a result, media organizations outside the borders of the US were able to broadcast footage of the bombing damage in Afghanistan released by the pro-Arab media, mainly Al Jazeera, but there was no such footage available from the US (Jasperson and El-Kikhia 2003).

The restrictions on freedom of speech were not all government-led, however. In the first years of the 'war on terror' there were appeals to the press to self-censor as a patriotic duty, albeit with governments armed with new powers to force them to comply through the above-mentioned legislation. For example, National Security Advisor Condoleezza Rice requested US networks not to air Osama Bin Laden's frequent taped 'messages' without prior official approval. This request was made on the grounds that the tapes could contain coded messages to al-Qaeda operatives and as a result might stir up more violence against Americans and recruit more followers (Krimsky 2002). The government denied that the request amounted to censorship, since the media organizations retained complete control over all editorial decisions. The White House, however, did not acknowledge that this control was compromised due to the strong pressure that the administration was putting on journalists to comply with the request. According to Michael Kinsley (cited in Graber 2003a: 36),

> journalists found it exceedingly difficult to challenge the government because the September attack was such a monstrous crime. Journalists who might be inclined to dissent feared the wrath of their readers and their editors and publishers, possibly leading to loss of their job. Such social pressures transformed White House requests into commands.

On an individual level, the post-9/11 era saw journalists treated as partisans, or even combatants, and deliberately targeted, both physically and legally. In Russia, for example, the dangers of reporting on the war in Chechnya were highlighted when the investigative journalist Anna Polytkovskaya was murdered in 2006. The link between her murder and her critical reporting on Chechnya has been the subject of much speculation (Heritage 2011; HRW 2007). In the US, the Bush administration was seen as markedly reluctant, even positively averse, to releasing information to the press when compared to previous administrations. There was a reclassification of information that had been in the public domain, reversing the presumption towards disclosure under the Freedom of Information Act and greatly restricting public access to presidential papers. The government also put significant pressure on investigative reporters to disclose their sources (HRW 2007). Despite the expectations of change and the promise of open government when President Obama came to office, a 2013 special report by the Committee to Protect Journalists claimed that

> the White House curbs routine disclosure of information and deploys its own media to evade scrutiny by the press. Aggressive prosecution of leakers of classified information and broad electronic surveillance programs deter government sources from speaking to journalists.
>
> *(Downie Jr. 2013)*

In the words of the *New York Times*' public editor Margaret Sullivan, Obama's administration is 'turning out to be the administration of unprecedented secrecy and of unprecedented attacks on a free press' (Sullivan 2013). But this is not just a US issue. Before 9/11, legal voids, arbitrary appointments of state media chiefs, physical attacks, trials and a lack of transparency characterized media environments in many parts of the world. Post-9/11, these trends have continued or even worsened. In the 2013 World Press Freedom Index (titled 'Dashed Hopes after Spring'), Reporters without Borders (2013) concluded that Syria is the deadliest country for journalists, but they found significant repression, arrest and suppression of reporters in Bahrain, Yemen, Oman, Vietnam, Azerbaijan, Eritrea and Belarus, too.

Freedom of speech in cyberspace

For many, the advent of the internet seemed to herald infinite possibilities for freedom of speech to flourish, and even threaten authoritarian regimes that would find it difficult to stop their citizens reading uncensored information from across the globe. What appeared to be an information Utopia, however, has quickly become populated, dominated and controlled by older power systems and interests (see the second case study on p. 144 concerning 'whistle-blowers'). States have moved quickly to attempt to fence and filter the internet; and new technologies, rather than enabling freedom of speech, are instead fuelling an explosion of state surveillance, often justified in the name of counter-terrorism. As UN Special Rapporteur on Freedom of Expression Frank La Rue (2011) reported, 'Governments are using increasingly sophisticated technologies and tactics which are often hidden from the public to censor online content and monitor and identify individuals who disseminate critical or sensitive information, which frequently lead to arbitrary arrests and detention.'

The 'war on terror' might not have been the immediate cause of this trend towards restriction of the internet and the proliferation of surveillance through modern technology, but it became one of the chief catalysts. The fight against terrorism became the most commonly invoked rationale when states censored internet publications – replacing the previous emphasis on child pornography. Corporations willingly participated in the fencing and filtering of access. The 'Great Firewall of China' is an excellent example of this, with Yahoo!, Microsoft and Google all censoring their search engines and even providing user information to the Chinese authorities.

However, these same companies, and many others, have shown themselves willing to form a broad coalition to fight for freedom of expression on the internet if they feel governments are going too far with regulation. This was demonstrated in the international reaction to the US Congress's introduction of two bills: the Stop Online Piracy Act (SOPA) and the Preventing Real Online Threats to Economic Creativity and Theft of Intellectual Property Act (PIPA) of 2011. The bills had global implications, not least because of the possibility of an international equivalent – ACTA (the Anti-Counterfeiting Trade Agreement), created through a multilateral agreement including the EU. On 18 January 2012 more than 7,000 online companies initiated a 'blackout' of their websites in protest. They were concerned that the extra powers that these laws provided to protect against copyright infringement (and to force search engines and service providers to take down sites) would limit 'online freedoms'. Meanwhile, a coalition of European NGOs complained that ACTA would 'profoundly restrict the fundamental rights and freedoms of European citizens, most notably the freedom of expression and communication privacy'.[2] Ultimately, ACTA was rejected by the European Parliament neutering its global ambitions, but significant concerns remain about the ways in which states are balancing new technologies with human rights when it comes to freedom of expression and the right to privacy. As the UN Special Rapporteur on Freedom of Expression said in his 2013 report, states must 'update their understandings and regulation of communications surveillance and modify their practices in order to ensure that individuals' human rights are respected and protected' (La Rue 2013).

This chapter now explores two case studies that demonstrate the tension between security and freedom of speech: the Danish cartoons controversy; and the 'whistle-blowing' of Edward Snowden.

Case study: Danish cartoons

On 30 September 2005 the Danish newspaper *Jyllands-Posten* published 12 cartoons depicting the Muslim Prophet Mohammed. The cartoons were selected from those submitted to the publication following a competition. The newspaper's cultural editor at the time, Fleming Rose (2006), explained that the competition was organized 'in response to several incidents of self-censorship in Europe caused by widening fears and feelings of intimidation in dealing with issues related to Islam' post-9/11. It is not surprising, given Islamic traditions which forbid representations of the Prophet, that many people considered the cartoons offensive and even derogatory. This was heightened by the fact that some of the cartoons associated Mohammed, and by extension all Muslims, with terrorism. Almost 100 complaints were received almost immediately, and thereafter the reaction developed into a gathering of 3,500 Muslims in Copenhagen to demonstrate against the publication of the cartoons.

The issue became a global one when 11 ambassadors from Muslim states wrote to the Danish Prime Minister, Anders Fogh Rasmussen, requesting a meeting to discuss the cartoons. His refusal to meet was justified on the grounds of free speech and his government's unwillingness to influence editorial opinion. In the weeks and months that followed, other newspapers and magazines around the world chose to republish the cartoons. By the end of February 2006, at least 143 papers in 56 countries had published all or some of the sketches (Strömbäck *et al.* 2008). Meanwhile, in response, the Danish embassies in Damascus and Beirut were attacked and set on fire, the Danish flag was burnt in Hebron and Nablus, public condemnations of the cartoons were made, foreign states closed their embassies in Copenhagen, and there were often violent threats, protests and demonstrations throughout the Middle East and Asia, resulting in several deaths. *Jyllands-Posten* apologized for hurting Muslim feelings, but maintained that it did 'not apologise for printing the cartoons. It was our right to do so' (Rose, cited in Browne 2006).

The publication of the cartoons triggered a world-wide dispute between the advocates of free speech and those arguing for restraint. But, as Human Rights Watch (2007: 71) points out, 'The discourse on whether the media had a right to publish the cartoons became confused with whether the media were right to do so.' The underlying motive of the commissioning editor was to make a point about self-censorship in Denmark resulting in Danish writers and artists becoming reluctant to write or speak openly about Islam or Muslim immigration to Denmark. In doing so, the newspaper was drawing upon one of the fundamental principles of Western democracy – freedom of speech. Defending his decision to publish, Rose (2006) claimed:

> I acknowledge that some people have been offended by the publication of the cartoons, and *Jyllands-Posten* has apologized for that. But we cannot apologize for our right to publish material, even offensive material.

On a separate occasion, he asserted: 'Religious feelings cannot demand special treatment in a secular society. In a democracy one must from time to time accept criticism or become a laughingstock' (Rose, cited in Belien 2005). *Jyllands-Posten*'s editor-in-chief at the time, Carsten Juste, used similar arguments when saying: 'We live in a democracy. That's why we can use all the journalistic methods we want to. Satire is accepted in this country, and you can make caricatures' (Juste, cited in Belien 2005).

Freedom of expression was also invoked by the Danish prime minister in his letter to ambassadors:

> The Danish society is based on respect for freedom of expression, on religious tolerance and on equal standards for all religions. The freedom of expression is the very foundation of the Danish democracy. The freedom of expression has a wide scope and the Danish government has no means of influencing the press. However, Danish legislation prohibits acts or expressions of blasphemous or discriminatory nature. The offended party may bring such acts or expressions to court, and it is for the courts to decide in individual cases.
>
> *(Rasmussen 2005)*

The publication of the cartoons was legally acceptable under Danish law, regardless of whether they were seen as offensive, provocative, insulting or blasphemous by some readers. There was some consensus among Muslim and non-Muslim audiences that their publication was indeed offensive, insulting or provocative; but a small minority of more extreme Muslims demanded violent punishment (and even execution) of those who published the cartoons. Thus, their appearance in the press raised questions about the limits of freedom of speech. As a limited human right, legitimate restrictions on freedom of speech are outlined in a number of international covenants and conventions, as discussed earlier in this chapter. These documents do indeed allow the right to say things that are offensive or provocative, but they do not stretch to the right to defame, insult, intimidate or incite violence. However, as O'Neill (2006) points out, 'These supposed distinctions are inevitably unclear because interpretations of speech acts vary with audiences.' Still, the criticism of the cartoons and their publication rarely suggested that they might provoke discrimination or violence against Muslim communities; rather, they focused on equality issues in Western societies more generally (HRW 2007).

The central issue was whether the notion of free speech had been used as a smokescreen for the vilification of Muslims, with Modood (2006: 6) remarking that 'Europe has to choose which is more important, the right to ridicule Muslims or the integration of Muslims', and asking whether the intolerant attitudes displayed towards Muslims were anti-religious or racist. Some, such as Bleich (2006: 17), saw clear signs of racism and an attitude that bore

> all the earmarks of classic racialization: namely the essentializing of an entire group of people based on a primordial identity marker, and the classification of such a group as inherently dangerous and inferior.

Others focused on the lack of limits on freedom of speech on the grounds of religion (Modood 2006). It was in this context that the Danish authorities' unwillingness either to take action against *Jyllands-Posten* or to apologize was contrasted with the proliferation of Holocaust-denial laws and blasphemy laws protecting Christianity in some European countries. Europe was seen as secular with embedded and established Christian values, and because of this hypocritical in its reaction to the publication of the cartoons.

In response to such accusations, in 2007 Human Rights Watch declared:

> While critics are right to point to the selectivity of existing European blasphemy laws in protecting only Christianity, the key question here is why any religious system should be legally shielded from criticism or even ridicule when political beliefs, aesthetic views, or cultural opinions are not. Speech which targets religious believers for criminal acts should not be protected, but speech which derides only religious ideas should not be punished.
>
> *(HRW 2007: 11)*

Framing the controversy

Aside from the freedom of speech debate provoked by the publication of the cartoons, a second dimension of the controversy became the actual media coverage and the framing of this debate in the Western and non-Western media. For the foreign media, the furious reactions and threats of violence that emerged several months after the publication of the cartoons were far more newsworthy than *Jyllands-Posten*'s decision to publish the sketches in the first place. It was only then that the controversy became a 'serendipitous global news event' (Craft and Waisbord 2008: 133), with coverage increasing dramatically between January and March 2006 (Strömbäck *et al.* 2008).

According to Larsen and Seidenfaden (cited in Strömbäck *et al.* 2008), three main broad frames were employed to make sense of the case. The first of these was the freedom of speech, propagated by *Jyllands-Posten* itself and the Danish government. It viewed the Mohammed cartoons debate in terms of freedom of speech and the press in opposition to self-censorship in response to the fear of Islam. According to this frame, the debate was about having or not having freedom of speech, without looking specifically at what it is and how it works in practice. The second frame was labelled the 'clash of civilizations', following Huntington's (1993) concept. In this perspective, the cartoons debate was seen as part of an ongoing struggle between two inherently different cultures – the Western Christian world and the Islamic world – and their associated value systems. The third frame – the intolerance frame – highlighted that the cartoons were the latest example of anti-Islamic sentiment in Denmark and pointed out that the problem was not so much their publication, but rather Danish intolerance towards the Muslim minority.

Strömbäck *et al.* (2008) analysed the use of all three of these frames in the leading newspapers in the US and Sweden. They found that the freedom of speech frame was more common in the *New York Times* while the intolerance frame was more prevalent in *Dagens Nyheter*. The Swedish newspaper – which is a high-quality daily – also contained more coverage of the topic and used a more negative tone, whereas the American paper was more sympathetic towards *Jyllands-Posten* and the

Danish government. The study stressed the importance of distance when reporting an international issue, both in terms of higher reliance on government sources and the need for the issue to involve conflicts that are easily understandable and can be visualized. There is a clear preference for frames that fit existing schemas, and in the case of geographical, cultural and social proximity news media devote more attention and framing is influenced by struggles played out between domestic actors.

The results of a study focusing on Argentinian and US press also identified the presence of the freedom of speech frame with both absolutist and social responsibility positions, alongside the 'clash of civilizations' frame (Craft and Waisbord 2008). It also suggested that the media in the two countries adopted the same frames common in the European press – familiar and already at hand – and thus encouraged more distance in the coverage, failing to connect the issues under discussion to important domestic political and journalistic subjects. On the back of this Craft and Waisbord (2008: 146) concluded that 'it remains questionable whether such occasions are moments for cosmopolitan participation in public spaces that transcend the national'.

Looking specifically at the Danish frames of understanding of the publication of the cartoons and the events that followed them, Hervik (2008) identifies three frames that partially overlap with those suggested for the international media. The first – freedom of speech – coincides with Larsen and Seidenfaden's first frame. However, Hervik extends it to include the 'clash of civilizations' frame as well. The second frame specifically presents the controversy as relating to freedom of speech as a human right with limitations, highlighting the notions of human rights, understanding, respect and sensibility and thus considering the publication as an 'unnecessary and premature act'. The final frame focused attention on the demonization of Muslims, rather than freedom of speech – while it criticized *Jyllands-Posten* and the government for their handling of the controversy, and the latter for arguably escalating the issue, it also defended the right to freedom of speech. Hervik's (2008: 60) study found that the first frame – which he labels 'free speech is the issue, and it is a Danish one' – dominated the domestic news coverage, just as it was dominant in the Western media coverage in general.

Case study: Whistle-blowing

This chapter's second case study examines an instance of whistle-blowing – the disclosure of classified documents to the press by the former CIA employee and National Security Agency (NSA) contractor Edward Snowden in 2013. Among the newspapers that have published some of the information provided by Snowden are the *Guardian* in the UK, the *Washington Post* and the *New York Times* in the US, and *Der Spiegel* in Germany. The details released have revolved primarily around the NSA's mass surveillance programme and, to a lesser extent, its counterpart agencies in Britain, Israel, Canada, Australia and Norway. Following these revelations, Snowden requested and was granted asylum in Russia. At the time of writing (late 2013), he was still in that country.

According to Snowden (cited in Greenwald *et al.* 2013), his 'sole motive' for leaking the documents was 'to inform the public as to that which is done in their name and that which is done against them'. The disclosures understandably fuelled debates over mass surveillance, government secrecy, and the balance between national security and information privacy. Responses have included a debate in the US Congress over an Intelligence and Oversight Surveillance Reform Act to limit the powers of the country's security agencies; Brazil cancelled a state visit to the US in protest against American spying on its government and private companies; and in Germany the media expressed outrage at a foreign power's infringement of German citizens' privacy (including the tapping of Chancellor Angela Merkel's phone).

The use of surveillance by security agencies is nothing new. A US Senate committee researched government surveillance practice from President Franklin D. Roosevelt to President Richard Nixon and concluded that 'too many people have been spied upon by too many Government agencies and too much information has been collected' (cited in Fraleigh and Tuman 2011: 104). However, after 9/11 there seemed to be a surge in surveillance activity, with President Bush signing a secret order in 2002 authorizing the NSA to 'eavesdrop on US citizens' by monitoring their emails, phone calls and other communications, 'despite previous legal prohibitions against such domestic spying' (Eggen 2005). The administration kept the details of this programme secret and insisted that it was 'carefully targeted at terrorists' (Gorman 2008). Snowden's leaked documents revealed that the security agencies have access not only to so-called 'metadata' (who called whom and when) but to the content of a huge amount of phone calls, internet searches and online transactions made by ordinary citizens in their own and other countries. Those who defend this level of state surveillance argue that such intrusion is necessary in order to catch terrorists and criminals and point out that terrorist plots have been foiled and many human lives saved as a result. However, as Jacobs and Wright (2013: 434) point out,

> [E]ven if it is true that some lives may be saved, does this justify the mass invasion of privacy which it entails? What is the trade-off of values and principles here? ... More importantly, there really are slippery slopes here ... Law abiding citizens may not have anything to fear now, but under other circumstances these surveillance capabilities could well be used against entirely legitimate political and cultural activities.

Still, one cannot but agree with the remark that 'Perhaps the most shocking revelation to emerge from the publication of the US National Security Agency (NSA) and GCHQ documents disclosed by the American whistleblower Edward Snowden is that Britain appears not to be shocked at all' (Jacobs and Wright 2013: 433).[3] Unlike the debates in other countries about intelligence agencies collecting information on the phone calls, emails and internet use of private citizens, in the UK the prime focus was on a single newspaper – the *Guardian* – that published information based on the NSA documents leaked by Snowden. The editor, Alan Rusbridger, appeared before a parliamentary committee on 3 December 2013 to defend the *Guardian*'s decision to publish the Snowden information amid accusations from MI5, MI6 and the government that the newspaper had put national security at risk by doing so. Thus, in the UK, the debate became about whether the actions of the *Guardian* were in the public interest by holding the authorities to account for their actions or reckless behaviour that endangered national security. This echoed the long-standing tensions relating to the freedom of speech and national security that were examined earlier, and raised new questions about the current status of freedom of speech in Britain. A *New York Times* editorial boldly claimed that 'British press freedom [is] under threat' (Board 2013). The accusations levelled against the *Guardian* in Britain were juxtaposed with the treatment of the press in Germany, where *Der Spiegel* did not incur any 'government bullying', and in the US, where the *New York Times* published similar material in the belief 'that the public has a clear interest in learning and debating about the NSA's out-of-control spying on private communications' (Board 2013). The editorial concluded that British journalists' ability to do their job effectively was under serious threat. These differing reactions can be put down to the lack of constitutional guarantees for press freedom in the UK (unlike in the US, for example), the political climate in the aftermath of the Leveson Inquiry into press standards, and the specific cultural context.

Concern about freedom of speech in Britain was also expressed by UN Special Rapporteur on Freedom of Opinion and Expression Frank La Rue, who stressed, 'The protection of national security secrets must never be used as an excuse to intimidate the press into silence and backing off from its crucial work in the clarification of human rights violations.' Similarly, UN Special Rapporteur on Human Rights and Counter-terrorism Ben Emmerson declared, 'Under no circumstances, journalists, members of the media, or civil society organizations who have access to classified information on an alleged violation of human rights should be subjected to intimidation and subsequent punishment' (both cited in OHCHR 2013).

Support for the *Guardian* has come from other journalists as well, such as one of the reporters who uncovered Watergate, Carl Bernstein, who wrote an open letter to Rusbridger after the latter's appearance before the parliamentary committee referring to it as:

> something quite different in purpose and dangerously pernicious: an attempt by the highest UK authorities to shift the issue from government policies and excessive government secrecy in the United States and Great Britain to the conduct of the press – which has been quite admirable and responsible in the case of the *Guardian*.
>
> *(Bernstein, cited in Boffey 2013)*

More support has come from the Index on Censorship (cited in Boffey 2013):

> The *Guardian* has also lived up to the responsibility of a free press to reveal facts and issues of interest to the public. A British newspaper should be able

to report on these issues without fear of retribution. But comments made by politicians and the security services may have led many round the world to question Britain's commitment to press freedom.

Rusbridger himself defended his newspaper's publication of the information provided by Snowden by explicitly referring to freedom of expression and the freedom of the press in Britain: 'we have that freedom to write, and report, and to think and we have some privacy, and those are the concerns which need to be balanced against national security, which no one is underestimating' (Rusbridger, cited in Boffey 2013).

Conclusions

Freedom of speech is unlike other human rights. For those living in liberal democracies who have the benefit of a free press, it becomes an invisible protector, enabling the democratic process to operate and keeping power in check. The suppression of freedom of speech is almost always associated with authoritarianism and the abuse of other human rights.

However, this chapter has demonstrated that even in liberal democratic states there are a host of questions relating to the limits that might be imposed on this right, particularly considering the challenges associated with the emergence of multicultural societies. The contrasting European and US approaches to 'hate speech' demonstrate that there is no universal agreement on where the boundaries of free speech should be set, even among liberal states, and historical political factors (such as the US Constitution and the Holocaust in Europe) clearly still have significant influence on where the line is drawn. The case studies presented here serve to illustrate these tensions, in particular the difficulty in squaring freedom of speech with freedom of religion, and the importance of an unfettered mainstream media in attempts to bring abuses of power to light.

Questions

- What are the benefits of freedom of speech for society?
- What is the tension between freedom of expression and other human rights?
- How does freedom of speech relate to stronger and weaker forms of cosmopolitan thought?
- What are the best arguments for justifying limitations to freedom of speech in the media?

Notes

1 www.freedomhouse.org/about-us.
2 http://freeknowledge.eu/acta-a-global-threat-to-freedoms-open-letter.
3 GCHQ stands for Government Communications Headquarters.

Further reading

Bleich, E. 2006. 'On democratic integration and free speech: response to Tariq Modood and Randall Hansen'. *International Migration* 44(5): 17–22.

Chang, N. 2002. *Silencing Political Dissent. How Post-September 11 Anti-terrorism Measures Threaten Our Civil Liberties*. New York: Seven Stories Press.

Cohen, N. 2013. *You Can't Read This Book: Censorship in an Age of Freedom*. London: Fourth Estate.

Fraleigh, D. M. and J. S. Tuman. 2011. *Freedom of Expression in the Marketplace of Ideas*. London: Sage.

Kierulf, A. and H. Ronning (eds). 2009. *Freedom of Speech Abridged? Cultural, Legal and Philosophical Challenges*. Goteborg: Nordicom.

Modood, T. 2006. 'The liberal dilemma: integration or vilification?' *International Migration* 44(5): 4–7.

Smolla, R. A. 1992. *Free Speech in an Open Society*. New York: Alfred A. Knopf.

Useful websites

www.freedomhouse.org (Freedom House)
www.article19.org (Article 19)
www.hrw.org (Human Rights Watch)
www.liberty-human-rights.org.uk (Liberty)
www.amnesty.org (Amnesty International)
www.indexoncensorship.org (Index on Censorship)
www.aclu.org (American Civil Liberties Union)
www.theguardian.com/media/2006/feb/05/religion.news ('Timeline: A History of Free Speech')
www.ifex.org (International Freedom of Expression Exchange)
http://freespeechdebate.com/en (Free Speech Debate)

8

TORTURE

Introduction

Torture is allegedly one of the most common violations of human rights (Schulz 2013: 312). According to Amnesty International, in 2012 torture took place in 112 countries around the world (AI 2013). As a practice, it is hardly new. Throughout history, torture has been widely accepted and used as a legitimate means of obtaining evidence, confessions and intelligence. In addition, it has been used as an official form of punishment and even a permissible form of revenge (Buchanan 2013; Moss 2011; O'Byrne 2003; Schulz 2013). During the period when torture was not outlawed, it did not need to be hidden. Today, however, it is prohibited by international law and national legal systems. The right to be free from torture is arguably one of the most widely recognized and accepted of all human rights: 'No other practice except slavery is so universally and unanimously condemned in law and human convention' (Shue 1978: 124).

Nevertheless, despite this apparent moral commitment to protect people from torture (and other inhuman and degrading treatment or punishment), it still happens. Moreover, the evidence suggests that it is carried out by both repressive regimes and liberal democratic states. Since the end of the Second World War, some of the notable Western countries who have been accused of using torture are the UK in Kenya and Northern Ireland; France in Vietnam and Algeria; Israel in the occupied territories; and the US in Vietnam, Central America, Afghanistan and Guantanamo Bay (Bellamy 2006b; Lukes 2006; Moss 2011). Amnesty International's reports regularly document torture taking place in parts of Latin America, Asia, the Middle East and Africa – with countries such as Brazil, Guatemala, El Salvador, Honduras, China, Burma, Bangladesh, India, Jordan, Sierra Leone, Liberia, Zimbabwe, South Africa, Iran and Egypt all implicated. The report of the UN's Commission of Inquiry on Human Rights in the Democratic People's Republic of Korea (2014) recorded systematic use of torture in that country (one of the many human rights violations committed there).

This is just the most recent confirmation of the continuing presence of the practice in the world today. Perhaps understandably, its use is now largely hidden – conducted in secret locations and not advertised to the general public. Overwhelmingly, governments around the world publicly disavow torture. When some use it, they deny doing so and sometimes attempt to revise accepted understandings of what constitutes it (Bellamy 2006b). Even those who are willing to defend the practice agree that 'it should be employed only rarely and within strict limits' (Schulz 2013: 312).

Investigative journalism therefore has an important role to play in uncovering instances of torture, which links back to the notion of the media acting as a 'watchdog', an observer of the state. However, the difficulty of arguments over the limited use of torture (normally in 'exceptional circumstances') means that the way in which the issue is framed and understood is very relevant, as are the ways in which states' justifications for its use are presented and challenged. This has led to considerable scrutiny of the media's performance in upholding this particular human right (e.g. Graber and Holyk 2009; Umansky 2006).

As in the other chapters, this topic will be discussed in general terms, and in the context of two case studies – the revelations regarding the US military's use of torture at Abu Ghraib prison and the use of extraordinary rendition and extradition of terror suspects. First, though, we must examine the human rights background to the prohibition of torture.

Torture and human rights

Torture is widely considered a 'crime against humanity', and a number of international declarations, resolutions and conventions expressly prohibit it. Arguably the most significant, as it inspired the inclusion of similar articles in later documents, is the UDHR. Article 5 declares clearly that 'No one shall be subjected to torture or to cruel, inhuman or degrading treatment or punishment.' But even before this there had been a process that sought to prohibit the use of torture. This was through the 1929 Geneva Convention on the Treatment of Prisoners of War, which covered treatment of prisoners of war and civilians during wartime and prohibited in absolute terms the cruel and inhuman treatment of captives. This and the other Geneva conventions agreed between 1864 and 1949 established that prisoners of war and wounded combatants should be protected from: murder; discrimination based on race, religion, sex and similar criteria; mutilation, cruel treatment and torture; humiliating and degrading treatment; and sentencing or execution without a fair trial. They also forbid torture, mutilation, rape, slavery, arbitrary killing, genocide, crimes against humanity (which include forced disappearance and deprivation of humanitarian aid) and war crimes (which include apartheid, biological experiments, hostage-taking, attacks on cultural objects and depriving people of the right to a fair trial) against anybody in any area of armed conflict.

In addition to the Geneva Conventions and the UDHR, in 1966 the ICCPR also outlawed torture. Its Article 7 uses the same wording as Article 5 of the UDHR, but adds a clause prohibiting medical and scientific experimentation. Importantly, the ICCPR also establishes that the prohibition of torture stands even in times of 'public emergency which threatens the life of the nation' (Article 4). Similar prohibition of torture is included in regional human rights treaties, such as the European Convention on Human Rights (1950), the European Convention for the Prevention of Torture and Inhuman or Degrading Treatment or Punishment (1987), the African Charter on Human and Peoples' Rights (1969), the American Convention on Human Rights (1969) and the Inter-American Convention to Prevent and Punish Torture (1985).

In 1984, as a result of pressure from a number of NGOs, notably the campaigns of Amnesty International earlier in that decade, the UN Convention against Torture and Other Cruel, Inhuman or Degrading Treatment or Punishment (CAT) was adopted and became the primary international document governing torture and ill-treatment. By the end of 2013, it had 154 signatories. Article 2 of the CAT prohibits torture in absolute terms: 'No exceptional circumstances whatsoever, whether a state of war or a threat of war, internal political instability or any other public emergency, may be invoked as a justification of torture.' Article 1 provides international law's first explicit definition of what constitutes torture:

> any act by which severe pain or suffering, whether physical or mental, is intentionally inflicted on a person for such purposes as obtaining from him or a third person information or a confession, punishing him for an act he or a third person has committed or is suspected of having committed, or intimidating or coercing him or a third person, or for any reason based on discrimination of any kind, when such pain or suffering is inflicted by or at the instigation of or with the consent or acquiescence of a public official or other person acting in an official capacity.

According to this definition, torture involves pain or suffering, be it physical or mental (although often it will have elements of both). This has to be inflicted for a specific purpose and with the involvement of a public/state official. The pain or suffering has to be severe and intentionally inflicted.

As with many other aspects of the human rights regime, states have repeatedly attempted to circumvent these conventions, or have tried to avoid falling foul of those they have signed up to through creative interpretation. Such nuanced readings of the conventions are then often tested through challenges in the courts. The 1978 decision of the European Court of Human Rights in *Ireland v. United Kingdom* is a good example. It established a difference between torture and cruel and degrading treatment, ruling that 'five techniques' – wall-standing, hooding, subjection to noise, deprivation of sleep, and deprivation of food and drink – constitute the latter, not the former (Carey *et al.* 2010: 73). Despite this ruling, however, two questions remained. At what point do pain and suffering become 'severe'? And might specific acts that stop short of causing life-threatening pain still constitute torture? These issues became central to the alleged use of torture by the Bush administration in the context of the 'war on terror', as will be examined later in this chapter.

Importantly, in addition to the obligation to refrain from torture themselves, the CAT obliges states to take action to prevent acts of torture from occurring on their territory and to criminalize and punish those who practise it. It also prohibits states from extraditing individuals to locations where they might be tortured and, upon receipt of the appropriate request, to extradite those accused of torture to other countries who seek to punish acts of torture. As will be seen later, some of these aspects of states' responsibilities were not adhered to in the context of the CIA programme of extraordinary renditions, which is the subject of the second case study in this chapter.

Arguments for and against torture

Considering that torture is now legally prohibited and that there is a broad consensus that it is morally wrong (Sussman 2005), one might ask how there could be any significant debate over its usage. However, contemporary debates have explored whether torture can be justified in exceptional, one-off or emergency situations, and even whether it should be legalized to extract life-saving information from known terrorists in countries where there is an ongoing terrorist threat (Moss 2011: 92). The argument that torture is defensible – and even morally obligatory – under a narrow set of circumstances is generally based on a cost–benefit analysis: many lives could be saved by torturing a single person (see, e.g., Elshstain 2002; Parry 2004; Posner 2002; Shue 2002). Dershowitz (2002) has defended the licensing of torture in extraordinary cases when interrogational torture is – or is regarded to be – the least bad option, provided that appropriate mechanisms for accountability are in place. He advocates 'torture warrants', obtained from a judge, which would limit the brutal treatment to the minimum necessary to extract the necessary information and also reduce the instances of torture as a whole. Gross (2002) also argues that in exceptional circumstances public officials – the torturers themselves or the authorities who have directed them – might step outside the legal framework. There is a significant risk that they will face legal consequences, but there is also hope, presumably, that they will be legally (if not morally) excused retrospectively. These extraordinary cases and exceptional circumstances are usually associated with the so-called 'ticking-bomb scenario'. This raises the question of whether it is justified to use whatever coercive means is necessary against a person held in custody who is believed to know the whereabouts of a bomb that, if detonated, would kill hundreds or thousands of people.

While from a simple cost–benefit analysis this might seem like a relatively easy question to answer, there are strong arguments against allowing torture even in emergency and exceptional situations. First, as Schulz (2013: 320) points out, in real life a 'pure' ticking-bomb scenario is 'extraordinarily rare'. In such a pure scenario the authorities would have to know with absolute certainty that the suspect(s) knew where the bomb was hidden, that torture was an effective means of obtaining accurate information quickly, that the amount of pain inflicted was the minimum necessary to get the suspect(s) to talk, and that innocent people who would have died will be saved. Many critics argue that very few situations satisfy all of these criteria, so the ticking-bomb scenario is an improbable and artificial construct (Brecher 2010; Ramsay 2006). Second, it is not always easy to know who has the vital information and who does not, which could lead to the wrong person being questioned and potentially an innocent person being tortured (Carey et al. 2010). Third, there is the danger of a slippery slope: once torture is allowed under very limited conditions, there could be a temptation to expand either the number of people tortured or the circumstances in which torture is allowed (Brecher 2007; Ramsay 2006). As Bellamy (2006b: 142) notes, once 'the practice becomes normalised, the threshold for its use drops from the need to extract information necessary to save lives to the desire to extract expedient information'.

Three further arguments are employed to support torture's prohibition. First, there is no irrefutable evidence that torture always works. On the contrary, it quite likely that torture is a rather ineffective means of obtaining information, since a prisoner in excruciating pain is likely to tell interrogators anything they want to hear (Brecher 2010). This point is acknowledged even by those who practise torture. Former director of the CIA Porter Goss (cited in Klein 2005), speaking in front of the US Senate Intelligence Committee in February 2005, admitted that torture 'doesn't work. There are better ways to deal with captives.' Similarly, a memo written by an FBI official in Guantanamo (declassified in 2005) claimed that extreme coercion produced 'nothing more than what FBI got using simple investigative techniques' (Klein 2005). Second, and significantly, considering the legal provisions outlined earlier in this chapter, the use of torture involves breaching inalienable rules-of-war constraints guaranteeing immunity for non-combatants. Finally, it could be argued that a general right to torture cannot be defended in a morally consistent way: claiming a moral right to torture prisoners to extract essential military information creates a precedent that others may use in different contexts and for different reasons (Bellamy 2006b: 124).

Torture and the 'war on terror'

The absolute prohibition of torture came under particular strain – both morally and legally – in the context of the 'war on terror' announced by President George W. Bush following the terrorist attacks of 11 September 2001. While US law relating to torture did not change after 9/11, a significant new phase of debate began in the United States about how to define torture, and whether physical and psychological stress methods that fall outside of that definition are acceptable. Attempts were made to define torture in a narrow way, 'to reduce the scope of what is meant by torture and degrading treatment, as well as to define a category of detainees who can be subjected to coercive methods of interrogation' (Foot 2006: 132–133). The reason for these changes was the assertion that torture was an essential tool for fighting terrorism and a legitimate means of extracting information vital for the protection of US citizens; that, without torture, the state would be unable to protect its citizens or undertake all of its counter-terrorism measures (Allhoff 2009; Bakir 2013; Bellamy 2006b).

These post-9/11 moves can be linked to two earlier developments that shed some light on the US government's attitude towards this issue. First, during the Cold War, the CIA's secret *Kubark Counterintelligence Interrogation* manual (1963) codified the application of psychological torture, consisting of sensory deprivation and self-inflicted pain. It surfaced publicly in 1997 without provoking much public reaction (Margulies 2006; McCoy 2006; Sands 2009). Second, when President Reagan endorsed the Convention against Torture in 1988 he attached a number of reservations and exceptions with the result that 'mental harm' was narrowly redefined – sensory deprivation (hooding), self-inflicted pain (stress positions) and disorientation (isolation and sleep denial) were all excluded from the US definition (McCoy 2006).

Post-9/11, the torture debate centred on the 'semantic manoeuvres' of the Bush administration (Allhoff 2009: 266). But given that torture had previously triggered widespread revulsion (Peirce 2010), its practice by US forces as an officially sanctioned information-gathering strategy in the war on terror still signified a major transformation. The explanation for this shift relates to the internal logic of the broader discourse of the war on terror upon which the torture policy was founded (Jackson 2007). The 'void of meaning' (Campbell 2002) created by the events of 9/11 was filled by the Bush administration with a politically driven narrative that became dominant in the public interpretation of the terrorist attacks (Jackson 2005: 31). Jackson (2005) argues that the words chosen to label the events worked to enforce a particular interpretation and meaning, most significantly that the terrorist attacks were an 'act of war'. This politically constructed understanding of events normalized and justified the Bush administration's response. As Crelinsten (2003: 295) puts it, 'the practice of torture is only possible because reality is defined in such a way as to make it possible'. Because 9/11 was an act of war, a 'war on terror' appeared reasonable and logical. Alternative narratives and interpretations, and subsequently alternative responses, were thus excluded, denied or suppressed from very early on.

The war on terror narrative contained four key features (Jackson 2005: 29–58). First, 9/11 was constructed as an 'exceptional tragedy' and a 'grievous harm' through the use of such phrases as 'a national tragedy', a 'terrible national shock', 'so much suffering' and a 'nightmare'. The administration stressed that the day would never be forgotten because of the great suffering and grief experienced by the American people. This established United States' status as the primary victim. The overall emphasis and construction of an exceptional grievance subsequently helped to divest the nation of its moral responsibility for counter-violence.

Second, the attacks were presented as primarily an act of war rather than a crime against humanity or mass murder. In his first address to the nation, on 11 September 2011 itself, President Bush (2001a) declared, 'Today, our fellow citizens, our way of life, our very freedom came under attack in a series of deliberate and deadly terrorist acts.' Four days later, the term 'war' had already entered the public domain, with the President claiming, 'War has been waged against us by stealth and deceit' (Bush 2001b). In effect, this construction of the attacks as 'war' set the foundations for everything that followed.

The third feature of the narrative was the use of descriptions of the attacks that could easily fit into existing and very popular meta-narratives, starting with the Second World War (an analogy with Pearl Harbor reinforced the idea that the United States was engaged in a 'war') and the Cold War (an analogy with the struggle against communism made it easier to understand the terrible and fearful danger posed by terrorism and served to mobilize and organize the nation behind a common cause). There were also Manichean narratives of good versus evil told as the struggle of civilization against barbarism. Here, the attacks were constructed as an expression of the 'barbarous', 'uncivilized' world and as a part of a long-running struggle between savagery and civility. This sub-narrative also had the benefit of differentiating strongly between 'us' and 'them' – 'we' are the civilized ones who use violence only in pursuit of just and good goals, while 'they' are clearly uncivilized, savage people who have no respect for human life. The discourse was also connected to narratives relating to globalization, with the attacks constructed as an attack on globalisation and world economic progress. This made them seem reactionary, anti-modern, and a treat to the entire global economic system that underpins 'our way of life'.

Connected with the above, the fourth feature of the war on terror narrative was a fascination with the reason for the attacks. Discussion of this topic generally confirmed existing narratives about the United States and its place in the world. The attacks were understood as stemming from the nature of the terrorists themselves (as barbarians, totalitarian and expansionist), on the one hand, and the virtue of the US as a symbol of freedom and democracy, on the other. This had the advantage of diverting attention away from alternative explanations that might have highlighted US foreign policy failures or global development strategies as possible triggers. By positioning the aims of the attacks firmly in this context, an aggressive counter-attack could be presented as the only possible way to prevent the terrorists from 'winning', and as the best way to react to the global terrorist threat.

Enacting the torture policy

This official public discourse 'set the logic and possibilities of policy formulation' and 'helped to create the wider legitimacy and social consensus that was required to enact the torture policy' (Jackson 2007: 354). Specifically, the Bush administration secretly redefined torture, disregarding prohibitions in both US and international law and claiming that the coercive techniques it endorsed fell short of torture (Wolfendale 2009); it introduced a new category of detainees so that the Geneva Conventions would not apply; and it secretly outsourced torture by using extraordinary rendition, 'black sites' and secret prisons.

Intelligence gathered from interrogation of suspected terrorists was seen as essential for fighting the war on terror and for preventing future attacks, so from 2002 onwards intense debates took place over the methods of interrogation among government attorneys in the Office of Legal Counsel (OLC) of the Department of Justice, who worked closely with the White House (Bakir 2013; Lukes 2006). The US Department of the Army's *Field Manual 34-52*, which came into effect in 1992, contained guidelines for American military interrogators and prohibited the use of coercive techniques, in part 'because they produce low quality intelligence' (see McCoy 2006; Rose 2004a). However, in the new context of the war on terror, these were dismissed as insufficient and ineffective. The now-infamous 'torture memos' provided the Bush administration's answer to the question of how far American military and intelligence personnel could go when interrogating terror suspects. The first memo, the 'Bybee report' – after Jay Bybee, Assistant Attorney General for the OLC, 2001–2003 – redefined torture so narrowly that almost any coercive interrogation technique would not be categorized as such (Margulies 2006: 91). It stipulated that,

> for an act to constitute torture as defined in Section 2340 [the federal torture statute], it must inflict pain that is difficult to endure. Physical pain amounting to torture must be equivalent in intensity to the pain accompanying serious physical injury, such as organ failure, impairment of bodily function, or even death. For purely mental pain or suffering to amount to torture under Section 2340, it must result in significant psychological harm of significant duration, e.g., lasting for months or even years.
>
> *(Bybee 2002a: 1)*

As such, according to Bybee, only the most extreme acts were impermissible. Lesser acts of cruel, inhuman or degrading treatment were now not seen as violating the Convention against Torture. Beyond that, in the context of the US Constitution, the President, as Commander-in-Chief, is not bound by domestic or international prohibitions against torture. Similarly, if authorized by the President, interrogators can escape prosecution by the Justice Department: they are permitted to violate the prohibition on torture if they believe it is necessary as a lesser evil to prevent a direct or imminent threat to the US and its citizens.

The second Bybee memo focused on the enhanced interrogation techniques proposed by the CIA and specifically addressed the issue of waterboarding – a controversial technique used in the war on terror that simulates drowning. Famously, President Bush himself publicly defended the decision to use waterboarding on the basis that it had saved lives (Kornblut 2010). (He also added that his lawyers had informed him it was a legal practice.) The second Bybee memo concluded that the technique would not inflict the 'severe physical pain or suffering' prohibited in the Convention against Torture because it does not inflict actual physical harm or physical pain. It also argued that any physical effects would not continue for a 'protracted period of time', meaning that waterboarding fell outside the generally accepted definition of torture (Bybee 2002b: 11).

Understandably, the United States' reassessment of what does – and what does not – constitute torture was met with a wave of international criticism. The UN High Commission for Human Rights emphasized that 'there can be no doubt that the prohibition on torture and cruel, inhuman and degrading treatment is non-derogable under international law'. Human Rights Watch pointed out that the United States had previously denounced as torture the methods it was now defending when they had been used by other countries (Ramsay 2006: 106). In June 2004, following the Abu Ghraib revelations, the first torture memo was withdrawn (Goldsmith 2007). A replacement memo, drafted in December 2004, rescinded the narrow torture definition from 2002 and returned to the internationally recognized definition of intentionally inflicting significant pain or putting someone in fear of serious physical injury (Margulies 2006). The new memo also did not grant the President authority to ignore the torture ban in his role as Commander-in-Chief, in contrast to the earlier one. However, the existing approved interrogation techniques were not affected by the new document (Goldsmith 2007).

A second focus of the Bush administration's efforts in the war on terror related to the status of prisoners. Article 17 of the third Geneva Convention (1949) declares, 'No physical or mental torture, nor any other form of coercion, may be inflicted on prisoners of war to secure from them information of any kind whatever.' To circumvent this protection, and to deprive suspected terrorists of their rights, a new concept – 'illegal enemy combatant' (as opposed to the traditional prisoner of war) – was introduced. Thus, by denying suspected terrorists prisoner-of-war status, the Bush administration hoped to make Article 17 inapplicable. The revision of the established norms was announced in January 2002 by Alberto Gonzales, in his role as White House legal counsel, who claimed that 'The war on terror is a new kind of war … this new paradigm renders obsolete Geneva's strict limitation on questioning of enemy prisoners and renders quaint some of its provisions' (cited in Ramsay 2006: 106). This argument followed the official political rhetoric very closely: the threat and the response to that threat were 'new' and unprecedented and required a 'new paradigm' if the terrorists were to be defeated (Jackson 2007: 356). This rhetorical construction was necessary to overcome the inherent contradiction between declaring a 'war' and invoking national self-defence on the basis of international law and at the same time denying the applicability of the laws of war to captured fighters. The thinking was that if this 'new kind of war' were being fought by 'enemy combatants' rather than recognized soldiers, then the internationally agreed protections would cease to apply and none of the traditional rules would need to be followed.

According to this reconceptualization, detainees captured in Afghanistan were not entitled to the protections of the Geneva Conventions. The right to prisoner-of-war status and the protections outlined in Article 3 prohibiting 'cruel treatment and torture' under any circumstances and banning 'outrages upon personal dignity, in particular humiliating and degrading treatment' were deemed not to apply to them (Margulies 2006: 55). The inapplicability of the Geneva Conventions was based on the fact that al-Qaeda was a non-state actor and not a signatory to any treaty, while the 'nature of the conflict' – between a 'nation state and a non-governmental organization' – meant it did not come under the auspices of Article 3 (Bakir

2013: 68; Margulies 2006: 56–59; McCoy 2006). These arguments, alongside the new, narrow definition of torture, were used to excuse the ill-treatment of detainees and allow it to continue. As a result, places like Bagram Air Base in Afghanistan, Guantanamo Bay in Cuba and Abu Ghraib prison in Iraq have become synonymous with the torture of prisoners.

Given that the Geneva Conventions make it illegal to ask another party to torture prisoners, and illegal for the United States to gather information through the use of torture, the third strand of the Bush administration's war on terror was equally controversial. It involved the indefinite detention of suspects at Guantanamo Bay prison, secret detention facilities known as 'black sites' that were run outside the law by the CIA, and detention sites in North Africa and the Middle East run by foreign security forces, to which the CIA had access, but was always able to deny any direct American involvement (Bakir 2013: 80). The practice of extraordinary rendition, the subject of the second case study in this chapter, became one of the methods used by the CIA to avoid legal limitations and oversight when interrogating detainees. While the US acknowledged the existence of 'rendition to justice', whereby suspects were apprehended and transported to the United States or other countries for trial or questioning, the practice of extraordinary rendition, which involved the risk of torture, was formally denied by the Bush administration for years (Carle 2011; Grey 2006).

The administration was able to employ these techniques because, in the words of Allhoff (2009: 267), 'a practice that had previously been highly proscribed has now been met with more sympathy, at least in some circles'. Indeed, after 9/11, it seems that both the military personnel who carried it out and the wider US public came to view torture as acceptable. In 2005, it was reported that most Americans (and a majority of people in Britain, France and South Korea) thought that torturing terrorist suspects was justified at least in rare instances (Associated Press 2005), although this 'consensus' has since been challenged (see the second case study, below). To achieve this tacit acceptance, the Bush administration effectively went through the steps of torture training suggested by Crelinsten (2003). This involved rewriting laws (or at least reinterpreting them), creating a new language and vocabulary, redefining social relations, and channelling all of these processes of transformation through the mass media (as will be discussed in the next section). Ultimately, this convinced US society to accept torture as a legitimate tactic in the fight against terrorism, at least temporarily. As Crelinsten (2003: 295–296; emphasis in the original) says, 'to enable torture to be practiced *systematically* and *routinely*, not only do torturers have to be trained and prepared, but wider elements of society must also be prepared and, in a sense, trained to accept that such things go on'.

The political discourses identified by Jackson (2005) and discussed earlier were essential for the creation of the necessary political legitimacy and social consensus required to carry out the Bush administration's policies properly. They effectively helped to construct a new social reality:

> in order to enact the agreed-upon torture policy, administration officials had to deconstruct existing social reality with its conventional morality

> prohibiting torture and replace it with a new 'torture-sustaining' reality based
> upon a set of new morality-defining narratives.
>
> *(Jackson 2007: 359)*

The overarching narratives used and continuously reproduced as part of the war on terror were twofold. First, there was the depiction of a powerful, threatening enemy whose very existence justified the use of extraordinary measures against it. Crucially, this enemy was also dehumanized, making it undeserving of normal human rights protection. This first narrative was built around the US administration's claims that terrorism posed not simply a threat of sudden violent death, but a 'threat to *civilization*', a 'threat to the very essence of what you do', a 'threat to our *way of life*', and a threat to 'the peace of *the world*' (Jackson 2007: 358; emphases in the original). The threat of terrorism was presented as supremely catastrophic and the terrorists themselves as highly sophisticated, cunning and extremely dangerous.

The second narrative constructed the terrorists as evil-doers, savages and barbarians, cruel and inhuman. It relied on words and phrases such as 'evil', 'the very worst of human nature', 'no faith', 'no religion', 'animals', 'inhuman', 'cancer' and 'parasites' (Jackson 2005: 59–76). This language established clear boundaries between 'them' and 'us', and served to dehumanize and demonize the enemy to such an extent that any counter-violence towards them would appear acceptable and proportionate. The wide acceptance of such a language, including by the mass media, no doubt had an impact on how soldiers and prison guards talked and thought about their enemies, and on how they treated them, as the case study on Abu Ghraib will demonstrate later. Importantly, this pattern of defining the enemy as alien to the dominant culture – as 'them', not 'us' – is not unique to the war on terror; rather, it occurs frequently. Moreover, the scapegoating of a particular subgroup is generally seen as a social conditon conducive to the rise of torture (Staub 1990: 49–50). In the words of Schulz (2013: 317):

> Those who are labelled outsiders, as having violated our most sacred values, can be thought to have sacrificed their claim to the protection of rights, including their right to be regarded as human.

Crelinsten (2005: 76–77) also sees this dehumanization of an outsider group as central to the institutionalization of torture, but includes some additional factors. These are the framing of a situation as a national emergency or a perceived threat to security; the need to process large numbers of suspects; the authorization to violate standard social norms; and the presence of a 'sacred mission' in whose name anything becomes acceptable. The war on terror, and the narrative constructed around it, satisfied all of these conditions.

The role of the media

Several years after the death of Osama Bin Laden, and with the phrase 'war on terror' no longer on the lips of the US president, the 'orthodox' account that the media failed to alert the general public to the abuses that were being carried out has now been joined by what historians would call a revisionist view of media performance.

The standard view is that although the global media played a role in exposing political scandals relating to Guantanamo, Abu Ghraib, secret detention centres and extraordinary rendition, it took far too long for these stories to enter the mainstream:

> When the record on torture coverage is examined in detail, an ambiguous picture emerges: in the post-9/11 days, some reporters offered detailed accusations and reports of abuse and torture, only to be met with scepticism by their own editors. Stories were buried, played down, or ignored – a reluctance that is much diminished but still bubbles up with regard to the culpability of policymakers.
>
> *(Umansky 2006: 18)*

Graber and Holyk (2009) examined all the complaints that had been made about the media (incomplete coverage, avoidance of certain words, such as 'torture', over-reliance on official sources, lack of critical voices or quality investigative journalism) and found a mixed picture. They conducted content analysis of newspapers in the UK, Canada, Israel and the US for a six-month period in 2006. The results offered some support for the orthodox view of the media's failure to cover the issue of torture: they showed that stories tended to be based on government versions of events and there was a shortage of good investigative journalism; also, the coverage was incomplete and the word 'torture' was often avoided. Interestingly, Graber and Holyk noted that the media was more willing to cover events that implicated other countries in the use of torture. However, against this critical view of media performance, they found that counter-arguments were present and some non-official sources were used. These mixed results were explained by the pressure of commercial constraints and difficulties in distinguishing between the legal and illegal treatment of detainees (Graber and Holyk 2009: 240–241), which meant that large amounts of information about torture remained unpublished.

For John Tulloch, a professor of media studies who was injured by the London bombings in 2005 (inadvertently becoming part of the story of the war on terror), the dynamic day-by-day revelations about victims and perpetrators can become an additional trauma for those involved. However, he found that subsequent stories about the torture of prisoners allowed the UK media to play a much more critical role. He argues that torture represents a particularly stark expression of (Foulcauldian) bio-politics – an example of the state employing disciplinary institutions and instruments to exert power and control over the human body. However, this can also be subverted by the way it is presented in the media. In a critical media environment, news of torture can be used to challenge legitimacy: images of torture were used by the left-wing media in the UK to parody and expose the abuse of power, question political leadership and challenge the validity of the foreign policy initiated and executed by Blair and Bush (Tulloch 2009: 213–215).

This was possible partly because of the shocking and graphic nature of the pictures that were leaked from Abu Ghraib prison (see case study below). If torture is reported in a non-visual way, however, there is much greater scope for audiences to react sympathetically, to either the victim or the perpetrator. Psychologists have long been interested in framing's impact on social norms, and many researchers have used acceptance of torture as a test. Thus, the framing of torture in the media becomes crucial to the level of torture which the public are willing to accept takes place 'in their name', or through their own state's security apparatus.

There are some interesting psychological effects when it comes to perceptions of torture. The election of President Obama in succession to President Bush was widely seen as coinciding with a shift in US public opinion from 'torture works' to 'torture is un-American' (Koppelman 2009). However, a study of US public opinion regarding torture between the years 2001 and 2009 concluded that the majority of the US public was actually against torture, so the mis-reporting of this added to a 'false consensus' in the public debate on the topic (Gronke *et al.* 2010). Audiences are more willing to accept the use of torture if it is presented as a long-standing policy, rather than something new and different from what has gone before (Crandall *et al.* 2008).

The cultural studies literature has attempted to shed light on the legitimizing force of ideas and acts contained in popular media, such as film and TV. The use of torture by the character Jack Bauer in the Fox TV series *24* has become emblematic of this debate, particularly as former President Bill Clinton cited the show and the plight of its protagonist when discussing the consequences of sanctioning torture. Fears over the negative impacts of depictions of torture in US films and TV shows prompted Human Rights First to launch a campaign – the Primetime Torture Project – that was designed to educate both soldiers and the creative industries about the consequences and 'realities' of torture.[1] A study of the use of *24* in mediated political discourse found its overall impact was neutral (Tenenboim-Weinblatt 2009), with both sides in the political debate using its fictional characters to support their positions:

> proponents of torture used *24* as evidence that supported torture, whereas opponents of torture presented the show as either a fantasy that had no bearing on the actual effectiveness and morality of torture or, alternatively, as being a cause of positive attitudes toward torture or even of actual interrogation techniques.
>
> *(Tenenboim-Weinblatt 2009: 382)*

The mediation of debates over the use of torture is now considered in the context of two case studies in which factual accounts of harsh treatment had considerable political consequences.

Case study: Abu Ghraib

Images of US soldiers torturing Iraqi detainees at Abu Ghraib prison in Iraq, which would soon become 'iconic' (Higham and Stephens 2004), were first broadcast on the CBS television network on 28 April 2004. A few days later, they were published in the *New Yorker*. These images broke the Abu Ghraib story around the world and gave impetus to the investigation of what had happened there. Significantly, it was a kind of 'citizen journalism' because US soldiers took the photographs on their own digital cameras for their own use.

While the Abu Ghraib photos were shocking and compelling in their own right, they fed into the existing debate about the United States' treatment of detainees abroad and the use of torture as a component of the war on terror (Berger 2007). They raised questions about the extent of the violence, the involvement of military commanders, wider US government attitudes and the country's policy on torture. This was particularly significant in terms of the impact the story would have on US foreign policy, its international support, and the reactions of the Iraqi population (Andén-Papadopoulos 2008; Carlson 2009). The Bush administration responded by launching a systematic effort to blame what happened in Abu Ghraib on a 'few bad apples' and to protect the officials who had established the policy from scrutiny and punishment. This was absolutely necessary if the initial Manichean frame of the war on terror – of good versus evil (see Entman 2004; Kellner 2005) – was to survive. It was in this context that the images became the centre of a political framing contest that raised questions about the media's ability to challenge official government narratives (Bennett *et al.* 2006; Andén-Papadopoulos 2008).

The photos depicted physically coerced and sexually humiliated detainees watched over by smiling American soldiers at Abu Ghraib prison. Their broadcast provoked an immediate world-wide reaction and a public outcry that stretched 'well beyond the Middle East to public opinion among European allies, including countries in the US led coalition' (Wright 2004). The images 'ignited a global firestorm', 'caused international embarrassment for the United States and cast a shadow over the war in Iraq' (Ricchiardi and Cirillo 2004: 25, 24). They also provided visual support for a story that had remained hidden from public view up to that point. By the time the story broke, Guantanamo Bay had been functioning as a detention centre for over two years, and the 'torture–intelligence nexus' (Bakir 2013) was fully operational. The photographic and documentary evidence that emerged from Abu Ghraib was not fully controlled by the government elite, as digital cameras in the hands of military personnel were the primary source. Thereafter, news organizations independently disseminated the photos and advanced the story by publishing the images and offering their interpretations of them (Bennett *et al.* 2006: 315; Smith and Dionisopoulos 2008).

On the surface, then, as Berger (2007: 226) suggests, it would appear that the Abu Ghraib photographs had a great impact. They not only performed an undisputable and undeniable information function but became a 'bargaining chip' in the battle for greater public oversight and increased transparency and accountability in US-run prisons. Arguably, they also brought to the surface abuse that at the time many people already suspected was occurring at other institutions. This included secret CIA-run prisons in Eastern Europe and elsewhere (Priest 2005) and terror suspects placed in the custody of allied countries with no provisions against torture

(Mayer 2005; Qureshi 2009; see also the second case study, below). Solaroli (2011: 249) goes even further by arguing that the Abu Ghraib photographs

> helped crystallize an already existing discourse that was critical of the US foreign policy in Iraq, and forced public attention on wider questions of the Bush administration's handling of prisoners and political legitimacy in the 'war on terror', by functioning themselves as means of resistance to the acts they represented, and by de-constructing and re-articulating the hegemonic Iraqi war narrative of American liberation and moral superiority.

Therefore, this seems to be a prime example of the media using its influence to safeguard human rights. After all, the publication of the Abu Ghraib photographs set in motion a series of internal military inquiries and congressional hearings, and thereafter greater attention was paid to the treatment of prisoners elsewhere (Bennett *et al.* 2006).

The causal impact of the media images on their own, however, is widely disputed. For some commentators, the context and the narrative framing of these images were more important than the images themselves (Griffin 2004; Zelizer 2004). As Andén-Papadopoulos (2008: 6) argues, in the Abu Ghraib case the relevance, representativeness and causes of the images were far from obvious when they appeared, which left the door open for alternative 'framings'. The two media organizations that originally broke the story illustrate this very well, as they offered two contrasting accounts of what could be seen in the photographs. CBS's *60 Minutes II* largely repeated the Bush administration's key argument that the images represented evidence of the misconduct of a small group of morally corrupt individuals. Thus, the programme framed Abu Ghraib as an isolated case of abuse resulting from (mis)management, rather than policy failure. Seymour Hersh, on the other hand, in a three-part series of articles in the *New Yorker*, put forward a critical counter-frame by suggesting that policies formulated by Washington elites led directly to the violations in Abu Ghraib (Hersh 2004b, 2004c, 2004d). Hersh not only offered new details and context to explain the causes of the scandal but focused on why American soldiers photographed themselves smiling and posing with their victims. He put forward the argument that photography was 'part of the dehumanizing interrogation process', where the visual documentation added to the shame embedded in the torture (Hersh 2004a: 38). This echoed Sontag's (2004) claim that 'the horror of what is shown in the photographs cannot be separated from the horror that the photographs were taken' in the first place.

The logic of cascading activation (Entman 2004: 7) highlights the importance of the early news media coverage and the frame it imposes as guiding responses to all future reports. Following this logic, these two competing narratives effectively shaped the debate over the content, meaning and implications of the Abu Ghraib photographs. Both of them contradicted the Bush administration's frame on Iraq and threatened to delegitimize the Manichean dichotomy within which the whole war on terror was situated. As part of this, the US was portrayed as a 'good' nation, reluctant to engage in war but willing to use force to ensure victory over a savage enemy (Entman 2004; Kellner 2005). The appearance of the Abu Ghraib images undermined and challenged this and 'represented a potential violation of the Manichean frame' (Smith and Dionisopoulos 2008: 309), a 'frame break' (Goffman 1974). In this context, the administration could offer only one interpretation of the events at the prison, for no matter how appalling the bad behaviour of a few soldiers might seem, the damage caused by this framing could be contained (Danner 2004b). To achieve this, the government drew the 'focus on [to] the photographs – the garish signboards of the scandal – and not the scandal itself' (Danner 2004a), highlighting the actions of the American soldiers but obscuring the wider political and military issues.

Bennett *et al*. (2006) show that the Abu Ghraib story was quickly and over-whelmingly framed as 'regrettable' abuse on the part of a handful of troops. The word 'torture' barely appeared in the news coverage, and only slightly more often in editorials. The US mainstream media allowed the Bush administration's 'isolated abuse' frame to dominate its news bulletins and articles and did not offer the public a coherent alternative frame (in contrast to the alternative press, which in many cases did adopt the torture frame). This happened despite considerable photographic and documentary evidence and the critical statements of governmental and non-governmental actors. Among these were credible accounts from independent journalists supporting a torture frame (Danner 2004a, 2004b; Hanley 2003; Hersh 2004a, 2004b, 2004c, 2004d) as well as government-commissioned investigative reports on the conditions in US detention centres (Danner 2004a; Schlesinger 2004). As Entman points out, 'the coverage did not completely converge on the inter-pretation of the White House … [as] journalists (and elites) frequently explored the responsibility of … higher-ups in the administration and military, and the existence of similar incidents at other US military prisons'. However, he continues, 'That is not to say there was as much focus on those giving as on those just following orders' (Entman 2006: 216).

This kind of coverage leads to the conclusion that 'The early limited appearance of the torture frame followed by its quick demise suggests that event-driven frames, particularly in matters of high consequence, are seriously constrained by mainstream news organizations' deference to political power' (Bennett *et al*. 2006: 481). Bennet *et al*. (2006) suggest that this deference and the media's inability or unwillingness to construct a coherent challenge to the administration's claims about its policy on torturing detainees were due to the lack of consistent counter-framing by high-level officials. Thus, the case of Abu Ghraib can be seen as offering empirical support for the rules of indexing, whereby news framing depends on the unity of the official position. If there is no disagreement or strong differences of opinion among the political elite, critical counter-frames can be stifled; alternatively, if there is a serious official debate, counter-frames may come to the fore (Bennett *et al*. 2006; Bennett 1990; Hallin 1986; Mermin 1999). This lack of frame contestation among mainstream US political leaders in response to Abu Ghraib has been challenged (Rowling *et al*. 2011), but the overwhelming reliance on official sources in news coverage is widely confirmed, thus allowing the administration to shape the discourse surrounding Abu Ghraib (Andén-Papadopoulos 2008; Jones and Sheets 2009; Rowling *et al.* 2011). Rowling *et al.* (2011: 1058) highlight 'the White House's position atop the framing hierarchy and the cultural resonance of the frames they constructed[, which] … gave them the power to set frames that cascaded past congressional challenges, into the press, and, eventually, to the public'. Thus, whether it is explained through indexing or cascading activation, the US media's deferential role in the case of Abu Ghraib seems beyond doubt.

In contrast, Jones and Sheets (2009) found that foreign news outlets were much more likely to characterize what happened at Abu Ghraib as torture, although this largely depended on the nation's level of social identification with the US. So, while German, Italian and Spanish journalists tended to label the events at the prison 'torture' rather than 'abuse' or 'mistreatment', Australian, British and Canadian reporters were found to be closer to the characterizations employed by their US counterparts, avoiding 'torture' and preferring the more ambiguous terms of 'abuse' and 'mistreatment'.

Case study: 'Extraordinary' rendition and 'ordinary' extradition

'Extraordinary' rendition

It is now widely known that after the 9/11 terrorist attacks the CIA developed a 'global spider's web' (Marty 2006) of secret detention centres. Known as 'black sites', these centres housed people who had been arrested and deported without undergoing any legal process through a practice known as 'extraordinary rendition'. Effectively, the CIA kidnapped individuals in one country and then flew them to another, where they would be interrogated and often tortured. The US had employed extraordinary rendition for the interrogation of suspected terrorists ever since the 1980s, but the numbers involved had always been very small; after 9/11, use of the practice increased dramatically. A report by the Open Society Justice Initiative catalogued 136 individual cases spanning 54 countries, but it is highly likely that there were more (Singh 2013: 6).

One of the many problems with secret detention and extraordinary rendition, from a human rights perspective, is the possibility that the detainees will be subjected to torture (Moss 2011: 166–168). Many of the countries involved were known to employ interrogation methods that would amount to torture. This meant that extraordinary rendition was often in direct contravention of Article 3 of the UN Convention against Torture, which states: 'No State Party shall expel, return or extradite a person to another State where there are substantial grounds for believing that he would be in danger of being subjected to torture.' This expands upon the general right of freedom from torture contained in Article 5 of the UDHR and Article 3 of the ECHR.

The detailed information we now have about these secret operations has been amassed through the efforts of several national and intergovernmental organizations that undertook investigations into the CIA's activities. However, those investigations were first triggered by the actions of individual journalists and the publication of their articles by prominent national newspapers, as well as the campaigns of human rights NGOs (Satterthwaite 2006). Stephen Grey's book *Ghost Plane* (Grey 2006) provides a compelling narrative of the investigative journalist's work and demonstrates the effort needed to uncover what the CIA was doing, often at personal risk, through the collection of vast amounts of information, such as data on international aircraft movements.

The initial response from most governments was to deny any involvement in the CIA's programme, but the publication of parallel investigations by journalists in many different countries in late 2005 generated intense pressure on parliaments and bureaucracies to launch inquiries. These inquiries ultimately unlocked Pandora's box. Revelations about secret prisons had been published as early as 2002 by the *Washington Post* (Priest and Gellman 2002); two years later, reports of British government involvement in the 'legal black hole' of US detention centres also appeared (Rose 2004b). It soon became clear that Guantanamo was but 'one island in a global penal archipelago' (Kaplan 2005: 831). In early 2005 the number of reports began to grow, with Matias Valles (2005) revealing the CIA's use of airports in the Balearic Islands and articles in Ireland's *Village* magazine detailing its use of Shannon airport (February/March 2005). However, it was a 1 November *Washington Post* article on secret prisons in Eastern Europe (Priest 2005), followed closely by a Human Rights Watch report (HRW 2005), that finally gave the story irresistible momentum (Priest 2005). An avalanche of stories followed across Europe – for instance, in the UK's *Guardian*, Germany's *Handelsblatt* and *Berliner Zeitung* (24 and 25 November) and France's *Le Figaro* (2 December).

Since these revelations first appeared in the media, it has been Western and Northern European governments, and the government of Canada, that have made the most progress in uncovering the details of extraordinary rendition, 'echoing a geographic pattern familiar from other human rights contexts' (Boon *et al.* 2010: vii). Council of Europe reports (e.g. Marty 2006) were followed by various national reports (e.g. ISC 2007), although there remain a host of unanswered questions, such as how governments actually benefited from their complicity in US-led torture (Hirsch 2011). While Western European countries have sought to demonstrate transparency following the revelations about extraordinary rendition, countries in Central and Eastern Europe have been more mixed in their responses. Poland and Lithuania, for example, initially denied any involvement, but eventually (and slowly) took steps to uncover the activities and improve accountability. Government and opposition in Romania, by contrast, participated in an inquiry that simply 'white-washed government officials of any wrongdoing' (Carey 2013: 449).

'Ordinary' extradition

When it comes to legal forms of extradition, such as the cases of Abu Hamza and Abu Qatada, similar human rights issues are to the fore, but the media has a very different role to play. It sheds considerable light on the importance of human rights issues in extradition cases, and demonstrates how these are often downplayed in favour of national security concerns in public debates. Both Abu Hamza and Abu Qatada were resident in the UK and subject to extradition requests from foreign powers that were challenged through numerous appeals hearings which eventually reached the ECtHR in Strasbourg. These were two among a series of decisions where the ECtHR overturned the UK House of Lords on cases relating to national security (Michaelsen 2012: 763).

Abu Hamza was arrested in the UK in 2004. Although the initial case against him was dropped, the US accused him of a number of crimes relating to terrorist activities, including setting up a terrorist training camp. It subsequently sought his extradition from the UK (also in 2004), but the process was significantly delayed because of a series of appeals based on human rights arguments – for example, over his possible detainment in a 'supermax' prison such as ADX Florence, located in Fremont County, Colorado (Moss 2009; Wagner 2010). Eventually, in 2010, the appeal reached the ECtHR on the basis that it contravened Article 3 of the ECHR. After assurances that Abu Hamza would not be subjected to inhumane treatment (for instance, a guarantee that he would be able to make a claim through the US legal system), the court finally allowed the extradition to take place in 2012. The case was highly publicized in the UK media, which focused on jokes about Abu Hamza's physical appearance (he had lost an eye and both arms in an explosion), calculations about how much his case was costing the 'British taxpayer' (e.g. Doyle 2012), and lengthy discussions about the role of the ECtHR once it finally rejected his fight against extradition (e.g. Rozenburg 2012; West 2012).

The UK granted Abu Qatada refugee status in 1994, but he was arrested in 2002 under the Anti-terrorism, Crime and Security Act (2001). He was never formally charged, however, and was released under a 'control order' under the Prevention of Terrorism Act (2005). Around this time, a Jordanian court convicted him (in his absence) of conspiracy to carry out terror attacks, which resulted in Jordan submitting a request to the UK for his extradition (Michaelsen 2012). The UK agreed to the request after an MOU (memorandum of understanding) had been agreed that stipulated Abu Qatada would not suffer torture or ill-treatment on his return to Jordan. The adequacy of this MOU was challenged in several appeals against extradition, first in the UK courts and eventually at the ECtHR. These were again based on Article 3 of the ECHR. The ECtHR acknowledged that torture was 'widespread and routine' in Jordan, but it was satisfied that the MOU addressed these issues. However, it found that extradition would contravene Abu Qatada's right to a fair trial because evidence against him was likely to be gathered via torture (contravening Article 6 of the ECHR) (Early and Garlicki 2012). Therefore, a further agreement between the two countries relating to how the trial would proceed (any information gathered through torture would be inadmissible) was necessary before he was finally extradited in 2013.

As with the Abu Hamza case, there was intense media scrutiny of this case and the ECtHR's judgements, leading to a political backlash over Britain's human rights obligations. Difficulties in deporting a foreign national connected naturally with widespread concerns over the government's (in)ability to control migration flows more generally. Home Secretary Theresa May and Justice Minister Chris Grayling both expressed frustration over the ECtHR's intervention, and their statements were linked to discussions over a 'renegotiation' of the UK's membership of the Council of Europe.

Taken together, these examples show contrasting roles for the media when it comes to its impact on human rights. The reports of extraordinary rendition across the world applied pressure that resulted in national and international inquiries. The simultaneous publication of articles in many European countries was also significant. It suggested the existence of a nascent global public sphere, where revelations in one country enabled and encouraged investigations in another. However, it is unclear whether these were motivated by human rights concerns. For many of the publications involved, the central issue in the story of extraordinary rendition was not the torture of detainees but rather the trampling of national sovereignty by an 'imperialist' power (the CIA). Nevertheless, the end result was a strengthening of international norms. While the human rights of the individuals involved were secondary to national security concerns in the media reports, ultimately the existence of the international human rights regime was what enabled the subsequent national and international inquiries to hold governments to account.

The comparison with legal forms of extradition provides an interesting contrast, as here governments have the opportunity to manipulate and shape media coverage through the release of specific information about suspects. In the cases of Abu Hamza and Abu Qatada, the guilt or innocence of the individuals concerned was almost completely forgotten as the impact on international norms came to dominate the coverage. The media became a forum for discussions that challenged the very legitimacy of the human rights regime.

Conclusions

As with genocide, the prohibition of anything that can be defined as 'torture' is now a foundational component of the international human rights regime. This is one of the reasons why governments are so keen to avoid using the word, and especially to avoid accusations that they have utilized torture, which has led to battles over semantics and the introduction of euphemisms such as 'enhanced interrogation techniques'. The media has been central in efforts to eradicate torture in liberal democratic states, which has resulted in notable successes as well as scandals, such as those described in the case studies here. However, as human rights organizations have reported, torture and degrading treatment of prisoners remains commonplace in many parts of the world. Moreover, the network of detention centres used in the system of extraordinary rendition demonstrates that states such as the US are very well aware of the locations and governments that will carry out torture if and when required.

The norm against torture, as with many other human rights norms, is particularly vulnerable to the forces of securitization – where officials highlight an existential threat to demand 'exceptional' measures that allow them to override normal processes and safeguards and extend the powers of the state. The media is often a crucial component when it comes to convincing the public of both the existential threat and the need for special powers to combat it. This is why it is so important for an independent media, protected by the right of freedom of expression, to recognize when states are attempting to break their human rights obligations and then hold them to account. The case studies presented here underline the potential power of the media when it can be demonstrated that torture is taking place, but they also show how difficult it can be for individuals to piece together the necessary proof in the face of governments' determined efforts to maintain secrecy. Moreover, they remind us of the dangers and costs when whistle-blowers are silenced or the findings of investigative journalists remain unpublished and unknown.

Questions

- What are the main problems when it comes to providing a definition of 'torture'?
- Can the use of torture ever be justified on the basis of security threats?
- Why was the Convention against Torture adopted in 1984 when the practice had already been prohibited through the earlier Geneva Conventions?
- What are the ways in which the media might play a role in the state's justification of torture?

Note

1 www.humanrightsfirst.org/our-work/law-and-security/torture-on-tv/what-can-be-done.

Further reading

Andén-Papadopoulos, K. 2008. 'The Abu Ghraib torture photographs: news frames, visual culture, and the power of images'. *Journalism* 9(1): 5–30.

Bennett, W. L., R. G. Lawrence and S. Livingston. 2006. 'None dare call it torture: indexing and the limits of press independence in the Abu Ghraib scandal'. *Journal of Communication* 56(3): 467–485.

Brecher, B. 2007. *Torture and the Ticking Bomb*. Oxford: Blackwell.

Danner, M. 2004. *Torture and Truth: America, Abu Ghraib, and the War on Terror*. New York: New York Review Books.

Dershowitz, A. 2002. *Why Terrorism Works: Understanding the Threat, Responding to the Challenge*. New York: Yale University Press.

Grey, S. 2006. *Ghost Plane: The True Story of the CIA Torture Program*. New York: St Martin's Press.

Hersh, S. 2004. *Chain of Command: The Road from 9/11 to Abu Ghraib*. New York: HarperCollins.

Jackson, R. 2005. *Writing the War on Terror: Language, Politics and Counter-Terrorism*. Manchester: Manchester University Press.

Levinson, S. (ed.). 2002. *Torture: A Collection*. Oxford: Oxford University Press.

Moss, K. 2011. *Balancing Liberty and Security: Human Rights, Human Wrongs*. Basingstoke: Palgrave Macmillan.

Useful websites

www.amnesty.org (Amnesty International)
www.hrw.org (Human Rights Watch)
www.omct.org (World Organisation Against Torture)
www.cvt.org (Centre for Victims of Torture)
www.freedomfromtorture.org (Freedom from Torture)
www.apt.ch (Association for the Prevention of Torture)
www.ohchr.org/en/hrbodies/cat/pages/catindex.aspx (Committee against Torture)
http://tortureaccountability.org (Center for Torture Accountability)
www.atlas-of-torture.org (Atlas of Torture)

9

CONCLUSION

Media and human rights: cosmopolitan promise or deficit?

This book began with the claim that human rights have become more newsworthy and more intensely present in the media. Why is this important? How much should we care about the extent to which the media reports on human rights, the consistency and breadth of that coverage, or its quality and accuracy? The evidence presented in this book suggests strongly that the answer to these questions depends on the position that is adopted with regards to, first, conceptualizing the media and its role in society, and, second, the significance of human rights for the individual and society, and the ways in which these norms should be developed within the international states system.

There can be only very basic or general agreement on what international human rights are because deep political questions surround every aspect of this putative regime, and indeed each human right itself. The tensions around the universality of human rights, their enforcement and monitoring, and the role of the individual states and international organizations in this process inevitably inform any discussions about the role of the media in protecting and promoting human rights. Given the varied nature of human rights and the range of dilemmas and challenges associated with them, the specific political dimensions and debates cannot be ignored when analysing the media–human rights nexus. This book has argued for a balanced approach to the relationship between the two – one that is based on an understanding of both the media's dynamics and the nature of and key debates relating to each particular human rights issue. In light of the existing complexities and controversies surrounding every human right, the way that different kinds of human rights are discussed and communicated (or ignored and evaded) becomes all the more important, and meaningful.

If we agree that there is no single, unified understanding of human rights, then we accept the constructed and contingent nature of human rights as a concept. But this does not completely dissolve the importance of human rights. There is basic agreement and consensus that human rights have a place in the international system. There is, however, significant disagreement on the wording, the scope, the power and the enforcement of each individual human right, as illustrated in each of the chapters in Part III. The point here is that accepting the constructed nature of human rights does not concede the radical post-modern accusation of 'Western ideological imperialism'. It is more accurate to describe debates over human rights as falling within a spectrum of weaker and stronger forms of cosmopolitanism. Analysis of the practice of communication around human rights thus becomes an important window through which to interrogate different ways of thinking about this regime and to understand how it is both derivative of and subject to broader political and societal tensions and cleavages. This book has attempted to supply the necessary tools with which to construct such an analysis by developing a framework with which to connect this spectrum of positions or perspectives on the international human rights regime with the ways in which the media plays, and is perceived to play, a role.

The material presented in the preceding chapters has been framed by a qualitative and case-study approach that draws on research from a range of different conceptual and theoretical traditions. This interdisciplinary approach has at least three benefits. First, it provides a theoretically informed understanding that seeks to offer a straight-forward way of combining contemporary media analysis with debates around the politics of human rights. Second, it problematizes the way we think about both human rights and the media, avoiding their treatment as unified and 'monolithic' concepts. Third, it creates a framework that may then be applied to a systematic empirical analysis of human rights debates in the media. This means connecting some rather abstract philosophical questions (relating to the evolving meaning of cosmopolitanism in the modern world) to practical questions about the role of the media in society, and using these two 'axes' to comprehend contemporary debates over human rights. This concluding chapter takes the opportunity to reconsider the questions that were raised at the start of the book, and apply them to the case studies comparatively in the context of the analytical framework sketched out in the first part of the book.

Introducing the cosmopolitan 'lens' for understanding the relationship between the media and human rights, Chapter 3 suggested a positive correlation between a stronger cosmopolitan normative position and a more optimistic view of the media as a force for transforming and constructing global values (Figure 3.1). How does this fit with the evidence from the case studies presented in the rest of the book? The most obvious observation is that this correlation creates a gap which emerges between the expectations and the capabilities of the media when it comes to human rights. Instead of a cosmopolitan 'promise', there is a 'cosmopolitan deficit' (see Figure 9.1).

Those who are more optimistic about the potential of the media to bring about a more cosmopolitan global society are likely to be most critical of actual media performance, which, as the case studies demonstrate, often falls well short of cosmopolitan aspirations. Of course, the notion of a deficit makes sense only from

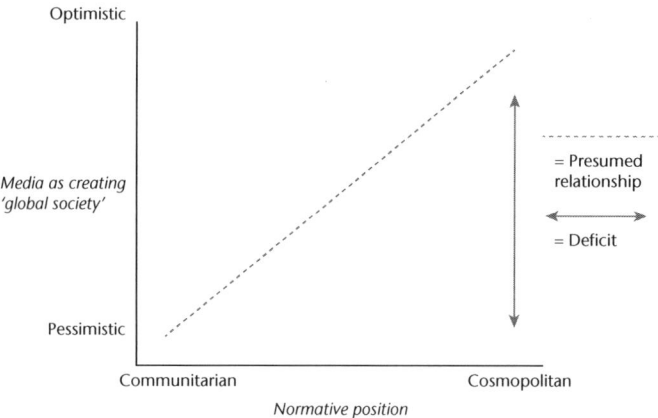

FIGURE 9.1 The cosmopolitan deficit

the perspective of someone holding such a position. Weak cosmopolitan, or communitarian, understandings of global justice are more likely to be satisfied with the media's performance when it comes to human rights, and the ways in which the topics covered in this book are addressed. For stronger cosmopolitans, this state of affairs produces the cognitive dissonance that permeates much academic writing about human rights and the media. Cognitive dissonance refers to the problem of maintaining two conflicting ideas inside one's head at the same time. In this case, the ideas are: a strongly cosmopolitan desire for a world governed by universal values; and a knowledge of the media as a system that is strongly communitarian and nationalistic in its outlook and position.

A variable deficit

Alongside the connection with different normative positions, this book has linked the media's role with a detailed understanding of how international human rights were created and how they have evolved over time. This helps to provide further insights into the contours of this deficit. Ten case studies relating to humanitarian intervention, genocide, asylum and immigration, freedom of speech, and torture have been examined. Individually and together, they illustrate key aspects of the nexus between the media and human rights, but they also demonstrate that the gap (or disconnect) between the cosmopolitan promise and reality is highly variable across different human rights.

The best way to describe this effect is to modify and expand upon the concept of 'indexing' that is usually associated with Bennett (1990). Bennett argued that media criticism of government policy could be linked to the extent to which there is dissensus in the political elite: the greater the conflict in the corridors of power, the more opportunities the media has to present alternative, and critical, voices. In the context of the evidence presented here, there is an additional kind of indexing – where media performance can be linked to the inherent characteristics of the formal framework of human rights. The case studies examined here demonstrate that some human rights are less controversial, disputed or challenged on cultural relativity grounds than others. In other words, they are more widely accepted as universal human rights, and states have signed up to more binding agreements about them. These tend to be the human rights in which the media has the potential to play a more active role in generating attention and holding governments to account; although they do so only infrequently – a kind of punctuated equilibrium. Those human rights that touch upon questions of sovereignty and security tend to be guaranteed by weaker international agreements in terms of content and form, and fewer states adhere to them. Here the media usually avoids the language of human rights, and the deficit is likely to be wider – indexed to the gap between the human right (in an ideal sense) and the eventual form of international covenants and agreements that actually address it.

As the instances of torture, genocide and human suffering considered here reveal, media coverage is more likely to be empathetically framed towards the victims of genocide and humanitarian crises, although not all of them and not instantly. The media is also more likely to be critical and perform its watchdog role, as it did when uncovering the policy and practice of torture during the 'war on terror'. The problems it encounters when dealing with these stories reflect the tendency for governments to twist the language of detention and punishment to avoid use of the word 'torture' (Graber and Holyk 2009). However, the creation of a global scandal over Abu Ghraib demonstrates the ability for the media at least to punctuate the equilibrium. In comparison, the media's generally weak role in the case of human rights around immigration can be indexed to the partial and weak international legal framework that exists for these issues. There is widespread agreement on rights for refugees, but states have almost complete power over how these are implemented. The evidence here suggests that the media's role can be indexed to this state of affairs. The usual framing of this topic in the media – the language, concepts and definitions used predominantly in debates about immigrants, refugees and asylum-seekers – does not suggest a cosmopolitan concern for the 'other'. Rather, it echoes the general disregard for the rights of individuals who have crossed borders that is shown by states (normally in favour of the interests of security and prosperity in the receiving state). Similarly, the right to freedom of speech is complex and there are important national differences over implementation – for instance, in the US and Europe. This lack of a universal understanding backed by international law appears to affect and limit the role that the media can play.

Another type of indexing can be related back to the underlying fundamental human rights debates outlined in Chapter 1. For example, the choice to present arguments about freedom of speech through the prism of a threat to national security (to the state) or as a threat to the individual (from the state) is not accidental. It reflects different interpretations of the human rights framework – ranging from universalist to cultural relativist positions. The acceptance by many of the restriction, limitation and even sacrifice of freedom of speech demonstrates ambiguity in terms of a universal belief in the importance of this human right.

The first four case studies – the Kosovo conflict in 1999, the intervention in Libya in 2011, the genocide in Rwanda in 1994 and the ongoing conflict in Darfur – all relate to the issue of international humanitarian intervention. In these cases there are questions over the media's ability to raise awareness and inform the public debate with news of human rights abuses; there are also questions about the media's ability to bring human rights issues to the attention of policy-makers and its role in the making of foreign policy.

The intervention in Kosovo in 1999 is often linked with a new post-Cold War era of military humanitarianism as it was 'sold' to Western publics as a case of humanitarian intervention. Ever since, it has been cited on both sides of the argument regarding the existence, or non-existence, of a cosmopolitan international order. Cosmopolitan arguments were central to the arguments put forward to justify the intervention, but there was no authorization for the operation through the UN system. Despite some suggestions that the media might have played an independent role in creating the conditions for intervention, the evidence suggests that its coverage actually followed the arguments of political elites. The second case study, Libya in 2011, provides an interesting contrast to Kosovo, because on this occasion there was a UN Security Council resolution and thus an international legal basis for the intervention. Libya proves that the R2P doctrine can work, as long as the right combination of circumstances and political motivations is in place. As with Kosovo, the Western media was decidedly pro-intervention. Non-Western media organizations, such as Al Jazeera, arguably provided a more balanced assessment. Again in a similar way to Kosovo, the role of the media when it came to the political decision to intervene was ambiguous at best. There is insufficient evidence to support the notion of a causation. All that can be said is that there was clear alignment in both cases between the coverage provided by the Western media and the policies adopted by Western governments.

Whereas Kosovo and Libya prove that international interventions are possible, Rwanda (1994) and Darfur (2003 onwards) are examples of the international community demonstrably failing to meet the most basic cosmopolitan requirement to stop genocide from taking place. The deficit seems to be widest here, so why was the media's performance so poor? Ironically, the case for intervention was arguably stronger in these cases than in either Kosovo or Libya because of global commitments made with regard to genocide. The errors made over Rwanda led to numerous assertions that the international community would never allow such a situation to happen again, but Darfur proves that these were hollow promises. As with the first two case studies, there is a discernible correlation between the response of the international community and the quality and quantity of coverage in the global media. There are also similarities in both Darfur and Rwanda in terms of the framing of the conflicts, with the media guilty of promoting stereotypical Western understandings of Africa. However, while Darfur proves that genocide did not end with the twentieth century, it does perhaps demonstrate that some lessons were learnt from Rwanda: the media, encouraged by NGOs and human rights activists, has made significantly more effort to provide coverage; and politicians (including some from the US) have been more willing to use the word 'genocide'. Nevertheless, the rhetorical commitment to cosmopolitan values is insufficient to solve the problems on the ground. Darfur indicates that, while there is less of a deficit in terms of media performance, there is more of a gap when it comes to international enforcement of human rights.

Compared to the first four examples of intervention and non-intervention, the case studies in Chapter 6 on immigration and asylum show a different kind of deficit. The evidence from the UK and Bulgarian coverage of European mobility is that the media seems highly unlikely to link the issue with cosmopolitan values. Instead, it is complicit in the presentation of immigration issues as a question of communitarian priorities. In one sense, this echoes corresponding inadequacy at the level of international law when it comes to the right to migrate. This is perhaps more worrying, from the cosmopolitan perspective, when it comes to the field of asylum and refugees. This is because, in contrast to immigration, most states have signed up to international agreements on the treatment of refugees. On this issue the deficit is pronounced – there is very little evidence of the media holding governments to account, which is particularly problematic when those governments are pursuing very restrictive and prejudicial policies towards refugees. Some of these points are illustrated by the enormous challenge faced by the UNHCR when tasked with transmitting a global message based on cosmopolitan principles. The evidence from this case study highlights the importance of new media tools, but interestingly shows that there is still no easy answer to the difficulty of filtering messages through national policy debates and traditional media systems.

The case studies presented in Chapter 7 illustrate two very different challenges: to the cosmopolitan vision of an international order based on universal principles; and to the fundamental role played by the media in modern liberal democratic systems. The Danish cartoons case study demonstrates how difficult it is for contemporary multicultural societies to maintain or advance cosmopolitan principles while avoiding cultural relativism. This cosmopolitan deficit can be connected to inherent weaknesses in the international human rights regime – a foundational question for the universality of freedom of speech and its relationship with freedom of religion. The second case study demonstrates the value in prioritizing the former over the latter. While governments' treatment of whistle-blowers (certainly since the emergence of WikiLeaks) has often left a lot to be desired, the case of Edward Snowden demonstrates the benefits of safeguarding a robust right to freedom of expression. Here, the international press (in the shape of the *Guardian*, *Der Spiegel*, the *Washington Post* and the *New York Times*) fulfilled a vital function by publicizing the information Snowden had gathered. This proves that the media can utilize its right to freedom of speech to inform and protect other human rights. It underlines the importance of the media in the context of human rights, but also demonstrates the vulnerability of the press, especially when considering the political pressure faced by the *Guardian*. The contrasting ways in which the story played out in the US and the UK also show that freedom of speech is linked to and influenced by different state and media systems.

The final pair of case studies relate to the topic which has most exercised the minds of scholars working on the question of media and human rights over the last ten years – namely, the impact of the 'war on terror'. Both of them – Abu Ghraib and extraordinary rendition – can be analyzed in two basic ways. On the one hand, they can be seen as cases where the deficit grew dangerously wide. The media initially, and for several years thereafter, missed some serious human rights abuses – a problem that can be attributed to its unquestioning attitude towards government sources, and its 'rally round the flag' patriotism in the aftermath of 9/11. On the other hand, the global media scandals that developed following the eventual publication of these two stories perhaps provides evidence of the media's continuing ability to fulfil a watchdog role even in the context of serious security threats. As with the cases relating to immigration and asylum, the framing of stories emerges as crucial in how human rights are understood and discussed. The protection of human rights is not simply about informing: the framing of the Abu Ghraib story demonstrates that governments can still control the message even if they cannot control the messenger. These two cases now play dominant roles in the conventional narrative of human rights and the Western media in the twenty-first century.

Important questions remain about the role of the media since the 9/11 terrorist attacks, and particularly during the early years of the interventions in Iraq and Afghanistan. But the (subtle, yet significant) policy shifts over security in the international sphere more than ten years later, alongside some legislative roll-back, prompt new questions, too. Are we now in a post-post-9/11 era in terms of the media and human rights? Was the media's complicity in the rampant securitization that occurred in the first decade of the twenty-first century the start of a long phase in which governments have again gained the advantage in controlling the news and the message? Was it, alternatively, an anachronistic low point, a temporary lull or lapse in the global media's expansive march towards a more globalized and transparent communication future? Or was it a telling reminder of the media's inability or unwillingness to reach out to distant others and help to understand and secure universal values?

The ways in which human rights are discussed brings these questions into direct contact with politics – the ideal meets the non-ideal. The ideal of world citizenship associated with a cosmopolitan position is far from the non-ideal world that is divided into hundreds of nation-states of wildly varying power and resources. Systems of communication remain resolutely embedded in non-global social systems, usually framed by national political communities and, to a limited extent, wider transnational communities based on language. The ideal of human rights as universal values is often distant from the pragmatism of international politics, which is why the study of human rights in the media allows us to observe grand battles between world views and witness clashes between fundamental core principles.

BIBLIOGRAPHY

Agamben, G. 2005. *State of Exception*. Chicago: Chicago University Press.

Alden, E. 2009. *The Closing of the American Border: Terrorism, Immigration, and Security since 9/11*. New York: Harper Perennial.

Alia, V. and S. Bull. 2005. *Media and Ethnic Minorities*. Edinburgh: Edinburgh University Press.

Allern, S. 2002. 'Journalistic and commercial news values: news organizations as patrons of an institution and market actors'. *Nordicom Review* 23(1–2): 137–152.

Allhoff, F. 2009. 'The war on terror and the ethics of exceptionalism'. *Journal of Military Ethics* 8(4): 265–288.

Alozie, E. C. 2007. 'What did they say? African media coverage of the first 100 days of the Rwanda crisis'. In *The Media and the Rwanda Genocide*, A. Thompson (ed.) (pp. 211–230). London: Pluto Press.

Alston, P. 1990. 'US ratification of the covenant on economic, social and cultural rights: the need for an entirely new strategy'. *American Journal of International Law* 84(2): 365–393.

Alston, P. 2006. 'Reconceiving the UN human rights regime: challenges confronting the new UN Human Rights Council'. *Melbourne Journal of International Law* 7: 185–224.

Amnesty International (AI). 2010. *'Libya of Tomorrow': What Hope for Human Rights?* London: Amnesty International Publications.

Amnesty International (AI). 2012. *Libyan Rendition Case Shows It's Time for UK to Come Clean*. London: Amnesty International Publications.

Amnesty International (AI). 2013. *Amnesty International Report 2013*. London: Amnesty International Publications.

Andén-Papadopoulos, K. 2008. 'The Abu Ghraib torture photographs: news frames, visual culture, and the power of images'. *Journalism* 9(1): 5–30.

Anderson, P. J. 2007a. 'Challenges for journalism'. In *The Future of Journalism in the Advanced Democracies*, P. J. Anderson and G. Ward (eds) (pp. 51–72). Aldershot: Ashgate Publishing.

Anderson, P. J. 2007b. 'Competing models of journalism and democracy'. In *The Future of Journalism in the Advanced Democracies*, P. J. Anderson and G. Ward (eds) (pp. 39–49). Aldershot: Ashgate Publishing.

Anheier, H., M. Glasius and M. Kaldor. 2001. 'Introducing global civil society'. In *Global Civil Society 2001*, H. Anheier, M. Glasius and M. Kaldor (eds) (pp. 3–22). Oxford: Oxford University Press.

Annan, K. 1999a. Statement by UN Secretary General Kofi Annan on the occasion of World Press Freedom Day.

Annan, K. 1999b. 'Two concepts of sovereignty'. *The Economist*, 16 September.

Apodaca, C. 2007. 'The whole world could be watching: human rights and the media'. *Journal of Human Rights* 6(2): 147–164.

Archibugi, D. 2004. 'Cosmopolitan guidelines for humanitarian intervention'. *Alternatives* 29(1): 1–22.

Arendt, H. 1962. *The Origins of Totalitarianism*. Cleveland and New York: Cleveland World Publishing Co.

Article 19. n.d. *National Security*. London: Article 19.

Article 19. 1996. *The Johannesburg Principles on National Security, Freedom of Expression and Access to Information*. London: Article 19.

Article 19. 2008. *Expert Meeting on the Links between Articles 19 and 20 of the ICCPR: Freedom of Expression and Advocacy of Religious Hatred that Constitutes Incitement to Discrimination, Hostility or Violence*. Geneva: UN HCHR.

Associated Press. 2005. 'Poll finds broad approval of terrorist torture'. 9 December

Azadovskii, K. and B. Egorov. 2002. 'From anti-Westernism to anti-Semitism'. *Journal of Cold War Studies* 4(1): 66–80.

Bacevich, A. J. and E. A. Cohen. 2001. 'Introduction: strange little war'. In *War over Kosovo: Politics and Strategy in a Global Age*, A. J. Bacevich and E. A. Cohen (eds) (pp. ix–xiv). New York: Columbia University Press.

Bader, V. 2005. 'The ethics of immigration'. *Constellations* 12(3): 331–361.

Bagaric, M. and J. Morss. 2005. 'State sovereignty and migration control: the ultimate act of discrimination'. *Journal of Migration and Refugee Issues* 1(1): 25–50.

Bahador, B. 2007. *The CNN Effect in Action: How the News Media Pushed the West toward War in Kosovo*. Basingstoke: Palgrave Macmillan.

Bahador, B. 2011. 'Did the global war on terror end the CNN effect?' *Media, War & Conflict* 4(1): 37–54.

Bakir, V. 2013. *Torture, Intelligence and Sousveillance in the War on Terror: Agenda-building Strategies*. Farnham: Ashgate.

Balabanova, E. 2007. *Media, Wars and Politics: Comparing the Incomparable in Western and Eastern Europe*. London: Ashgate.

Balabanova, E. 2010. 'Media power during humanitarian interventions: is Eastern Europe any different from the West?' *Journal of Peace Research* 47(1): 71–82.

Balabanova, E. 2011. 'Media and foreign policy in Central and Eastern Europe post 9/11: in from the cold?' *Media, War & Conflict* 4(1): 69–82.

Balabanova, E. and A. Balch. 2010. 'Sending and receiving: the ethical framing of intra-EU migration in the European press'. *European Journal of Communication* 25(4): 382–397.

Balch, A. 2010. *Managing Labour Migration in Europe: Ideas, Knowledge and Policy Change*. Manchester: Manchester University Press.

Balch, A. and E. Balabanova. 2011. 'A system in chaos? Knowledge and sense-making on immigration policy in public debates'. *Media, Culture and Society* 33(6): 885–904.

Balch, A., E. Balabanova and R. Trandafoiu. 2014. 'A Europe of rights and values? public debates on Sarkozy's Roma affair in France, Bulgaria and Romania'. *Journal of Ethnic and Migration Studies* 40(8): 1154–1174.

Bardos, G. 2003. 'International policy in Southeastern Europe: a diagnosis'. In *Yugoslavia Unraveled: Sovereignty, Self-Determination, Intervention*, R. Thomas (ed.) (pp. 139–163). Oxford: Lexington.

Barnett, M. 2002. *Eyewitness to a Genocide: The United Nations and Rwanda*. Ithaca: Cornell University Press.

Barroso, J. M. 2014. Speech of the President of the European Commission to the European Parliament.

Barry, B. 2011. 'Libya's lessons'. *Survival: Global Politics and Strategy* 53(5): 5–14.

Bartrop, P. and S. Totten. 2004. 'The history of genocide: an overview'. In *Teaching about Genocide: Issues, Approaches, and Resources*, S. Totten (ed.) (pp. 23–56). Greenwich: Information Age Publishing.

Beardsworth, R. 2011. *Cosmopolitanism and International Relations Theory*. Cambridge: Polity Press.

Beckett, C. and J. Ball. 2012. *WikiLeaks: News in the Networked Era*. Cambridge: Polity Press.

Beitz, C. 2009. *The Idea of Human Rights*. Oxford: Oxford University Press.

Belien, P. 2005. 'Jihad against Danish newspaper'. *Brussels Journal*, 22 October.

Bell, D. A. 1996. 'The East Asian challenge to human rights: reflections on an East West dialogue'. *Human Rights Quarterly* 18(3): 641–667.

Bellamy, A. J. 2002. *Kosovo and International Society*. Basingstoke: Palgrave Macmillan.

Bellamy, A. J. 2004. 'Ethics and intervention: the "humanitarian exception" and the problem of abuse in the case of Iraq'. *Journal of Peace Research* 41(2): 131–147.

Bellamy, A. J. 2006a. *Just Wars: From Cicero to Iraq*. Cambridge: Polity Press.

Bellamy, A. J. 2006b. 'No pain, no gain? Torture and ethics in the war on terror'. *International Affairs* 82(1): 121–148.

Bellamy, A. J. 2006c. 'Whither the responsibility to protect? Humanitarian intervention and the 2005 World Summit'. *Ethics and International Affairs* 20(2): 143–169.

Bellamy, A. J. 2008. *Responsibility to Protect*. Cambridge: Polity Press.

Bellamy, A. J. 2013. 'Peace operations and humanitarian intervention'. In *Issues in 21st Century World Politics*, M. Beeson and N. Bisley (eds) (pp. 106–119). London: Palgrave Macmillan.

Bellamy, A. J. and N. J. Wheeler. 2008. 'Humanitarian intervention in world politics'. In *The Globalization of World Politics: An Introduction to International Relations*, 4th edn, J. Baylis, S. Smith and P. Owens (eds) (pp. 522–539). Oxford: Oxford University Press.

Bellamy, A. J. and P. D. Williams. 2011. 'The new politics of protection? Côte d'Ivoire, Librya and the responsibility to protect' *International Affairs* 87(4): 825–850.

Benhabib, S. 2004. *The Rights of Others: Aliens, Residents and Citizens*. Cambridge: Cambridge University Press.

Bennett, W. L. 1990. 'Toward a theory of press–state relations in the United States'. *Journal of Communication* 40(2): 103–125.

Bennett, W. L. 2003. 'Communicating global activism: strengths and vulnerabilities of networked politics'. *Information, Communication and Society* 6(2): 143–168.

Bennett, W. L. and D. L. Paletz. 1994. *Taken by Storm: The Media, Public Opinion, and US Foreign Policy in the Gulf War*. Chicago: University of Chicago Press.

Bennett, W. L., R. G. Lawrence and S. Livingston. 2006. 'None dare call it torture: indexing and the limits of press independence in the Abu Ghraib scandal'. *Journal of Communication* 56(3): 467–485.

Berger, D. 2007. 'Regarding the imprisonment of others: prison abuse photographs and social change'. *International Journal of Communication* 1: 210–237.

Berry, V. and A. McChesney. 1988. 'Human rights and foreign policy-making'. In *Human Rights in Canadian Foreign Policy*, R. O. Matthews and C. Pratt (eds) (pp. 59–76). Kingston: McGill-Queen's University Press.

Blair, T. 1999a. 'Doctrine of the international community'. Speech to the Economic Club of Chicago, 22 April.

Blair, T. 1999b. 'A new generation draws the line'. *Newsweek*, 19 April.

Bleich, E. 2006. 'On democratic integration and free speech: response to Tariq Modood and Randall Hansen'. *International Migration* 44(5): 17–22.

Bleich, E. 2011. 'The rise of hate speech and hate crime laws in liberal democracies'. *Journal of Ethnic and Migration Studies* 37(6): 917–934.

Bob, C. 2014. 'The global battle over religious expression: Sweden's Åke Green Case in local and transnational perspective'. *Journal of Ethnic and Migration Studies* 40(2): 212–229.

Boffey, C. 2013. '*Guardian* and Snowden: Alan Rusbridger knocks MPs' questions out of the park – but he may be dismayed by police action'. *The Drum*, 4 December. Available at: www.thedrum.com/opinion/2013/12/04/guardian-and-snowden-alan-rusbridger-knocks-mps-questions-out-park.

Boomgaarden, H. G. and R. Vliegenthart. 2009. 'How news content influences anti-immigration attitudes: Germany, 1993–2005'. *European Journal of Political Research* 48(4): 516–542.

Boon, K. E., A. Huq and D. C. Lovelace (eds). 2010. *Terrorism: Commentary on Security Documents Volume 108: Extraordinary Rendition.* Oxford: Oxford University Press.

Booth, K. 2001. *The Kosovo Tragedy: The Human Rights Dimension.* London: Frank Cass.

Booth, R. 2013. 'Qatar World Cup 2022: 70 Nepalese workers die on building sites'. *Guardian*, 1 October.

Booth, R., O. Gibson and P. Pattisson. 2013. 'Qatar under growing pressure over workers' deaths as FIFA is urged to act'. *Guardian*, 2 October.

Borer, T. A. 2012a. '"Fresh, wet tears": shock media and human rights awareness campaigns'. In *Media, Mobilization, and Human Rights: Mediating Suffering*, T. A. Borer (ed.) (pp. 143–180). London: Zed Books.

Borer, T. A. 2012b. 'Introduction: willful ignorance – news production, audience reception, and responses to suffering'. In *Media, Mobilization, and Human Rights: Mediating Suffering*, T. A. Borer (ed.) (pp. 1–41). London: Zed Books.

Boyle, K. 2001. 'Hate speech – the United States versus the rest of the world?'. *Maine Law Review* 53(2): 488–502.

Branton, R. P. and J. Dunaway. 2009. 'Slanted newspaper coverage of immigration: the importance of economics and geography'. *Policy Studies Journal* 37(2): 257–273.

Brecher, B. 2007. *Torture and the Ticking Bomb.* Oxford: Blackwell Publishing.

Brecher, B. 2010. 'Torture and the "ticking bomb": fantasy and the so-called war on terror'. *At the Interface/Probing the Boundaries* 64: 17–34.

Brevini, B., A. Hintz and P. McCurdy (eds). 2013. *Beyond WikiLeaks: Implications for the Future of Communications, Journalism and Society.* Basingstoke: Palgrave Macmillan.

Brewer, P. R. and K. Gross. 2005. 'Values, framing, and citizens' thoughts about policy issues: effects on content and quantity'. *Political Psychology* 26(6): 929–948.

Brock, G. 2013. 'Rethinking the cosmopolitanism versus non-cosmopolitanism debate: an introduction'. In *Cosmopolitanism versus Non-cosmopolitanism: Critiques, Defenses, Reconceptualizations*, G. Brock (ed.) (pp. 1–34). Oxford: Oxford University Press.

Brown, G. W. 2010. 'Kant's cosmopolitanism'. In *The Cosmopolitanism Reader*, G. W. Brown and D. Held (eds) (pp. 45–60). Cambridge: Polity Press.

Brown, G. W. and D. Held. 2010. 'Editors' introduction'. In *The Cosmopolitanism Reader*, G. W. Brown and D. Held (eds) (pp. 1–14). Cambridge: Polity Press.

Browne, A. 2006. 'This is not just about cartoons, but standing up for our values'. *The Times*, 1 February.

Buchanan, A. 2013. 'Moral progress and human rights'. In *Human Rights: The Hard Questions*, C. Holder and D. Reidy (eds) (pp. 399–417). Cambridge: Cambridge University Press.

Buchanan, S., B. Grillo and T. Threadgold. 2003. *'What's the Story?': Results from Research into Media Coverage of Refugees and Asylum Seekers in the UK.* London: Article 19.

Bucher, J., L. Engel, S. Harfensteller and H. Dijkstra. 2013. 'Domestic politics, news media and humanitarian intervention: why France and Germany diverged over Libya'. *European Security* 22(4): 524–539.

Burke, E. 2006 (1790). *Reflections on the Revolution in France.* London: Pearson Longman.

Bush, G. W. 2001a. Address to the Nation.

Bush, G. W. 2001b. Remarks at the National Day of Prayer and Remembrance, National Cathedral, Washington, DC.

Buzan, B. 1983. *People, States and Fear: National Security Problem in International Relations.* Chapel Hill: University of North Carolina Press.

Buzan, B., O. Wæver and J. de Wilde. 1998. *Security: A New Framework for Analysis.* Boulder, CO: Lynne Rienner Publishers.

Bybee, J. 2002a. *Memorandum for Alberto R. Gonzales, Counsel to the President, Re: Standards of Conduct for Interrogation under 18 U.S.C. 2340–2340A.*

Bybee, J. 2002b. *Memorandum for John Rizzo, Acting General Counsel of the Central Intelligence Agency, Interrogation of al Qaeda Operative.*

Caliendo, S. M., M. P. Gibney and A. Payne. 1999. 'All the news that's fit to print? *New York Times* coverage of human rights violations'. *Harvard International Journal of Press/Politics* 4: 48–69.

Callamard, A. 2007. *Burying the Truth under the Cloak of National Security.* Report for Article 19. Available at: www.article19.org/resources.php/resource/2748/en/burying-the-truth-under-the-cloak-of-national-security.

Campbell, D. 2001. 'Time is broken: the return of the past in the response to September 11'. *Theory & Event* 5(4).

Campbell, D. 2007. 'Geopolitics and visuality: sighting the Darfur conflict'. *Political Geography* 26(4): 357–382.

Caney, S. 1997. 'Human rights and the rights of states: Terry Nardin on nonintervention'. *International Political Science Review* 18(1): 27–37.

Carens, J. H. 1987. 'Aliens and citizens: the case for open borders'. *Review of Politics* 49(2): 251–273.

Carey, H. F. 2013. 'The domestic politics of protecting human rights in counter-terrorism: Poland's, Lithuania's, and Romania's secret detention centres and other East European collaboration in extraordinary rendition'. *East European Politics and Societies* 27(3): 429–465.

Carey, S. C., M. Gibney and S. C. Poe. 2010. *The Politics of Human Rights: The Quest for Dignity.* Cambridge: Cambridge University Press.

Carle, G. L. 2011. *The Interrogator: An Education.* New York: Nation Books.

Carruthers, S. L. 2000. *The Media at War.* Basingstoke: Palgrave Macmillan.

Carruthers, S. L. 2011. *The Media at War*, 2nd edn. London: Palgrave Macmillan.

Carvalho, J. 2014. *Impact of Extreme Right Parties on Immigration Policy: Comparing Britain, France and Italy.* London: Routledge.

Casey, J. P. 2010. 'Open borders: absurd chimera or inevitable future policy?'. *International Migration* 48(5): 14–62.

Cassese, A. 1990. *Human Rights in a Changing World.* Cambridge: Polity Press.

Castles, S., H. de Haas and M. J. Miller. 2013. *The Age of Migration: International Population Movements in the Modern World*, 5th edn. Basingstoke: Palgrave Macmillan.

CEC. 2003. *Communication on Immigration, Integration and Employment.* Brussels: Commission of the European Communities, COM (2003) 336 Final.

Chalk, F. and K. Jonassohn. 1990. *The History and Sociology of Genocide: Analyses and Case Studies.* New Haven, CT: Yale University Press.

Chandler, D. 2000. 'International justice'. *New Left Review* 6: 55–66.

Chandler, D. 2002. *From Kosovo to Kabul: Human Rights and International Intervention.* London: Pluto Press.

Chandler, D. 2006. *From Kosovo to Kabul and Beyond: Human Rights and International Intervention*, 2nd edn. London: Pluto Press.

Chang, N. 2002. *Silencing Political Dissent: How Post-September 11. Anti-Terrorism Measures Threaten Our Civil Liberties.* New York: Seven Stories Press.

Chaon, A. 2007. 'Who failed in Rwanda, journalists or the media?'. In *The Media and the Rwanda Genocide*, A. Thompson (ed.) (pp. 160–166). London: Pluto Press.

Charny, I. W. (ed.). 1988. *Genocide: A Critical Bibliographic Review.* New York: Facts on File.

Chavez, L. R. 2001. *Covering Immigration: Popular Images and the Politics of the Nation.* Los Angeles: University of California Press.

Chesterman, S. 2001. *Just War or Just Peace? Humanitarian Intervention and International Law.* Oxford: Oxford University Press.

Chivvis, C. S. 2012. 'Libya and the future of liberal intervention'. *Survival: Global Politics and Strategy* 54(6): 69–92.

Chomsky, N. 1999. *The New Military Humanism: Lessons from Kosovo.* London: Pluto.

Chomsky, N. 2000. *Rogue States.* London: Pluto Press.

Chong, D. 2012. 'Framing strategies for economic and social rights in the United States'. In *Media, Mobilization, and Human Rights: Mediating Suffering*, T. A. Borer (ed.) (pp. 122–142). London: Zed Books.

Chopra, J. and T. G. Weiss. 1992. 'Sovereignty is no longer sacrosanct: codifying humanitarian intervention'. *Ethics and International Affairs* 6(1): 95–117.

Chouliaraki, L. 2006. *The Spectatorship of Suffering*. London: Sage.

Chouliaraki, L. 2008. 'The symbolic power of transnational media: managing the visibility of suffering'. *Global Media and Communication* 4(3): 329–351.

Chouliaraki, L. 2013. *The Ironic Spectator: Solidarity in the Age of Post-humanitarianism*. Cambridge: Polity Press.

Chouliaraki, L. and B. Blaagaard. 2013. 'Introduction'. *Journalism Studies* 14(2): 150–155.

Cisneros, J. D. 2008. 'Contaminated communities: the metaphor of "immigrant as pollutant" in media representations of immigration'. *Rhetoric and Public Affairs* 11(4): 569–601.

Clements, B. 2013. 'Public opinion and military intervention: Afghanistan, Iraq and Libya'. *Political Quarterly* 84(1): 119–131.

Cmiel, K. 2004. 'The recent history of human rights'. *American Historical Review* 109(1): 117–135.

Cohen, B. 1994. 'A view from the academy'. In *Taken by Storm: The Media, Public Opinion, and US Foreign Policy in the Gulf War*, W. L. Bennett and D. Paletz (eds) (pp. 8–11). Chicago: Chicago University Press.

Cohen, B. C. 1963. *The Press and Foreign Policy*. Princeton, NJ: Princeton University Press.

Cohen, N. 2013. *You Can't Read This Book: Censorship in an Age of Freedom*. London: Fourth Estate.

Cohen, S. 2011. *Folk Devils and Moral Panics: The Creation of the Mods and Rockers*. London: Routledge.

Cole, P. 2000. *Philosophies of Exclusion: Liberal Political Theory and Immigration*. Edinburgh: Edinburgh University Press.

Cole, W. M. 2010. 'No news is good news: human rights coverage in the American print media, 1980–2000'. *Journal of Human Rights* 9(3): 303–325.

Coliver, S. 1998. 'Commentary to: the Johannesburg principles on national security, freedom of expression and access to information'. *Human Rights Quarterly* 20(1): 12–80.

Cooper, A. F. and J. F. Turcotte. 2012. 'Celebrity diplomats as mobilisers? Celebrities and activism in a hypermediated time'. In *Media, Mobilization, and Human Rights: Mediating Suffering*, T. A. Borer (ed.) (pp. 181–204). London: Zed Books.

Cottle, S. 2008. *Global Crisis Reporting: Journalism in the Global Age*. Berkshire: Open University Press.

Cottle, S. 2009. 'Global crises in the news: staging new wars, disasters, and climate change'. *International Journal of Communication* 3: 494–516.

Cottle, S. 2011. 'Media and the Arab uprisings of 2011: research notes'. *Journalism* 12(5): 647–659.

Cottle, S. and M. Rai. 2008. 'Global 24/7 news providers: emissaries of global dominance or global public sphere?'. *Global Media and Communication* 4(2): 157–181.

Craft, S. and S. Waisbord. 2008. 'When foreign news remains foreign: cartoon controversies in the US and Argentine press'. In *Transnational Media Events: The Mohammed Cartoons and the Imagined Clash of Civilisation*, E. Eide, R. Kunelius and A. Phillips (eds) (pp. 133–148). Goteborg: Nordicom.

Cram, L. 2009. 'Introduction: banal Europeanism: European Union identity and national identities in synergy'. *Nations and Nationalism* 15(1): 101–108.

Crandall, C., S. Eidelman, L. J. Skitka and G. S. Morgan. 2008. 'Status quo framing increases support for torture'. *Social Influence* 1: 1–10.

Crelinsten, R. 2003. 'The world of torture: a constructed reality'. *Theoretical Criminology* 7(3): 293–318.

Crelinsten, R. 2005. 'How to make a torturer'. *Index on Censorship* 34(1): 72–77.

Crossman, R. 1977. *Diaries of a Cabinet Minister, Volume 3: Secretary of State for Social Services 1968–1970*. London: Hamish Hamilton/Jonathan Cape.

Curran, J. 2005. 'What democracy requires of the media'. In *The Press*, G. Overholser and K. Hall Jamieson (eds) (pp. 120–140). New York: Oxford University Press.

Daalder, I. H. 1999. 'And now, a Clinton Doctrine?' *Haagsche Courant*, 10 July.

Daadler, I. H. and M. E. O'Hanlon. 1999. 'Unlearning the lessons of Kosovo'. *Foreign Policy*, 116: 128–140.

Daalder, I. H. and M. E. O'Hanlon. 2000. *Winning Ugly NATO's War to Save Kosovo*. Washington, DC: Brookings Institution Press.

Daalder, I. H. and J. G. Stavridis. 2012. 'NATO's victory in Libya: the right way to run an intervention'. *Foreign Affairs* 91(2): 2–7.

Dahlgren, P. 2013. 'Online journalism and civic cosmopolitanism: professional vs. participatory ideals'. *Journalism Studies* 14(2): 156–171.

Dallaire, R. with B. Beardsley. 2003. *Shake Hands with the Devil: The Failure of Humanity in Rwanda*. Toronto: Random House Canada.

Daly, M. W. 2007. *Darfur's Sorrow: A History of Destruction and Genocide*. New York: Cambridge University Press.

Danner, M. W. 2004a. 'Abu Ghraib: the hidden story'. *New York Review of Books*, 7 October. Available at: www.nybooks.com/articles/archives/2004/oct/07/abu-ghraib-the-hidden-story/?page=1.

Danner, M. 2004b. *Torture and Truth: America, Abu Ghraib, and the War on Terror*. New York: New York Review Books.

Dannreuther, R. 2013. *International Security: The Contemporary Agenda*, 2nd edn. Cambridge: Polity Press.

Dauvergne, C. 1999. 'Amorality and humanitarianism in immigration law'. *Osgoode Hall Law Journal* 37(3): 598–623.

Davidson, J. W. 2013. 'France, Britain and the intervention in Libya: an integrated analysis'. *Cambridge Review of International Affairs* 26(2): 310–329.

Day, R. E. 2000. 'The "conduit metaphor" and the nature and politics of information studies'. *Journal of the American Society for Information Science* 51(9): 805–811.

Deibert, R. 2000. 'International plug'n play: citizen activism, the internet, and global public policy'. *International Studies Perspectives* 1(3): 255–272.

Delanty, G. 2006. 'The cosmopolitan imagination: critical cosmopolitanism and social theory'. *British Journal of Sociology* 57(1): 25–47.

Delanty, G. 2009. *The Cosmopolitan Imagination: The Renewal of Critical Social Theory*. Cambridge: Cambridge University Press.

Delgado, R. and J. Stefancic. 1997. *Must We Defend Nazis? Hate Speech, Pornography, and the New First Amendment*. New York: New York University Press.

Deng, F. M., S. Kimaro, T. Lyons, D. Rothchild and I. W. Zartman. 1996. *Sovereignty and Responsibility: Conflict Management in Africa*. Washington, DC: Brookings Institution Press.

Dershowitz, A. 2002. *Why Terrorism Works: Understanding the Threat, Responding to the Challenge*. New York: Yale University Press.

Des Forges, A. 2007. 'Call to genocide: radio in Rwanda, 1994'. In *The Media and the Rwanda Genocide*, A. Thompson (ed.) (pp. 41–54). London: Pluto Press.

Destexhe, A. 1995. *Rwanda and Genocide in the Twentieth Century*. London: Pluto Press.

Dhir, K. S. 2007. 'Stakeholder activisim through nonviolence'. *Corporate Communications: An International Journal* 12(1): 75–93.

Dieter, H. and R. Kumar. 2008. 'The downside of celebrity diplomacy: the neglected complexity of development'. *Global Governance* 14(3): 259–264.

Dittrich, L. 2009. 'Matt Damon: The celebrity shall save you'. *Esquire*, September: 118–125.

Donnelly, J. 2007. 'The relative universality of human rights'. *Human Rights Quarterly* 29(2): 281–306.

Donnelly, J. 2013a. *International Human Rights: Dilemmas in World Politics*, 4th edn. Boulder, CO: Westview Press.

Donnelly, J. 2013b. *Universal Human Rights in Theory and Practice*, 3rd edn. New York: Cornell University Press.

Douzinas, C. 2007. *Human Rights and Empire: The Political Philosophy of Cosmopolitanism*. London: Routledge-Cavendish.

Downie, L., Jr. 2013. *Special Report: The Obama Administration and the Press*. Report for the Committee to Protect Journalists. Available at: http://cpj.org/reports/2013/10/obama-and-the-press-us-leaks-surveillance-post-911.php.

Doyle, J. 2012. 'Hamza's failed bids to stay in UK cost us £1m: Justice Secretary orders immediate review following revelation'. *Daily Mail*, 7 November.

Doyle, M. 2007. 'Reporting the genocide'. In *The Media and the Rwanda Genocide*, A. Thompson (ed.) (pp. 145–159). London: Pluto Press.

Duffield, M. 2001. *Global Governance and the New Wars: The Merging of Development and Security*. London: Zed Books.

Duffy, B. and T. Frere-Smith. 2014. *Perceptions and Reality: Public Attitudes to Immigration*. London: Ipsos MORI Social Research Institute.

Dun, F. van. 2001. 'Human dignity: reason or desire? Natural rights versus human rights'. *Journal of Libertarian Studies* 15(4): 1–28.

Dunne, T. and M. Hanson. 2013. 'Human rights in international relations'. In *Human Rights: Politics and Practice*, 2nd edn, M. Goodhart (ed.) (pp. 42–57). Oxford: Oxford University Press.

Dussel, E. 2000. 'Europe, modernity, and Eurocentrism'. *Nepantla: Views from South* 1(3): 465–478.

Dworkin, R. 1986. *Law's Empire*. London: Fontana.

EACA. 2013. *Winners 2013*. Available at: http://act-responsible.org/ACT/EACAwinner13/eaca_winners13.htm.

Early, L. and L. Garlicki. 2012. 'Case of Othman (Abu Qatada) v. the United Kingdom European Court of Human Rights (Fourth Section) judgment'. *International Journal of Refugee Law* 24(2): 294–388.

Economist, The. 2011. 'David Cameron's war'. *The Economist*, 27 August.

Economist, The. 2013. 'Shutting down the internet: thou shalt not kill'. *The Economist*, 6 April.

Economist, The. 2014. 'Europe's populist insurgents: turning right'. *The Economist*, 4 January.

The Editorial Board. 2013. 'British press freedom under threat'. *New York Times*, 14 November.

Eggen, D. 2005. 'Bush authorized domestic spying'. *Washington Post*, 16 December.

Eke, C. 2008. 'Darfur: coverage of a genocide by three major US TV networks on their evening news'. *International Journal of Media and Cultural Politics* 4(3): 277–292.

Elder, M. 2013. 'Russia passes law banning gay "propaganda"'. *Guardian*, 11 June.

Ellinas, A. A. 2010. *The Media and the Far Right in Western Europe: Playing the Nationalist Card*. New York: Cambridge University Press.

Elshtain, J. B. 2002. 'Reflection on the problem of "dirty hands"'. In *Torture: A Collection*, S. Levinson (ed.) (pp. 77–89). Oxford: Oxford University Press.

Entman, R. 1993. 'Framing: toward clarification of a fractured paradigm'. *Journal of Communication* 43(4): 51–58.

Entman, R. 2004. *Projections of Power: Framing News, Public Opinion, and US Foreign Policy*. Chicago: University of Chicago Press.

Entman, R. 2006. 'Punctuating the homogeneity of institutionalized news: abusing prisoners at Abu Ghraib versus killing civilians at Fallujah'. *Political Communication* 23(2): 215–224.

Entman, R., J. Matthes and L. Pellicano. 2009. 'Nature, sources, and effects of news framing'. In *The Handbook of Journalism Studies*, K. Wahl-Jorgensen and T. Hanitzsch (eds) (pp. 175–190). London: Routledge.

European Parliament. 2013. *European Parliament Resolution on Qatar: Situation of Migrant Workers*. Brussels and Strabourg: European Parliament, 2013/2952(RSP).

Evans, G. 2008. *The Responsibility to Protect: Ending Mass Atrocity Crimes Once and for All*. Washington, DC: Brookings Institution Press.

Fabbrini, S. 2007. *Compound Democracies: Why the United States and Europe Are Becoming Similar*. Oxford: Oxford University Press.

Fair, J. E. and L. Parks. 2001. 'Africa on camera: television news coverage and aerial imaging of Rwandan refugees'. *Africa Today* 48(2): 35–57.

Falk, R. 2003. 'Humanitarian intervention: a forum'. *Nation*, 14 July.

Fein, H. 1990. 'Genocide: a sociological perspective'. *Current Sociology* 38(1): 1–126.

Fine, R. 2003. 'Kant's theory of cosmopolitanism and Hegel's critique'. *Philosophy and Social Criticism* 29(6): 609–660.

Fine, R. 2009. 'Cosmopolitanism and human rights: radicalism in a global age'. *Metaphilosophy* 40(1): 8–23.

Finney, N. 2003. *The Challenge of Reporting Refugees and Asylum Seekers*. London: ICAR.

Flikschuh, K. 2011. 'On the cogency of human rights'. *Jurisprudence* 2(1): 17–36.

Flint, J. and A. de Waal. 2008. *Darfur: A New History of a Long War*. London: Zed Books.

Føllesdal, A. 2009. 'Universal human rights as a shared political identity: impossible? Necessary? Sufficient?' *Metaphilosophy* 40(1): 77–91.

Foot, R. 2006. 'Torture: the struggle over a peremptory norm in a counter-terrorist era'. *International Relations* 20(2): 131–151.

Forsythe, D. P. 2012. *Human Rights in International Relations*, 3rd edn. Cambridge: Cambridge University Press.

Foster, L. 2013. Interview with the author.

Fraleigh, D. M. and J. S. Tuman. 2011. *Freedom of Expression in the Marketplace of Ideas*. London: Sage.

Franck, T. M. 2001. 'Are human rights universal?' *Foreign Affairs* 80(1): 191–204.

Franklin, B. 1997. *Newszak and News Media*. London: Arnold.

Freedman, L. 2000. 'Victims and victors: reflections on the Kosovo war'. *Review of International Studies* 26: 335-358.

Freedom House. 2013. *Freedom of the Press 2013: Middle East Volatility amid Global Decline*. Available at: www.freedomhouse.org/sites/default/files/FOTP%202013%20Full%20Report.pdf.

Freeman, G. 1995. 'Modes of immigration politics in liberal democratic states'. *International Migration Review* 29(4): 881–902.

Freeman, M. 2011. *Human Rights: An Interdisciplinary Approach*, 2nd edn. Cambridge: Polity Press.

Frohardt, M. and J. Temin. 2003. *Use and Abuse of Media in Vulnerable Societies*. Washington, DC: United States Institute of Peace.

Fryberg, S. A., N. M. Stephens, R. Covarrubias, H. R. Markus, E. D. Carter, G. A. Laiduc, and A. J. Salido. 2012. 'How the media frames the immigration debate: the critical role of location and politics'. *Analyses of Social Issues and Public Policy* 12(1): 96–112.

Fukuyama, F. 1992. *The End of History and the Last Man*. New York: Avon.

Galtung, J. and M. H. Ruge. 1965. 'The structure of foreign news: the presentation of the Congo, Cuba and Cyprus crises in four Norwegian newspapers'. *Journal of Peace Research* 2(1): 64–90.

Gamson, W. and A. Modigliani. 1987. 'The changing course of affirmative action'. In *Research in Political Sociology*, R. Braungart and M. Braungart (eds) (pp. 137–177). Greenwich: Jai Press.

Garton Ash, T. 2000. 'The war we almost lost'. *Guardian*, 4 September.

Gellner, E. 1994. *Conditions of Liberty: Civil Society and Its Rivals*. New York: Allen Lane.

Gibbs, D. 2000. '*Realpolitik* and humanitarian intervention: the case of Somalia'. *International Politics* 37: 41–55.

Gilboa, E. 2005. 'The CNN effect: the search for a communication theory of international relations'. *Political Communication* 22(1): 27–44.

Gill, N. 2009. 'Whose "no borders"? Achieving border liberalization for the right reasons'. *Refuge* 26(2): 107–120.

Gitlin, T. 1980. *The Whole World Is Watching*. Berkeley: University of California Press.

Gladstone, R. 2014. 'Number of Darfur's displaced surged in 2013'. *New York Times*, 23 January.

Gladwell, M. 2010. 'Small change: why the revolution will not be tweeted'. *New Yorker*, 4 October.

Glasgow University Media Group (GUMG). 1985. *War and Peace News*. Milton Keynes: Open University Press.

Goff, P. 1999. *The Kosovo News and Propaganda War*. Vienna: Vienna International Press Institute.

Goffman, E. 1974. *Frame Analysis: An Essay on the Organization of Experience*. Cambridge, MA: Harvard University Press.

Golding, P. and P. Elliot. 1979. *Making the News*. London: Longman.

Goldsmith, J. 2007. *The Terror Presidency: Law and Judgment inside the Bush Administration*. London: W. W. Norton.

Goodhart, M. 2003. 'Origins and universality in the human rights debates: cultural essentialism and the challenge of globalization'. *Human Rights Quarterly* 25(4): 935–964.

Gorman, S. 2008. 'NSA's domestic spying grows as agency sweeps up data'. *Wall Street Journal*, 10 March.

Gourevitch, P. 1998. *We Wish to Inform You that Tomorrow We Will Be Killed with Our Families*. New York: Picador.

Gow, J. 2003. *The Serbian Project and Its Adversaries*. Montreal: McGill-Queen's University Press.

Gowing, N. 1994. *Real Time Television Coverage of Armed Conflicts and Diplomatic Crises: Does it Pressure or Distort Foreign Policy Decisions*. Working paper for Joan Shorenstein Center on the Press, Politics and Public Policy. Available at: http://shorensteincenter.org/wp-content/uploads/2012/03/1994_01_gowing.pdf.

Graber, D. 2003a. 'Terrorism, censorship and the 1st Amendment: in search of policy guidelines'. In *Framing Terrorism: The News Media, the Government, and the Public*, P. Norris, M. Kern and M. Just (eds) (pp. 27–42). London: Routledge.

Graber, D. 2003b. 'The media and democracy: beyond myths and stereotypes'. *Annual Review of Political Science* 6: 139–160.

Graber, D. and G. Holyk. 2009. 'What explains torture coverage during war-time? A search for realistic answers'. In *Terrorism and Torture: An Interdisciplinary Perspective*, W. G. K. Stritzke, S. Lewandowsky, D. Denemark, J. Clare and F. Morgan (eds) (pp. 221–245). Cambridge: Cambridge University Press.

Greenberg, J. and S. Hier. 2001. 'Crisis, mobilization and collective problematization: "illegal" Chineese migrants and the Canadian news media'. *Journalism Studies* 2(4): 563–583.

Greenwald, G., E. MacAskill and L. Poitras. 2013. 'Edward Snowden: the whistleblower behind the NSA surveillance revelations'. *Guardian*, 10 June.

Grey, S. 2006. *Ghost Plane: The True Story of the CIA Torture Program*. New York: St Martin's Press.

Griffin, M. 2004. 'Picturing America's "war on terrorism" in Afghanistan and Iraq: photographic motives as news frames'. *Journalism* 5(4): 381–402.

Gronke, P., D. Rejali, D. Drenguis, J. Hicks, P. Miller and B. Nakayama. 2010. 'US public opinion on torture, 2001–2009'. *PS: Political Science & Politics* 43(3): 437–444.

Gross, O. 2002. 'The prohibition on torture and the limits of the law'. In *Torture: A Collection*, S. Levinson (ed.) (pp. 229–253). Oxford: Oxford University Press.

Gruley, J. and C. S. Duvall. 2012. 'The evolving narrative of the Darfur conflict as represented in *The New York Times* and the *Washington Post*, 2003–2009'. *GeoJournal* 77: 29–46.

Grzyb, A. 2009a. 'Media coverage, activism, and creating public will for intervention in Rwanda and Darfur'. In *The World and Darfur: International Response to Crimes against Humanity in Western Sudan*, A. Grzyb (ed.) (pp. 61–91). Montreal: McGill-Queen's University Press.

Grzyb, A. (ed.). 2009b. *The World and Darfur: International Response to Crimes against Humanity in Western Sudan*. Montreal: McGill-Queen's University Press.

Guicherd, C. 1999. 'International law and the war in Kosovo'. *Survival* 41(2): 19–34.

Habermas, J. 1989. *The Structural Transformation of the Public Sphere*. Cambridge: Polity Press.

Hall, E. B. 1906. *The Friends of Voltaire*. London: Smith, Elder.

Hallin, D. 1986. *The Uncensored War: The Media and Vietnam*. Berkeley: University of California Press.

Hamelink, C. J. 1994. *The Politics of World Communication: A Human Rights Perspective*. London: Sage.

Hammarberg, T. 2011. 'Foreword: media freedom in Europe'. In *Human Rights and a Changing Media Landscape*, H. R. Writings (ed.) (pp. 7–20). Strasbourg: Council of Europe Publishing.

Hammond, P. 2000. 'Reporting "humanitarian" warfare: propaganda, moralism and NATO's Kosovo war'. *Journalism Studies* 1(3): 365–386.

Hammond, P. 2007. *Framing post-Cold War Conflicts: The Media and International Intervention*. Manchester: Manchester University Press.

Hammond, P. and E. Herman (eds). 2000a. *Degraded Capability: The Media and the Kosovo Crisis*. London: Pluto Press.

Hammond, P. and E. Herman. 2000b. 'Conclusions: first casualty and beyond'. In *Degraded Capability: The Media and the Kosovo Crisis*, P. Hammond and E. Herman (eds) (pp. 200–208). London: Pluto Press.

Hanley, C. J. 2003. 'Former Iraqi detainees tell of riots, punishment in the sun, good Americans, and pitiless ones'. Associated Press, 29 October.

Hannerz, U. 1996. *Transnational Connections: Culture, People, Places*. London: Routledge.

Hansen, R. 2000. *Citizenship and Immigration in Post-war Britain*. Oxford: Oxford University Press.

Harcup, T. and D. O'Neill. 2001. 'What is news? Galtung and Ruge revisited'. *Journalism Studies* 2(2): 261–280.

Harding, L. 2012. *Mafia State: How One Reporter Became an Enemy of the Brutal New Russia*. London: Guardian Books.

Harff, B. 2003. 'No lessons learned from the Holocaust? Assessing risks of genocide and political mass murder since 1955'. *American Political Science Review* 97(1): 57–73.

Harff, B. and T. R. Gurr. 1989. 'Victims of the state: genocides, politicides and group repression since 1945'. *International Review of Victimology* 1(1): 23–41.

Harrison, S., Z. Todd and R. Lawton. 2008. 'Talk about terrorism and the media: communicating with the Conduit Metaphor'. *Communication, Culture & Critique* 1(4): 378–395.

Hart, P. 2011. 'Media grade Obama's bombing'. *Extra!*, May.

Harvey, D. 2009. *Cosmopolitanism and the Geographies of Freedom*. New York: Columbia University Press.

Hawkins, V. 2004. *The Silence of the UN Security Council: Conflict and Peace Enforcement in the 1990s*. Florence: European Press Academic Publishing.

Hawkins, V. 2008. *Stealth Conflicts: How the World's Worst Violence Is Ignored*. Aldershot: Ashgate.

Hawkins, V. 2011. 'Media selectivity and the other side of the CNN effect: the consequences of not paying attention to conflict'. *Media, War & Conflict* 4(1): 55–68.

Hayter, T. 2003. 'No borders: the case against immigration controls'. *Feminist Review* 73(1): 6–18.

Hehir, A. 2008. *Humanitarian Intervention after Kosovo: Iraq, Darfur and the Record of Global Civil Society*. Basingstoke: Palgrave Macmillan.

Hehir, A. 2010. *Humanitarian Intervention: An Introduction*. Basingstoke: Palgrave Macmillan.

Hehir, A. 2013a. 'Introduction: Libya and the Responsibility to Protect'. In *Libya: The Responsibility to Protect and the Future of Humanitarian Intervention*, A. Hehir and R. Murray (eds) (pp. 1–14). Basingstoke: Palgrave Macmillan.

Hehir, A. 2013b. 'The permanence of inconsistency: Libya, the Security Council, and the Responsibility to Protect'. *International Security* 38(1): 137–159.

Heinze, E., and R. Freedman. 2010. 'Public awareness of human rights: distortions in the mass media'. *International Journal of Human Rights* 14(4): 491–523.

Held, D. 1995. *Democracy and the Global Order: From the Modern State to Cosmopolitan Governance*. Cambridge: Polity Press.

Held, D. 2003. *Cosmopolitanism: A Defense*. Cambridge: Polity Press.

Herf, J. 2006. *The Jewish Enemy: Nazi Propaganda during World War II and the Holocaust*. Cambridge, MA: Harvard University Press.

Heritage, T. 2011. 'Analysis: journalist's murder a test case for Russia's Putin'. Reuters, 6 October.

Herman, E. 2003. 'The propaganda model: a retrospective'. *Against All Reason*, 9 December.

Herman, E. and N. Chomsky. 1988. *Manufacturing Consent: The Political Economy of the Mass Media*. London: Vintage.

Herman, E. and D. Peterson. 2000. 'CNN: selling NATO's war globally'. In *Degraded Capability: The Media and the Kosovo Crisis*, P. Hammond and E. Herman (eds) (pp. 111–122). London: Pluto Press.

Hersh, S. 2004a. *Chain of Command: The Road from 9/11 to Abu Ghraib*. New York: HarperCollins.

Hersh, S. 2004b. 'Torture at Abu Ghraib: American soldiers brutalized Iraqis. How far up does the responsibility go?' *New Yorker*, 10 May: 42–50.

Hersh, S. 2004c. 'Chain of command: how the Department of Defense mishandled the disaster at Abu Ghraib'. *New Yorker*, 17 May: 38–43.

Hersh, S. 2004d. 'The gray zone: how a secret Pentagon program came to Abu Ghraib'. *New Yorker*, 24 May: 38–44.

Hervik, P. 2008. 'Original spin and its side effects: freedom of speech as Danish news management'. In *Transnational Media Events: The Mohammed Cartoons and the Imagined Clash of Civilisations*, E. Eide, R. Kurnelius and A. Phillips (eds) (pp. 59–80). Goteborg: Nordicom.

Higgins, P. 2008. 'Open borders and the right to immigration'. *Human Rights Review* 9: 525–535.

Higgins, R. 1973. 'The right in international law of an individual to enter, stay in and leave a country'. *International Affairs* 49(3): 341–357.

Higham, S. and J. Stephens. 2004. 'Punishment and amusement: documents indicate 3 photos were not staged for interrogation'. *Washington Post*, 22 May.

Hilsum, L. 1995. 'Where is Kigali?' *Granta* 51: 145–179.

Hilsum, L. 2012. *Sandstorm: Libya in the Time of Revolution*. London: Faber & Faber.

Hines, B. 2010. 'The right to migrate as a human right: the current Argentine immigration law'. *Cornell International Law Journal* 43(3): 472–511.

Hirsch, A. 2011. 'The stain of complicity in torture: the British lawyers who wrote the official guidance on complicity in torture for the war on terror bear a heavy responsibility'. *Guardian*, 18 January.

Hodge, C. 2000. 'Casual war: NATO's intervention in Kosovo'. *Ethics and International Affairs* 14: 39–54.

Hodkinson, P. 2011. *Media, Culture and Society: An Introduction*. London: Sage.

Hoge, J. F. 1994. 'Media pervasiveness'. *Foreign Affairs* 73: 136–144.

Höijer, B. 2004. 'The discourse of global compassion: the audience and media reporting of human suffering'. *Media, Culture and Society* 26(4): 513–531.

Hollifield, J. F. 1992. *Immigrants, Markets, and States: The Political Economy of Postwar Europe*. London: Harvard University Press.

Holzgrefe, J. L. and R. Keohane (eds). 2005. *Humanitarian Intervention: Ethical, Legal, and Political Dilemmas*. Cambridge: Cambridge University Press.

Human Rights Watch (HRW). 2000. 'Introduction'. In *World Report 2000*, Human Rights Watch (ed.). New York: Human Rights Watch. Available at: www.hrw.org/legacy/wr2k/Front.htm#TopOfPage.

Human Rights Watch (HRW). 2005. *Human Rights Watch Statement on US Secret Detention Facilities in Europe*. New York: Human Rights Watch.

Human Rights Watch (HRW). 2007. 'A shrinking realm: freedom of expression since 9/11'. In *World Report 2007*, Human Rights Watch (ed.) (pp. 63–86). New York: Human Rights Watch.

Huntington, S. 1993. 'The clash of civilizations?' *Foreign Affairs* 72(3): 22–49.

Ignatieff, M. 1997. *The Warrior's Honour: Ethnic War and the Modern Conscience*. New York: Henry.

Ignatieff, M. (ed.). 2001a. *Human Rights as Politics and Idolatry*. Princeton, NJ: Princeton University Press.

Ignatieff, M. 2001b. *Virtual War: Kosovo and Beyond*. London: Vintage Books.

Ignatieff, M. 2004. *The Lesser Evil: Political Ethics in an Age of Terror*. Toronto: Penguin.

Ilic, V. 2001. 'Yugoslavia: displacement from Kosovo: from patronage to self-help'. In *Caught between Borders: Response Strategies of Internally Displaced*, M. Vincent and B. R. Sorensen (eds) (pp. 250–265). London: Pluto Press.

Independent International Commission on Kosovo (IICK). 2000. *Kosovo Report*. Oxford: Oxford University Press.

Information Centre about Asylum and Refugees in the UK (ICAR). 2004. *Media Image, Community Impact*. London: ICAR.

Intelligence and Security Committee (ISC). 2007. *Rendition*. London: Intelligence and Security Committee.

International Commission of Inquiry on Darfur. 2005. *Report of the International Commission of Inquiry on Darfur to the United Nations Secretary-General*. Geneva: International Commission of Inquiry on Darfur.

International Commission on Intervention and State Sovereignty (ICISS). 2001. *The Responsibility to Protect*. Ottawa: International Development Research Centre.

International Council on Human Rights Policy (ICHRP). 2002. *Journalism, Media and the Challenge of Human Rights Reporting*. Geneva: ICHRP.

International Crisis Group (ICG). 2011. *Popular Protests in the Middle East and North Africa: Making Sense of Libya*. Brussels: ICG, Middle East/North Africa Report No. 107.

International Federation of Journalists. 1999. *The Role of Media in Promotion of Human Rights and Democratic Development in Africa*. Brussels: International Federation of Journalists.

International Press Institute (IPI). 2008. *IPI Watch List: Russia – June 2008 Update*. Vienna: International Press Institute.

Internews. 2012. *Speak up, Speak out: A Toolkit for Reporting on Human Rights Issues*. Washington, DC: Internews.

Jackson, R. 2005. *Writing the War on Terror: Language, Politics and Counter-Terrorism*. Manchester: Manchester University Press.

Jackson, R. 2007. 'Language, policy and the construction of a torture culture in the war on terrorism'. *Review of International Studies* 33(3): 353–371.

Jacobs, M. and T. Wright. 2013. 'Commentary: making sense of Snowden'. *Political Quarterly* 84(4): 433–435.

Jakobsen, P. V. 1996. 'National interest, humanitarianism or CNN: what triggers UN peace enforcement after the Cold War?' *Journal of Peace Research* 33(2): 205–215.

Jakobsen, P. V. 2000. 'Focus on the CNN effect misses the point: the real media impact on conflict management is invisible and indirect'. *Journal of Peace Research* 37(2): 131–143.

Jasperson, A. E. and M. O. El-Kikhia. 2003. 'CNN and Al Jazeera's media coverage of America's war on terror'. In *Framing Terrorism: The News Media, the Government, and the Public*, P. Norris, M. Kern and M. Just (eds) (pp. 113–132). London: Routledge.

Jatras, J. 2000. 'NATO's myths and bogus justifications for intervention'. In *NATO's Empty Victory: A Postmortem on the Balkan War*, T. G. Carpenter (ed.) (pp. 21–31). Washington, DC: Cato Institute.

Jewell, J. 2011. 'Libya: communicating intervention: how persuasive was media involvement?' *Intermedia* 39(3): 30–35.

Johnstone, D. 2000. 'NATO and the new world order: ideals and self-interest'. In *Degraded Capability: The Media and the Kosovo Crisis*, P. Hammond and E. Herman (eds) (pp. 7–18). London: Pluto Press.

Johnstone, D. 2002. *Fool's Crusade*. London: Pluto Press.

Jones, A. L. and R. E. Howard-Hassmann. 2005. 'Under strain: human rights and international law in the post 9/11 era'. *Journal of Human Rights* 4(1): 61–71.

Jones, P. 1994. *Rights*. Basingstoke: Macmillan.

Jones, S. 2008. 'Television news: geographic and source biases, 1982–2004'. *International Journal of Communication* 2: 223–252.

Jones, T. M. and P. Sheets. 2009. 'Torture in the eye of the beholder: social identity, news coverage, and Abu Ghraib'. *Political Communication* 26(3): 278–295.

Joppke, C. 1998. *Challenge to the Nation-state: Immigration in Western Europe and the United States*. Oxford: Oxford University Press.

Joyner, C. 2007. '"The Responsibility to Protect": humanitarian concern and the lawfulness of armed intervention'. *Virginia Journal of International Law* 47: 693–723.

Judah, T. 1999. 'Kosovo's road to war'. *Survival* 41(2): 5–18.

Judah, T. 2000. *Kosovo: War and Revenge*. New Haven, CT: Yale University Press.

Kaldor, M. 2003. *Global Civil Society: An Answer to War*. Cambridge: Polity Press.

Kaldor, M. 2010. 'Humanitarian intervention: towards a cosmopolitan approach'. In *The Cosmopolitanism Reader*, G. W. Brown and D. Held (eds) (pp. 334–350). Cambridge: Polity Press.

Kaldor, M. 2012. *New and Old Wars: Organised Violence in a Global Era*, 3rd edn. London: Polity Press.

Kaplan, A. 2005. 'Where is Guantanamo?' *American Quarterly* 57(3): 831–858.

Keane, F. 1996. *Season of Blood: A Rwandan Journey*. London: Penguin.

Kellner, D. 2005. *Media Spectacle and the Crisis of Democracy*. Boulder, CO: Paradigm.

Kellner, D. 2012. *Media Spectacle and Insurrection 2011: From the Arab Uprisings to Occupy Everywhere*. London: Bloomsbury.

Kessler, S. 2012. 'Amplifying individual impact: social media's emerging role in activism'. In *Media, Mobilization, and Human Rights: Mediating Suffering*, T. A. Borer (ed.) (pp. 205–215). London: Zed Books.

Kierulf, A. and H. Ronning (eds). 2009. *Freedom of Speech Abridged? Cultural, Legal and Philosophical Challenges*. Goteborg: Nordicom.

Kimani, M. 2007. 'RTLM: the medium that became a tool for mass murder'. In *The Media and the Rwanda Genocide*, A. Thompson (ed.) (pp. 110–124). London: Pluto Press.

Kim Dae, J. 1994. 'A response to Lee Kuan Yew: is culture destiny? The myth of Asia's anti-democratic values'. *Foreign Affairs* 73(6): 189–194.

King, R. and N. Wood. 2001. *Media and Migration*. London: Routledge.

Klang, M. 2004. 'Virtual sit-ins, civil disobedience and cyberterrorism'. In *Human Rights in the Digital Age*, M. Klang and A. Murray (eds) (pp. 135–145). London: Routledge.

Klein, N. 2005. 'The true purpose of torture: Guantanamo is there to terrorise – both inmates and the wider world'. *Guardian*, 14 May.

Knightley, P. 2004. *The First Casualty: The War Correspondent as Hero and Myth-Maker from the Crimea to Iraq*. Baltimore, MD: Johns Hopkins University Press.

Koppelman, A. 2009. 'Obama reframes the torture debate'. *Salon.com*. 30 April.

Kornblut, A. E. 2010. 'In interview, Bush defends Iraq war and waterboarding'. *Washington Post*, 9 November.

Krauthammer, C. 1999. 'The short, unhappy life of humanitarian war'. *National Interest* 57(5): 5–8.

Krimsky, G. A. 2002. 'The view from abroad'. *American Journalism Review*, January/February. Available at: www.ajr.org/article.asp?id=2444.

Kuper, L. 1981. *Genocide: Its Political Use in the Twentieth Century*. New Haven, CT: Yale University Press.

Kuper, L. 1985. *The Prevention of Genocide*. New Haven, CT: Yale University Press.

Kuperman, A. J. 2006. 'Suicidal rebellions and the moral hazard of humanitarian intervention'. In *Gambling on Humanitarian Intervention: Moral Hazard, Rebellion and Civil War*, T. Crawford and A. J. Kuperman (eds) (pp. 1–25). London: Routledge.

Kuperman, A. J. 2013. 'A model humanitarian intervention? Reassessing NATO's Libya campaign'. *International Security* 38(1): 105–136.

Kurasawa, F. 2004. 'A cosmopolitanism from below: alternative globalization and the creation of a solidarity without bounds'. *European Journal of Sociology/Archives* 45(2): 233–255.

Kyriakidou, M. 2009. 'Imagining ourselves beyond the nation? Exploring cosmopolitanism in relation to media coverage of distant suffering'. *Studies in Ethnicity and Nationalism* 9(3): 481–496.

Lagerkvist, J. 2012. 'The Wukan uprising and Chinese state–society relations: toward "shadow civil society"?' *International Journal of China Studies* 3(3): 345–361.

Lakoff, G. and S. Ferguson. 2006. *The Framing of Immigration*. Berkeley, CA: The Rockridge Institute.

Lang, K. and G. E. Lang. 1966. 'The mass media and voting'. In *Reader in Public Opinion and Communication*, 2nd edn, B. Berelson and M. Janowitz (eds) (pp. 455–472). New York: Free Press.

La Rue, F. 2011. *Report of the Special Rapporteur to the General Assembly on the Right to Freedom of Opinion and Expression Exercised through the Internet*. Geneva: United Nations Office of the High Commissioner on Human Rights, Report No. A/66/290. Available at: www.un.org/apps/news/story.asp?NewsID=40148#.U2YtascsiKw.

La Rue, F. 2013. *Report of the Special Rapporteur to the Human Rights Council on the Implications of States' Surveillance of Communications on the Exercise of the Human Rights to Privacy and to Freedom of Opinion and* Expression. Geneva: United Nations Office of the High Commissioner on Human Rights, Report No. A/HRC/23/40.

Lasswell, H. 1948. 'The structure and function of communication in society'. In *The Communication of Ideas*, L. Bryson (ed.) (pp. 37–51). New York: Institute for Religious and Social Studies.

Lasswell, H. 1971. *Propaganda Technique in World War I*. Cambridge, MA: MIT Press.

Lauren, P. G. 1998. *The Evolution of International Human Rights: Visions Seen*. Philadelphia: University of Pennsylvania Press.

LeBlanc, L. J. 1991. *Development of the Rule on Genocide*. Durham, NC: Duke University Press.

Lecheler, S. and C. H. De Vreese. 2010. 'Framing Serbia: the effects of news framing on public support for EU enlargement'. *European Political Science Review* 2(1): 73–93.

Leiken, R. 2005. 'Europe's angry Muslims'. *Foreign Affairs* 84(4): 120–135.

Lemarchand, R. 2009. 'The 1994 Rwanda genocide'. In *Century of Genocide: Critical Essays and Eyewitness Accounts,* S. Totten and W. S. Parsons (eds) (pp. 482–504). London: Routledge.

Lemkin, R. 1944. *Axis Rule in Occupied Europe*. Washington, DC: Carnegie Endowment for International Peace.

Lemkin, R. 1947. 'Genocide as a crime under international law'. *American Journal of International Law* 41(1): 145–151.

Lepard, B. 2002. *Rethinking Humanitarian Intervention: A Fresh Approach Based on Fundamental Ethical Principles in International Law and World Religions*. University Park: Pennsylvania State University.

Levin, L. 2012. *Human Rights: Questions and Answers*, 6th edn. Paris: UNESCO Publishing.

Levinson, S. (ed.). 2002. *Torture: A Collection*. Oxford: Oxford University Press.

Lewis, J., A. Williams and B. Franklin. 2008a. 'A compromised fourth estate? UK news journalism, public relations and news sources'. *Journalism Studies* 9(1): 1–20.

Lewis, J., A. Williams and B. Franklin. 2008b. 'Four rumours and an explanation: a political economic account of journalists' changing newsgathering and reporting practices'. *Journalism Practice* 2(1): 27–45.

Lindsey, R. A. 2013. 'What the Arab Spring tells us about the future of social media in revolutionary movements'. *Small Wars Journal*, 29 July.

Lippmann, W. 1922. *Public Opinion*. New York: Free Press.

Livingston, S. 1997. *Clarifying the CNN Effect: An Examination of Media Effects According to Type of Military Intervention*. Cambridge, MA: The Joan Shorenstein Barone Center on the Press, Politics and Public Policy at Harvard University.

Livingston, S. 2000. 'Media coverage of the war: an empirical assessment'. In *Kosovo and the Challenge of Humanitarian Intervention: Selective Indignation, Collective Action, and International Citizenship*, A. Schanabel and R. Thakur (eds) (pp. 360–384). Tokyo: United Nations University Press.

Livingston, S. and T. Eachus. 1995. 'Humanitarian crises and US foreign policy: Somalia and the CNN effect reconsidered'. *Political Communication* 12(4): 413–429.

Livingston, S. and T. Eachus. 1999. 'US coverage of Rwanda'. In *The Path of a Genocide*, H. Adelman and A. Suhrke (eds) (pp. 210–246). London: Transaction Publishers.

Louw, E. 2010. *The Media and Political Process*, 2nd edn. London: Sage.

Lu, C. 2006. *Just and Unjust Interventions in World Politics: Public and Private*. Basingstoke: Palgrave Macmillan.

Lukes, S. 2006. 'Liberal democratic torture'. *British Journal of Political Science* 36(1): 1–16.

Lull, J. 2007. *Culture-on-Demand: Communication in a Crisis World*. Oxford: Blackwell.

Lyons, G. and M. Mastanduno. 1995. 'Introduction: international intervention, state sovereignty, and the future of international society'. In *Beyond Westphalia: State Sovereignty and International Intervention*, G. Lyons and M. Mastanduno (eds) (pp. 1–20). Baltimore, MD: Johns Hopkins University Press.

McCombs, M. 2004. *Setting the Agenda: The Mass Media and Public Opinion*. Cambridge: Polity Press.

McCombs, M. and D. Shaw. 1972. 'The agenda-setting function of mass media'. *Public Opinion Quarterly* 36(2): 176–187.

McCorquodale, R. and R. Fairbrother. 1999. 'Globalisation and human rights'. *Human Rights Quarterly* 21(3): 735–766.

McCoy, A. W. 2006. *A Question of Torture: CIA Interrogation, from the Cold War to the War on Terror*. New York: Metropolitan Books.

MacIntyre, A. 1995. 'Is patriotism a virtue?'. In *Theorizing Citizenship*, R. Beiner (ed.) (pp. 209–228). Albany: State University of New York Press.

MacKinnon, R. 2009. 'China's censorship 2.0: how companies censor bloggers'. *First Monday* 14(2). Available at: http://dx.doi.org/10.5210/fm.v14i2.2378.

McLaughlin, G. 2002a. 'Rules of engagement: television journalism and NATO's "faith in bombing" during the Kosovo crisis, 1999'. *Journalism Studies* 3(2): 257–266.

McLaughlin, G. 2002b. *The War Correspondent*. London: Pluto Press.

McLuhan, M. 1964. *Understanding Media*. New York: Mentor.

Mcmahon, E. R. 2012. *The Universal Periodic Review: A Work in Progress*. Berlin: Friedrich Ebert Stiftung.

McNair, B. 2009. *News and Journalism in the UK*, 5th edn. London: Routledge.

McNair, B. 2011. *An Introduction to Political Communication*, 5th edn. London: Routledge.

McNulty, M. 1999. 'Media ethnicisation and the international response to war and genocide in Rwanda'. In *The Media of Conflict*, T. Allen and J. Seaton (eds) (pp. 268–286). London: Zed Books.

McPherson, E. 2010. *Human Rights Reporting in Mexico*. New York: Guilford Press.

McPherson, E. 2012. 'How editors choose which human rights news to cover: a case study of Mexican newspapers'. In *Media, Mobilization, and Human Rights: Mediating Suffering*, T. A. Borer (ed.) (pp. 96–121). London: Zed Books.

McQuail, D. 1994. *Mass Communication Theory*. London: Sage.

Malone, D. M. (ed.). 2004. *The UN Security Council: From the Cold War to the 21st Century*. Boulder, CO: Lynne Rienner Publishers.

Mamdani, M. 2007. 'The politics of naming: genocide, civil war, insurgency'. *London Review of Books*, 8 March.

Mandelbaum, M. 1999. 'A perfect failure: NATO's war against Yugoslavia'. *Foreign Affairs* 78(5): 2–8.

Margulies, J. 2006. *Guantanamo and the Abuse of Presidential Power*. London: Simon and Schuster.

Marty, D. 2006. *Alleged Secret Detentions and Unlawful Inter-state Transfers Involving Council of Europe Member States*. Strasbourg: Council of Europe, Parliamentary Assembly.

Matsuda, M. J., C. R. Lawrence III, R. Delgado and K. W. Crenshaw. 1993. *Words that Wound: Critical Race Theory, Assaultive Speech, and the First Amendment*. Boulder, CO: Westview Press.

Mayer, J. 2005. 'Outsourcing torture'. *New Yorker*, 14 February.

Mayroz, E. 2008. 'Ever again? The United States, genocide suppression, and the crisis in Darfur'. *Journal of Genocide Research* 10(3): 359–388.

Melvern, L. 2006. 'Rwanda and Darfur: the media and the Security Council'. *International Relations* 20(1): 93–104.

Melvern, L. 2007. 'Missing the story: the media and the Rwanda genocide'. In *The Media and the Rwanda Genocide*, A. Thompson (ed.) (pp. 198–210). London: Pluto Press.

Mendel, T. 2003. 'National security vs. openness: an overview and status report on the Johannesburg Principles'. In *National Security and Open Government: Striking the Right Balance* (pp. 1–32). Syracuse, NY: Campbell Public Affairs Institute.

Mermin, J. 1999. *Debating War and Peace: Media Coverage of US Intervention in the Post-Vietnam Era*. Princeton, NJ: Princeton University Press.

Metzl, J. 1996. 'Information technology and human rights'. *Human Rights Quarterly* 18(4): 705–746.

Michaelsen, C. 2012. 'The renaissance of non-refoulement? The Othman (Abu Qatada) decision of the European Court of Human Rights'. *International and Comparative Law Quarterly* 61(3): 750–765.

Midlarsky, M. 2005. *The Killing Trap: Genocide in the Twentieth Century*. New York: Cambridge University Press.

Mill, J. S. 1987 [1859]. *On Liberty*. Harmondsworth: Penguin.

Minear, L., C. Scott and T. G. Weiss. 1996. *The News Media, Civil War and Humanitarian Action*. London: Lynne Rienner Publishers.

Mitchell, J. 2014. 'Mediating cosmopolitanism: contests, ambiguities, critiques and questions'. In *Cosmopolitanism, Religion and the Public Sphere*, M. Rovisco and S. Kim (eds) (pp. 121–141). London: Routledge.

Modood, T. 2006. 'The liberal dilemma: integration or vilification?' *International Migration* 44(5): 4–7.

Moeller, S. 1999. *Compassion Fatigue: How the Media Sell Disease, Famine, War and Death*. New York: Routledge.

Morozov, E. 2011. *The Net Delusion: The Dark Side of Internet Freedom*. New York: Public Affairs Books.

Morris, J. 2013. 'Libya and Syria: R2P and the spectre of the swinging pendulum'. *International Affairs* 89(5): 1265–1283.

Morris, L. 2002. *Managing Migration: Civic Stratification and Migrants Rights*. London: Routledge.

Moss, K. 2009. *Security and Liberty: Restriction by Stealth*. London: Palgrave Macmillan.

Moss, K. 2011. *Balancing Liberty and Security: Human Rights, Human Wrongs*. Basingstoke: Palgrave Macmillan.

Motomura, H. 2006. *Americans in Waiting: The Lost Story of Immigration and Citizenship in the United States*. Oxford: Oxford University Press.

Münkler, H. 2004. *The New Wars*. London: Polity Press.

Murdie, A. 2009. 'The impact of human rights NGO activity on human rights practices'. *International NGO Journal* 4(10): 421–440.

Murray, R. W. 2013. 'Humanitarianism, responsibility or rationality? Evaluating intervention as state strategy'. In *Libya: The Responsibility to Protect and the Future of Humanitarian Intervention*, A. Hehir and R. Murray (eds) (pp. 15–33). Basingstoke: Palgrave Macmillan.

Mutua, M. 2001. 'Savages, victims, and saviours: the metaphor of human rights'. *Harvard International Law Journal* 42(1): 201–245.

Mutua, M. 2002. *Human Rights: A Political and Cultural Discourse*. Pennsylvania: University of Pennsylvania Press.

Naidoo, A. 2010. 'Activisim or slacktivisim: is the web making it too easy?' *Memebum*, 14 July.

National Union of Journalists (NUJ). 2005. *Fair Play: Refugees and Asylum Seekers in Scotland: A Guide for Journalists*. Scotland: Oxfam.

Nava, M. 2007. *Visceral Cosmopolitanism: Gender, Culture and the Normalization of Difference*. Oxford: Berg.

Negrine, R. and J. Stanyer (eds). 2007. *The Political Communication Reader*. Abingdon: Routledge.

Neuman, J. 1996. *Lights, Camera, War: Is Media Technology Driving International Politics?* New York: St Martin's Press.

Neuman, W. 2001. 'The impact of the new media'. In *Mediated Politics: Communication in the Future of Democracy*, W. L. Bennett and R. M. Entman (eds) (pp. 299–322). Cambridge: Cambridge University Press.

Nickel, H. W. 2007. *Making Sense of Human Rights*, 2nd edn. Oxford: Blackwell Publishing.

Nussbaum, M. 2010. 'Kant and cosmopolitanism'. In *The Cosmopolitanism Reader*, G. W. Brown and D. Held (eds) (pp. 27–44). Cambridge: Polity Press.

Nussbaum, M. and J. Cohen. 2002. *For Love of Country: Debating the Limits of Patriotism*. Boston, MA: Beacon Press.

Nye, J. 1999a. 'Redefining NATO's mission in the information age'. *NATO Review* 47: 12–15.

Nye, J. 1999b. 'Redefining the national interest'. *Foreign Affairs* 78(4): 22–35.

Oates, S. 2008. *Introduction to Media and Politics*. London: Sage.

O'Byrne, D. J. 2003. *Human Rights: An Introduction*. Harlow: Pearson Education.

Office of the High Commissioner for Human Rights (OHCHR). 2013. 'UK: "National security concerns must never justify intimidating journalists into silence", warn UN experts. Press release. Geneva: Office of the High Commissioner for Human Rights. Available at: www.ohchr.org/EN/NewsEvents/Pages/DisplayNews.aspx?NewsID=13678.

Okazaki, S. and C. Taylor. 2013. 'Social media and international advertising: theoretical challenges and future directions'. *International Marketing Review* 30(1): 56–71.

Omaar, R. and A. de Waal. 1993. 'Disaster pornography from Somalia'. *Media and Values* 61: 13–14.

O'Neill, O. 1975. 'Lifeboat Earth'. *Philosophy and Public Affairs* 4(3): 273–292.

O'Neill, O. 2006. 'A right to offend?' *Guardian*, 13 February.

O'Neill, W. G. 2002. *Kosovo: An Unfinished Peace*. London: Lynne Rienner Publishers.

Ong, J. C. 2009. 'Cultural studies: the cosmopolitan continuum: locating cosmopolitanism in media and cultural studies'. *Media, Culture and Society* 31(3): 449–466.

Orford, A. 2003. *Reading Humanitarian Intervention*. Cambridge: Cambridge University Press.

Osiatyński, W. 2009. *Human Rights and Their Limits*. Cambridge: Cambridge University Press.

O'Sullivan, D. 2000. 'Is the Declaration of Human Rights universal?' *International Journal of Human Rights* 4(1): 25–53.

Ovsiovitch, J. S. 1993. 'News coverage of human rights'. *Political Research Quarterly* 46: 671–689.

Pan, Z. and G. Kosicki. 1993. 'Framing analysis: an approach to news discourse'. *Political Communication* 10(1): 55–75.

Pape, R. A. 2012. 'When duty calls: A pragmatic standard of humanitarian intervention'. *International Security* 37(1): 41–80.

Park, D. 2002. 'Media, democracy, and human rights in Argentina'. *Journal of Communication Inquiry* 26(3): 237–260.

Parks, L. 2009. 'Digging into Google Earth: an analysis of "crisis in Darfur"'. *Geoforum* 40(4): 535–545.

Parry, J. T. 2004. 'Escalation and necessity'. In *Torture: A Collection*, S. Levinson (ed.) (pp. 145–164). Oxford: Oxford University Press.

Pearlman, A. 2012. 'The world's 7 worst internet censorships offenders'. *Global Post*, 4 April. Available at: www.globalpost.com/dispatches/globalpost-blogs/rights/the-worlds-7-worst-internet-censorship-offenders.

Pease, K. K. and D. P. Forsythe. 1993. 'Human rights, humanitarian intervention, and world politics'. *Human Rights Quarterly* 15(2): 290–314.

Peirce, G. 2010. *Dispatches from the Dark Side: On Torture and the Death of Justice*. London: Verso.

Peskin, V. 2008. *International Justice in Rwanda and the Balkans: Virtual Trials and the Struggle for State Cooperation*. New York: Cambridge University Press.

Philo, G., E. Briant and P. Donald. 2013. *Bad News for Refugees*. London: Pluto Press.

Pogge, T. 1994. 'Cosmopolitanism and sovereignty'. In *Political Restructuring in Europe: Ethical Perspectives*, C. Brown (ed.) (pp. 85–118). London: Routledge.

Posner, R. A. 2002. 'The best offense'. *New Republic*, 2 September.

Power, S. 2002. *'A Problem from Hell': America and the Age of Genocide*. London: Flamingo.

Preston, A. 1996. 'Television news and the Bosnian conflict: distance, proximity, impact'. In *Bosnia by Television*, J. Gow, R. Paterson and A. Preston (eds) (pp. 112–116). London: British Film Institute.

Priest, D. 2005. 'CIA holds terror suspects in secret prisons: debate is growing within agency about legality and morality of overseas system set up after 9/11'. *Washington Post*, 2 November.

Priest, D. and B. Gellman 2002. 'US decries abuse but defends interrogations: "stress and duress" tactics used on terrorism suspects held in secret overseas facilities'. *Washington Post*, 26 December.

Pritchard, K. J. 1991. 'Human rights: a decent respect for public opinion'. *Human Rights Quarterly* 13: 123–142.

Pruce, J. R. 2012. 'The spectacle of suffering and humanitarian intervention in Somalia'. In *Media, Mobilization, and Human Rights: Mediating Suffering*, T. A. Borer (ed.) (pp. 216–239). London: Zed Books.

Prunier, G. 2005. *Darfur: The Ambiguous Genocide*. Ithaca, NY: Cornell University Press.

Qureshi, A. 2009. *Rules of the Game: Detention, Deportation, Disappearance*. London: C. Hurst.

Ramos, H., J. Ron and O. N. T. Thoms. 2007. 'Shaping the Northern media's human rights coverage, 1986–2000'. *Journal of Peace Research* 44(4): 385–406.

Ramsay, M. 2006. 'Can the torture of terrorist suspects be justified?' *International Journal of Human Rights* 10(2): 103–119.

Ramsey, P. 2002. *The Just War: Force and Political Responsibility*. Lanham, MD: Rowman & Littlefield.

Rasmussen, A. F. 2005. Official response to ambassadors, 21 October.

Rawls, J. 1985. 'Justice as fairness: political not metaphysical'. *Phylosophy and Public Affairs* 14(3): 223–251.

Rawls, J. 1999. *The Law of Peoples*. Cambridge, MA: Harvard University Press.

Reddy, M. J. 1994. 'The Conduit Metaphor: a case of frame conflict in our language about language'. In *Metaphor and Thought*, A. Ortony (ed.) (pp. 164–201). Cambridge: Cambridge University Press.

Reeves, E. 2004. 'Secretary of State Colin Powell's genocide determination: what it does, and doesn't, mean for Darfur'. *H-Genocide*, 10 September.

Reisman, M. 1984. 'Reporting the facts as they are not known: media responsibility in concealed human rights violations'. *American Journal of International Law* 78: 650–652.

Reisman, M. 1985. 'Criteria for the lawful use of force in international law'. *Yale Journal of International Law* 10: 279–285.

Reporters without Borders. 2013. *World Press Freedom Index 2013: Dashed Hopes Follow Spring*. Paris: Reporters without Borders.

Ricchiardi, S. and M. Cirillo. 2004. 'Missed signals: why did it take so long for the news media to break the story of prisoner abuse at Abu Ghraib?' *American Journalism Review* 26: 22–30.

Richie, A. 1998. *Faust's Metropolis: A History of Berlin*. London: HarperCollins.

Robbins, B. 2012. *Perpetual War: Cosmopolitanism from the Viewpoint of Violence*. Durham, NC: Duke University Press.

Roberts, A. 1999. 'NATO's "humanitarian war" over Kosovo'. *Survival* 41(3): 102–123.

Roberts, A. 2000. 'The so called "right" to humanitarian intervention'. *Yearbook of International Humanitarian Law* 3: 3–51.

Robertson, A. 2010. *Mediated Cosmopolitanism: The World of Television News*. Cambridge: Polity Press.

Robertson, G. 2002. *Crimes against Humanity*. London: Penguin.

Robinson, P. 2001. 'Operation Restore Hope and the illusion of a news media driven intervention'. *Political Studies* 49(5): 941–956.

Robinson, P. 2002. *The CNN Effect: The Myth of News, Foreign Policy and Intervention*. London: Routledge.

Robinson, P. 2004. 'Researching US media–state relations and twenty-first century wars'. In *Reporting War: Journalism in Wartime*, S. Allan and B. Zelizer (eds) (pp. 96–112). London: Routledge.

Robinson, P. 2005. 'The CNN effect revisited'. *Critical Studies in Media Communication* 22(4): 344–349.

Robinson, P. 2012. 'News media and war'. In *The Sage Handbook of Political Communication*, H. A. Semetko and M. Scammell (eds) (pp. 342–355). London: Sage.

Ron, J., H. Ramos and K. Rodgers. 2005. 'Transnational information politics: NGO human rights reporting, 1986–2000'. *International Studies Quarterly* 49: 557–587.

Ronzitti, N. 1999. 'Lessons of international law from NATO's armed intervention against the Federal Republic of Yugoslavia'. *International Spectator* 34(3): 45–54.

Rose, D. 2004a. *Guantanamo: America's War on Human Rights*. London: Faber & Faber.

Rose, D. 2004b. 'Revealed: the full story of the Guantanamo Britons'. *Observer*, 14 March.

Rose, F. 2006. 'Why I published those cartoons'. *Washington Post*, 19 February.

Ross, C. 2006. 'Mass politics and the techniques of leadership: the promise and perils of propaganda in Weimar Germany'. *German History* 24(2): 184–211.

Rowling, C. M., T. M. Jones and P. Sheets. 2011. 'Some dared call it torture: cultural resonance, Abu Ghraib, and a selectively echoing press'. *Journal of Communication* 61(6): 1043–1061.

Rozenburg, J. 2012. 'European court makes the right call on Abu Hamza'. *Guardian*, 10 April.

Sachs, S. 2002. 'US defends the withholding of jailed immigrants' names'. *New York Times*, 21 May.

Sands, P. 2009. *Torture Team: Uncovering War Crimes in the Land of the Free*. London: Penguin.

Sandvig, H. 1988. 'The mass media and the United Nations in a human rights dilemma'. In *Human Rights and the Media*, A. Eide, A. Skogly and S. Skogly (eds) (pp. 52–70). Oslo: Norwegian Institute of Human Rights.

Satterthwaite, M. 2006. *Rendered Meaningless: Extraordinary Rendition and the Rule of Law*. New York: NYU School of Law.

Schabas, W. 2000. *Genocide in International Law: The Crime of Crimes*. Cambridge: Cambridge University Press.

Scheffler, S. 1997. 'Relationships and responsibilities'. *Philosophy and Public Affairs* 26(3): 189–209.

Schemer, C. 2012. 'The influence of news media on stereotypic attitudes toward immigrants in a political campaign'. *Journal of Communication* 62(5): 739–757.

Schimmel, N. 2009. 'Media accountability to investigate human rights violations'. *Peace Review: A Journal of Social Justice* 21: 442–447.

Schimmel, N. 2011. 'An invisible genocide: how the Western media failed to report the 1994 Rwandan genocide of the Tutsi and why'. *International Journal of Human Rights* 15(7): 1125–1135.

Schlesinger, J. R. 2004. *Final Report of the Independent Panel to Review DoD Detention Operations*. Washington, DC: Independent Panel to Review DoD Detention Operations.

Schofield, P. 2003. 'Jeremy Bentham's "Nonsense upon Stilts"'. *Utilitas* 15(1): 1–26.

Schulz, W. F. 2013. 'Torture'. In *Human Rights: Politics and Practice*, 2nd edn, M. Goodhart (ed.) (pp. 310–327). Oxford: Oxford University Press.

Scott, B. 2005. 'A contemporary history of digital journalism'. *Television and New Media* 6(1): 89–126.

Scruton, R. 1982. *A Dictionary of Political Thought*. London: Macmillan.

Seib, P. 2002. *The Global Journalist: News and Conscience in a World of Conflict*. Lanham, MD: Rowman & Littlefield.

Shah, D., M. Watts, D. Domke and D. P. Fan. 2002. 'News framing and cueing of issue regimes: explaining Clinton's public approval in spite of scandal'. *Public Opinion Quarterly* 66: 339–370.

Shaw, M. 1994. *Global Civil Society and International Relations*. London: Polity Press.

Shaw, M. 1996. *Civil Society and Media in Global Crises: Representing Distant Violence*. London: Pinter.

Shaw, M. 2003. *War and Genocide*. Cambridge: Polity Press.

Shaw, M. 2007. *What is Genocide?* Cambridge: Polity Press.

Shue, H. 1978. 'Torture'. *Philosophy and Public Affairs* 7(2): 124–143.

Shue, H. 1996. *Basic Rights: Subsistence, Affluence and US Foreign Policy*, 2nd edn. Princeton, NJ: Princeton University Press.

Shue, H. 2002. 'Torture'. In *Torture: A Collection*, S. Levinson (ed.) (pp. 47–60). Oxford: Oxford University Press.

Silverstone, R. 2007. *Media and Morality: On the Rise of the Mediapolis*. Cambridge: Polity Press.

Singh, A. 2013. *Globalizing Torture: CIA Secret Detention and Extraordinary Rendition*. New York: Open Society Justice Initiative, Open Society Foundations.

Skrbiš, Z., G. Kendall and I. Woodward. 2004. 'Locating cosmopolitanism: between humanist ideal and grounded social category'. *Theory, Culture and Society* 21(6): 115–136.

Skrbiš, Z. and I. Woodward. 2013. *Cosmopolitanism: Uses of the Idea*. London: Sage.

Slim, H. 2004. 'Dithering over Darfur? A preliminary review of the international response'. *International Affairs* 80(5): 811–828.

Slovic, P. 2007. '"If I look at the mass I will never act": psychic numbing and genocide'. *Judgement and Decision Making* 2(2): 79–95.

Smith, C. M. and G. N. Dionisopoulos. 2008. 'The Abu Ghraib images: "breaks" in a dichotomous frame'. *Western Journal of Communication* 72(3): 308–328.

Smith, R. W. 1987. 'Human destructiveness and politics: the twentieth century as an age of genocide'. In *Genocide and the Modern Age: Etiology and Case Studies of Mass Death*, I. Wallimann and M. N. Dobkowski (eds) (pp. 21–39). New York: Greenwood Press.

Smolla, R. A. 1992. *Free Speech in an Open Society*. New York: Alfred A. Knopf.

Soderlund, M. 2007. 'Role of news media in shaping and transforming the public perception of Mexican immigration and the laws involved'. *Law and Psychology Review* 31: 167–177.

Soh, C. S. 1996. 'The Korean "comfort women": movement for redress'. *Asian Survey* 36(12): 1226–1240.

Solana, J. 1999. 'NATO's success in Kosovo'. *Foreign Affairs* 78(6): 114–120.

Solaroli, M. 2011. 'Mediatized conflicts, performative photographs and contested memory: the Abu Ghraib scandal and the iconic struggle over the meanings of the "war on terror"'. *Global Media and Communication* 7(3): 245–250.

Sontag, S. 2003. *Regarding the Pain of Others*. New York: Farrar, Straus & Giroux.

Sontag, S. 2004. 'Regarding the torture of others'. *New York Magazine*, 23 May.

Soysal, Y. 1994. *Limits of Citizenship: Migrants and Postnational Membership in Europe*. Chicago: University of Chicago Press.

Staub, E. 1990. 'The psychology and culture of torture and torturers'. In *Psychology and Torture*, P. Suedfeld (ed.) (pp. 49–76). New York: Hemisphere.

Staub, E. 2013. 'A world without genocide: prevention, reconciliation, and the creation of peaceful societies'. *Journal of Social Issues* 69(1): 180–199.

Steinhauer, J. 2002. 'Records of 9/11 response not for public, city says'. *New York Times*, 23 July.

Straus, S. 2001. 'Contested meanings and conflicting imperatives: a conceptual analysis of genocide'. *Journal of Genocide Research* 3(3): 349–375.

Straus, S. 2005. 'Darfur and the genocide debate'. *Foreign Affairs* 84(1): 123–133.

Straus, S. 2013. 'Genocide and human rights'. In *Human Rights: Politics and Practice*, 2nd edn, M. Goodhart (ed.) (pp. 273–289). Oxford: Oxford University Press.

Street, J. 2011. Mass Media, Politics and Democracy, 2nd edn. Basingstoke: Palgrave Macmillan.

Strobel, W. P. 1997. *Late-breaking Foreign Policy: The News Media's Influence on Peace Operations*. Washington, DC: United States Institute of Peace.

Strömbäck, J. 2005. 'In search of a standard: four models of democracy and their normative implications for journalism'. *Journalism Studies* 6(3): 331–345.

Strömbäck, J., A. Shehata and D. V. Dimitrova. 2008. 'Framing the Mohammad cartoons issue: a cross-cultural comparison of Swedish and US press'. *Global Media and Communication* 4(2): 117–138.

Sullivan, M. 2013. 'Leak investigations are an assault on the press, and on democracy, too'. *New York Times*, 14 May.

Sussman, D. 2005. 'What's wrong with torture?' *Philosophy and Public Affairs* 33(1): 1–33.

Szerszynski, B. and J. Urry. 2002. 'Cultures of cosmopolitanism'. *Sociological Review* 50(4): 461–481.

Szerszynski, B. and J. Urry. 2006. 'Visuality, mobility and the cosmopolitan: inhabiting the world from afar'. *British Journal of Sociology* 57(1): 113–131.

Tai, Z. 2000. 'Media of the world and world of the media: a cross-national study of the rankings of the "top 10 world events" from 1988 to 1998'. *Gazette* 62(5): 331–353.

Tatum, D. C. 2010. *Genocide at the Dawn of the 21st Century: Rwanda, Bosnia, Kosovo, and Darfur.* New York: Palgrave.

Telegraph. 2014. 'Ukraine crisis: "We had to defend our citizens" says Russia'. *Telegraph,* 3 March.

Temple, M. 2006. 'Dumbing down is good for you'. *British Politics* 1(2): 257–273.

Tenenboim-Weinblatt, K. 2009. '"Where is Jack Bauer when you need him?" The uses of television drama in mediated political discourse'. *Political Communication* 26(4): 367–387.

Teresa, Mother. 1994. Letter to the US Supreme Court on Roe v. Wade. Available at: http://groups.csail.mit.edu/mac/users/rauch/nvp/roe/mothertheresa_roe.html.

Teson, F. 1997. *Humanitarian Intervention: An Inquiry into Law and Morality,* 2nd edn. Irvington-on-the-Hudson, NY: Transnational Publishers.

Teson, F. 2003. 'The liberal case for humanitarian intervention'. In *Humanitarian Intervention: Ethical, Legal and Political Dilemmas,* J. Holzgrefe and R. Keohane (eds) (pp. 93–129). Cambridge: Cambridge university Press.

Tester, K. 2001. *Compassion, Morality and the Media.* Philadelphia, PA: Open University Press.

Thomas, D. 2001. *The Helsinki Effect: International Norms, Human Rights, and the Demise of Communism.* Princeton, NJ: Princeton University Press.

Thompson, A. 2007. 'Introduction'. In *The Media and the Rwanda Genocide,* A. Thompson (ed.) (pp. 1–11). London: Pluto Press.

Thompson, M. 2009. 'Keeping Nick Griffin off air is a job for Parliament, not the BBC'. *Guardian,* 21 October.

Thussu, D. K. 2000. 'Legitimising "humanitarian intervention"? CNN, NATO and the Kosovo crisis'. *European Journal of Communication* 15(3): 345–361.

Thussu, D. K. 2003. 'Live TV and bloodless deaths: war, infotainment and 24/7 news'. In *War and the Media,* D. K. Thussu and D. Freedman (eds) (pp. 117–132). London: Sage.

Tomlinson, J. 1999. *Globalization and Culture.* Cambridge: Polity Press.

Totten, S. 2009. 'The Darfur Genocide'. In *Century of Genocide: Critical Essays and Eyewitness Accounts,* 3rd edn, S. Totten and W. S. Parsons (eds) (pp. 555–607). London: Routledge.

Totten, S. and P. R. Bartrop. 2009. 'The origin of the term genocide and the definition used in the UN Convention on the Prevention and Punishment of the Crime of Genocide'. In *The Genocide Studies Reader,* S. Totten and P. R. Bartrop (eds) (pp. 3–5). London: Routledge.

Totten, S. and E. Markusen. 2006. *Genocide in Darfur: Investigating the Atrocities in the Sudan.* New York: Routledge.

Tsutsui, K. and C. M. Wotipka. 2004. 'Global civil society and the international human rights movement: citizen participation in human rights international nongovernmental organizations'. *Social Forces* 83(2): 587–620.

Tuchman, G. 1978. *Making News: A Study in the Social Construction of Reality.* New York: Free Press.

Tulloch, J. 2009. 'Icons of fear: terrorism, torture, and the media'. In *Terrorism and Torture: An Interdisciplinary Perspective*, W. G. K. Stritzke, S. Lewandowsky, D. Denemark, J. Clare and F. Morgan (eds) (pp. 204–220). Cambridge: Cambridge University Press.

Umansky, E. 2006. 'Failures of imagination: American journalists and the coverage of American torture'. *Columbia Journalism Review* 45(3): 16–31.

UNHCR. 2012a. *2012 WRD Key Messages*. Geneva: UNHCR.

UNHCR. 2012b. *External Partner Brief: UNHCR's '1' Concept*. Geneva: UNHCR.

UNHCR. 2012c. *KPI Template 2012*. Geneva: UNHCR.

UNHCR. 2012d. *Summary of Major Stats from WRD 2012*. Geneva: UNHCR.

United Nations Centre for Human Rights (UNCHR). 1989. *World Public Information Campaign for Human Rights*, Vol. 8. Geneva: UN Centre for Human Rights.

United Nations Centre for Human Rights Commission of Inquiry on Human Rights in the Democratic People's Republic of Korea. 2014. *Report*. Geneva: Human Rights Council.

Valentino, B. 2004. *Final Solutions: Mass Killing and Genocide in the Twentieth Century*. Ithaca, NY: Cornell University Press.

Valles, M. 2005. 'La CIA usa Mallorca como base para sus secuestros por avion'. *Diario de Mallorca*, 12 March.

Valley, P. 2009. 'From A-lister to aid worker: does celebrity diplomacy really work?' *Independent*, 17 January.

Vandewalle, D. 2006. *A History of Modern Libya*. Cambridge: Cambridge University Press.

Verkhovsky, A. 2013. 'Religion rules'. *Index on Censorship* 42(4): 36–40.

Vick, D. W. 2004. 'Regulating hatred'. In *Human Rights in the Digital Age*, M. Klang and A. Murray (eds) (pp. 41–53). London: Routledge.

Vlieger, A. 2012. 'Domestic workers in Saudi Arabia and the Emirates: trafficking victims?' *International Migration, IOM – International Organisation for Migration* 50(6): 180–194.

Vreese, C. H. de. 2005. 'News framing: theory and typology'. *Information Design Journal + Document Design* 13(1): 51–62.

Wagner, A. 2010. 'Worries over US justice system as Abu Hamza extradition delayed'. UK Human Rights Blog.

Wagner, A. 2012. 'More press nonsense, this time on human rights damages'. UK Human Rights Blog.

Wagner, A. 2013a. 'No, the *Sun*, the Human Rights Act is not the EU'. UK Human Rights Blog.

Wagner, A. 2013b. '*Times* on the legal naughty step for bizarre "right to marry" headline splash'. UK Human Rights Blog.

Wahl-Jorgensen, K. and T. Hanitzsch (eds). 2009. *The Handbook of Journalism Studies*. London: Routledge.

Waisbord, S. 2008. 'News coverage of the Darfur conflict: a conversation with Jan Eliasson, United Nations Special Envoy to Darfur'. *International Journal of Press/Politics* 13(1): 75–80.

Waldorf, L. 2006. 'Mass justice for mass atrocity: rethinking local justice as transitional justice'. *Temple Law Review* 79(1): 1–88.

Waldron, J. 2000. 'What is cosmopolitan?' *Journal of Political Philosophy* 8(2): 227–243.

Wall, M. 2007. 'An analysis of news magazine coverage of the Rwanda crisis in the United States'. In *The Media and the Rwanda Genocide*, A. Thompson (ed.) (pp. 261–276). London: Pluto Press.

Walzer, M. 1983. *Spheres of Justice: A Defense of Pluralism and Equality*. New York: Basic Books.

Walzer, M. 1992. *Just and Unjust Wars*. New York: Basic Books.

Weiss, T. 2004. 'The sunset of humanitarian intervention? The responsibility to protect in a unipolar era'. *Security Dialogue* 35(2): 135–153.

Weiss, T. 2011. 'RtoP alive and well after Libya'. *Ethics and International Affairs* 25(3): 287–292.

Weiss, T. G. 2010. *Humanitarian Intervention*. Cambridge: Polity Press.

Weissbrodt, D. 2008. *The Human Rights of Non-Citizens*. Oxford: Oxford University Press.

Welch, D. (ed.). 2013. *Propaganda, Power and Persuasion*. London: British Library.

Welsh, J. 2011. 'Civilian protection in Libya: putting coercion and controversy back into RtoP'. *Ethics and International Affairs* 25(3): 255–262.

West, E. 2012. 'The ECHR is right about Abu Hamza, but Britain still needs to leave'. *Telegraph*, 10 April.

Wheeler, N. J. 2000. *Saving Strangers: Humanitarian Intervention in International Society*. Oxford: Oxford University Press.

Wodak, R. 2008. '"Us" and "them": inclusion and exclusion – discrimination via discourse'. In *Identity, Belonging and Migration*, G. Delanty, R. Wodak and P. Jones (eds) (pp. 54–77). Liverpool: Liverpool University Press.

Wolfendale, J. 2009. 'Torture lite and the normalisation of torture'. *Ethics and International Affairs* 29(1): 47–61.

Wolfers, A. 1962. *Discord and Collaboration: Essays on International Politics*. Baltimore, MD: Johns Hopkins University Press.

Wolfsfeld, G. 1997. *The Media and Political Conflict: News from the Middle East*. Cambridge: Cambridge University Press.

Wood, E. M. 2000. 'Kosovo and the new imperialism'. In *Masters of the Universe? NATO's Balkan Crusade*, T. Ali (ed.) (pp. 190–200). London: Verso.

Wright, R. 2004. 'In US, seeking to limit damage'. *Washington Post*, 4 May.

Zakaria, F. 1994. 'Culture is destiny: a conversation with Lee Kuan Yew', *Foreign Affairs* 73(2): 109–126.

Zelizer, B. 2004. 'When war is reduced to a photograph'. In *Reporting War: Journalism in Wartime*, S. Allan and B. Zelizer (eds) (pp. 115–135). London: Routledge.

Zhang, X. and W.-Y. Lin. 2014. 'Political participation in an unlikely place: how individuals engage in politics through social networking sites in China'. *International Journal of Communication* 8: 21–42.

Zimmerman, C. 2006. 'From propaganda to modernization: media policy and media audiences under National Socialism'. *German History* 24(3): 431–454.

INDEX

Entries in *italics* refer to figures; entries in **bold** refer to tables.

Printed in Great
Britain
by Amazon